W9-CON-768

JARVIS STREET

Also by Austin Seton Thompson
Spadina, A Story of Old Toronto

Jarvis Street

❧ A STORY OF TRIUMPH AND TRAGEDY ❧

AUSTIN SETON THOMPSON

PERSONAL LIBRARY PUBLISHERS

Toronto

Personal Library, Publishers
Suite 439, 17 Queen Street East
Toronto, Canada M5C 1P9

Publisher: Glenn Edward Witmer
Editor: Jennifer Glossop
Production Editor: Mark Eric Miller
Composition: CompuScreen Typesetting Ltd.
A PEPPERMINT DESIGN

Distributed to the trade by
John Wiley and Sons Canada Limited
22 Worcester Road
Rexdale, Ontario M9W 1L1

Canadian Cataloguing in Publication Data

Thompson, Austin Seton.
  Jarvis Street

Includes index.
ISBN 0-920510-15-9

1. Toronto, Ont.—Streets—Jarvis Street—History.
2. Jarvis family.   I. Title.

FC3097.67.T54   971.3′541   C80-094671-5
F1059.5.T6875J37

Printed and bound in Canada

For my wife

JOAN

Contents

Foreword

Jarvis Street has always been the raffish street in Toronto. Let Yonge be the longest, University Avenue the widest, Bay Street the richest; Jarvis has always retained its own flavour.

No wonder. Jarvis took its name from a raffish founder. The original Jarvis came to Canada as one of three officials in the office of the first lieutenant-governor, John Graves Simcoe, hoping to make his military pension liveable by the fees from his office. Alas, the fees were never so much as were expected and the only assets Jarvis built up were blocks of land assigned to him in the new settlement of Toronto. His son was also preferred to an appointment within the Family Compact and he too got into difficulties as chief superintendent of Indian Affairs in the fledgling province.

By the time both father and son were out of office, there were questionable, but substantial, debts against them, each in his own time. It was to satisfy those debts that Jarvis Street was originally built. In order to do this, it was equally typical of the family that the younger Jarvis had to demolish his own commodious house, since the best layout for the land necessitated the street going straight through his living room.

The original intention for Jarvis Street was for mechanics and what we would now call blue collar workers to live at the southern end; the commercial middle-class in the middle; and in the north, up to what is now Bloor Street, the wealthy, who had obtained their wealth either in trade or the professions.

The way in which the land sold very slowly until one of the real merchant princes of Toronto took a substantial interest, not only makes for good reading, but is a remarkable commentary on development, whether in the 19th century or the present.

Austin Thompson's family have been part of the Toronto scene for almost as many generations as the Jarvises. He therefore knows at first hand what he is writing about, which gives even the historical background an intimate and family flavour. But he is also alert to the architectural values of his subject, as well as the social nuances.

It is these nuances which give the street its character, and a walk up Jarvis Street nowadays is to pass through a sort of microcosm of urban Canada. At the southern end the mechanics have all gone, but city-controlled housing now fills what had been an industrial wasteland. Anchoring Jarvis at Front Street is the St. Lawrence Market and St. Lawrence Hall. The Hall, after extensive restoration, is now the home of the National Ballet of Canada. With the boom in fancy eating, the Market is full of genuine farmers and earnest gourmets every Saturday morning.

The same variety is shown further up the street where the CBC has its rattle-trap headquarters and produces most of the programmes seen nationally in this country. Those programmes are conceived and planned in a house which even a girls' school left over fifty years ago as being inadequate. Yet not far from it, on the opposite side of the street, is a remarkably trim and austere building for the armed forces—the Moss Park Armouries. For a non-military nation such as we have always been, it is funny to have such palatial headquarters for them and such ramshackle accommodation for the creative side of the country.

Going further north, we have Jarvis Collegiate Institute, a great training ground for many of Canada's leading figures in the last 100 years, and on the other side of the street, just before it ends, the national headquarters of the Anglican Church.

Sprinkled in between all this are, in the southern quadrant, a few seedy rooming houses, a home for alcoholics and, in the northern part, residences for the students of the National Ballet School and three or four immense apartment buildings, for which the old Massey mansion now serves as a restaurant.

With the Celebrity Club and the Keg Mansion at one end, and some lesser eating places at the other, with a sprinkling of hotels no longer of the dubious quality that they once were, Jarvis Street is still a vibrant, living street. To walk along it is to feel that vibrance and to know that though it is not a neighbourhood in the sense that Cabbagetown is, it is a street of character and importance in Canadian history.

From vegetables to ballet, from the houses of merchant princes to mechanics' tenements, from the Baptist Church to the CBC, Jarvis Street has run the gamut of our lives. Austin Thompson, by putting it in its context and meticulously tracing its development, has shown us this, of which before we were never so aware.

Garden Island, Kingston   Arnold Edinborough
August, 1980

List of Illustrations

Acknowledgements

Since the early part of this book is concerned with the settlement period of Toronto, I must first acknowledge the very considerable help I have derived from both volumes of Edith G. Firth's *Town of York*. Her excellent collection of documents, supported by commentaries, has proven an invaluable guide in the preparation of this work.

In considering the land holdings of the principal characters in this book, and the numerous transactions arising from them, I have been greatly assisted by Joseph Haughey, Land Registrar for the City of Toronto. His expert knowledge has been indispensable, and I offer him my warmest thanks for his unfailing courtesy and patience.

In 1976, as this book was in progress, Douglas Leighton, chairman of the Department of History, Huron College, University of Western Ontario, delivered a paper to the Canadian Historical Association on the subject, *The Compact Tory as Bureaucrat: Samuel Peters Jarvis and the Indian Department, 1837-1845*. Since Jarvis's dismissal as chief superintendent of the Indian Department was the main cause of the subdivision and sale of his hundred-acre park lot on Queen Street and the laying out of Jarvis Street, I am naturally grateful that Mr. Leighton has granted me permission to quote freely from his valued paper and to incorporate his independent findings into my own background material dealing with the early development of Jarvis Street. I am happy to acknowledge his generosity.

In the field of original research, I also wish to express my thanks to Paul Bircher for his willing and tireless help. It has been said that as history recedes, the myths grow larger. In the case of some of Toronto's most cherished myths, he has assisted me greatly in trying to reverse this process.

A number of people have been generous in sharing with me their expert knowledge of certain specialized subjects that have required consideration. For their help I especially offer my thanks to Dr. Lorne P. Laing and Robert D. W. Band, both of Toronto, to Donald Love of London, Ontario, and Mrs. Helen Redman of Midland, Ontario. I am grateful, too, to William Robertson, who has assisted me with much of the photography connected with this book, and to my son Evan, for reading critically each chapter as it progressed and making many valuable suggestions. And, finally, my special thanks to Mary Heather who typed the manuscript with care, tact, and patience.

A number of the Jarvis Street scenes illustrated in this book have been reproduced from *Toronto Old and New*, published in Toronto in 1891 by The Mail Printing Company.

A.S.T.

CHAPTER ONE

The King's Men

On February 25, 1791, Prime Minister William Pitt rose in the British House of Commons to announce that the House was about to consider legislation to divide the old Province of Quebec into two provinces. They were to be named Upper and Lower Canada. As he spoke, the mood of the English people was fretful. After suffering the humiliating loss of their American colonies a few years before, Englishmen were now being forced to focus their gaze across the Channel where rapidly escalating events in revolutionary France were already threatening England's social stability. In the light of their past experience with America and their present concerns with France, the British parliamentarians would have been forgiven if they had dealt with the proposed Canadian legislation in a superficial or casual way. They did not. The debate, in fact, was long and bitter, and didn't end until June 10 when King George III was asked to give his royal assent to the Constitutional Act.

Few pieces of colonial legislation have ever occupied the attention of so gifted an array of British politicians. The 1790's were Westminster's golden age of oratory. It was the age of Burke and Fox and Sheridan and Pitt. And historians were to argue later among themselves as to which of them was the greatest performer. It was agreed that Edmund Burke's speeches, after they had been polished for publication, ranked higher in literary content than the others, but his speaking style was said to be less effective in the House of Commons than those of his famous contemporaries. In the matter of improvisation, Charles William Fox excelled. He could come straight to the House from gambling at the fashionable Brooks's Club and enter at once into a complex debate with gusto and wit. Dressed casually in a faded, blue frock-coat and buff breeches, however, his figure was clumsy, his appearance unattractive. On the other hand, Richard Brinsley Sheridan, the Irish playwright, stood highest for his brilliant wit. His

1

cultivated, musical voice, it was said, exercised an "inconceivable attraction" for the members of the House of Commons, most of whom were highly critical connoisseurs of the art of public debate. But, in the final analysis, austere, celibate, hard-drinking William Pitt was acknowledged to rank first. Schooled from infancy by his father, the great Earl of Chatham, Pitt always spoke with clarity and precision. Habitually dressed in a sombre black frock-coat with a light waistcoat and cuffs of white lace, he projected an unyielding image of authority and dignity. Even William Hazlitt, the acerbic English essayist who disliked Pitt intensely, conceded that "he perhaps, hardly ever uttered a sentence that was not perfectly regular and connected. In this respect, he not only had the advantage over his contemporaries, but perhaps no one that ever lived equalled him in this singular faculty." As is often the case with men of unusual fluency, Pitt's flights into the realms of irony and sarcasm were effortless, and they never failed to delight his colleagues. On one occasion, for example, after listening impatiently to the hopelessly confused speech of an opponent, he remarked dryly to the House that "it was not, I presume, designed for a complete and systematic view of the subject."[1]

While Westminster's principal actors were debating the King's Canadian legislation, another group of men, destined to play important roles on a distant stage in Upper Canada, was waiting impatiently in England for the Act to be passed, and their appointments to government office confirmed. Among them were Colonel John Graves Simcoe, who was to become the first lieutenant-governor of the new province; Peter Russell, who had been promised the important post of receiver-general of revenue; and William Jarvis who was to fill the office of secretary and registrar of the province. They had all seen service in the American Revolutionary War.

For Simcoe, who was then thirty-nine years old and a member of the House of Commons for the riding of St. Mawes in Cornwall, and whose wife, a woman of means, had purchased the *Wolford* estate near Honiton, Devonshire, in 1784, an appointment to a vice-regal post in the Canadian wilderness was simply a further step in the development of an already successful career. It would not be correct to assume, however, that his brief term in Parliament had added much lustre to his reputation, although the time that he spent there was useful in bringing him into contact with many of the leading men of his time. In point of fact, he is known to have addressed the House on only one occasion, and that was during the bitter debate on Warren Hasting's clouded administration in India. Unhappily for Simcoe, the restless and critical House found his remarks memorable only because of Edmund Burke's devastating rebuttal of them. As a soldier habitually silent in Parliament, Simcoe was unwise to have chosen that heated occasion to present himself as a target for a marksman like Burke.[2]

Outside Parliament, Simcoe found surer and more familiar ground when he busied himself in writing a military memoir of the corps he had commanded with distinction in the Revolutionary War. He called it, quite explicitly, *A Journal of the Operations of The Queen's Rangers from the End of the Year 1777 to the Conclusion of the Late American War.* It was published privately in Exeter in 1787, and he later sent copies of it to the King and several government officials. There can be little doubt that the publication of the *Journal*, which drew attention not only to his military service in North America but to his knowledge of conditions there as well, enhanced his chances of winning a high office for himself in Canada. He desired such an appointment intensely, and he had no hesitation in saying so. When he wrote to the under-secretary of state on December 3, 1789, to enclose a copy of his *Journal*, after urging the abolition of the "miserable feudal system of old Canada," he added a significant sentence: "I should be happy to consecrate myself to the service of Great Britain in that country in preference to any situation of whatever emolument or dignity." That his appointment as lieutenant-governor had been settled even before the required legislation had been introduced is revealed in a letter he wrote to Lord Grenville, Secretary of State, on December 24, 1790. In it he asked his Lordship to instruct his under-secretary to obtain "a *Canvas House* similar to that sent with the Governor of Botany Bay," to enable him to move conveniently about the province, and act as a "faithful reporter to Your Lordship thereon."[3]

Unlike Colonel Simcoe, Russell and Jarvis were men of relatively limited means, subsisting narrowly on their government pensions. They were more interested in full-time employment, a government job with a steady income, than they were in clearing career paths for themselves in a pioneer settlement. Other visions also danced in their heads: there would be free lands awarded them in Canada and a satisfying flow of fees from their offices. For them, Simcoe's lofty concept of consecration "to the service of Great Britain" was muted by the forces of economic necessity.

Peter Russell, an Irish bachelor of fifty-eight, was the sole support of his half-sister Elizabeth, a spinster, to whom he was deeply attached. She was to accompany him to Canada and keep house for him. While he had earlier served for some years as an officer in the British Army, during the Revolutionary War he held a civilian appointment in New York on the headquarters staff of General Sir Henry Clinton, the British commander-in-chief. At the end of hostilities in 1781, after Lord Cornwallis, Clinton's second-in-command, had surrendered at Yorktown, Virginia, to the combined French and American forces, Russell returned to England with Clinton and set about trying to find work for himself. To fill in the time, he is said to have collaborated with Clinton in producing *A Narrative of the Campaign of 1781 in North America*, which was critical of Lord Cornwallis and stirred up considerable controversy. While Russell was well connected, being a distant relative of the Duke of Bedford, it was not until 1791, as the legislation for the creation of Upper Canada was being guided through the House by William Pitt, that he was at last assured of an appointment in the colony. He probably owed his appointment as much to the influence of Sir Henry Clinton as to anybody else. On the other hand, William Jarvis had Colonel Simcoe to thank for his good fortune in obtaining an important appointment in the new province.

Simcoe accomplished this by simply writing to Henry Dundas, later Lord Melville, who was then the home secretary and Pitt's closest friend. In his letter of August 12, 1791, Simcoe recommended Jarvis as "Secretary and Clerk of the Council as held by Mr. Odell in New Brunswick."[4] In fact, Jarvis was appointed "Secretary and Register of the Province," at an annual salary of £300. *Register* was the old form of the modern word *registrar*, and had the same meaning. Colonel Simcoe's interest in Jarvis, of course, arose from their association in the Queen's Rangers. In his *Journal*, Simcoe had recorded a skirmish in Virginia that occurred on the road between Williamsburg and Jamestown. "The whole of the loss of the Queen's Rangers," he wrote, "amounted to ten killed, and twenty-three wounded; among the latter was Lt. Swift Armstrong and Ensign Jarvis, acting with the grenadiers." At that time in the British Army, the rank of ensign was held by a junior officer whose duty it was to carry the flag of a regiment or company into action.

William Jarvis was born in Stamford, Connecticut, on September 11, 1756, where his father, Samuel, was the town clerk. Little is known of William's life until he joined Simcoe's Rangers. Following the end of the Revolutionary War, he made his way to England, probably in 1783, and joined a growing number of American Loyalists in their quest for compensation for the ruinous property losses they had suffered as a result of their support of the King's cause in North America.

While William Jarvis appears to have settled happily into English life, and is said to have belonged to a local militia regiment, most of the Loyalists didn't feel at home in England. They finally came to regard themselves as unwelcome exiles. They were particularly disturbed by the brutal prize fights and the physical violence that was resorted to in English parliamentary elections. One observer wrote:

> While London was too large for them, the countryside, especially in winter, was too bleak. Seeking moderate-priced and medium-sized places, the restless Loyalists searched for English counterparts of their hospitable American towns and usually never found them. The dialects of parts of England and Scotland were hard for them to understand, as were the sometimes coarse and forbidding features of many of the local people. The class system also appeared unjust to the Americans and they could not understand the attention paid to the various ranks of royalty. For example, in New England it was perfectly respectable for educated men to be engaged in trade, but in old England, the upper classes looked down upon such former colonial merchants as Samuel Curwen. When Curwen explained that he had also been a judge of the admiralty court, his social stature grew.[5]

Some of the American exiles worked together to present a petition to parliament in support of their claims, and they also circulated pamphlets in which they argued their "incontestible right to restitution." Many banded together as well in state groups in order to establish their local property losses in America. The Virginians and South Carolinians, for instance, set up committees to examine in detail the financial statements of refugees from their states with a view to discovering the amount of relief that might reasonably be requested from Great Britain. Other exiles, mainly the clergy, drew upon their religion for consolation in their time of trial. The Reverend Samuel Peters, D.D., for example, formerly of Connecticut, exclaimed to a half-empty church, "We have Jacob's Ladder to climb to heaven on—at its Top we shall meet and find Tranquility durable as Eternity. . . . Viewing this happy Prospect I am content in Hope, and in my Fortune."[6] Encouraged perhaps by Dr. Peters' blissful affirmation of faith, William Jarvis married his daughter, Hannah Owen, in London's St. George's Church, Hanover Square, on December 12, 1785. Hannah was born in Hebron, Connecticut, in 1763, but because of her father's notorious Royalist sympathies, they were forced to flee to England in 1774, before the actual outbreak of hostilities.

All in all, William Jarvis's nine-year sojourn in England worked out better for him than for many of his exiled compatriots. He seems to have adjusted happily to English life and to have escaped the acute financial stress that afflicted so many of the Loyalists. As evidence of this fact is a grateful letter that his older sister Polly wrote to him from New Brunswick in November 1787. Her husband, Tyler Dibblee, a Stamford attorney, had been a fervent Loyalist, and after escorting his wife and two children to St. John in 1783, he had committed suicide, crushed by the losses and hardships he had suffered in the Revolutionary War. Polly wrote: "I have received your two Letters and the Trunk, and I feel the good effects of the Clothes you sent me and my Children, and I value them to be worth more than I should have valued a thousand Pounds Sterling in the year 1774. . . . I wish every possible happiness may attend you and your amiable Wife and Child—and my Children have sense enough to know they have an Uncle Billy, and beg he will always remember them as they deserve."[7]

At the time Polly wrote her letter, William's first child, a boy whom he named Samuel Peters for his father-in-law, was just ten months old, having been born on January 24, 1787. The following year, William's family was increased by the arrival of his first daughter, Maria Lavinia, and in 1790 a second daughter, Augusta, was born.

Jarvis was a devoted and indulgent parent. In an age when society expected a father to be detached from the day-to-day lives of his children, Jarvis seemed to like nothing better than to be with them. He called them his "lambs," and tender-hearted sentimentality appeared always to pervade his relationship with them. It is hardly surprising, therefore, to find that towards the end of his stay in England he commissioned a large portrait in oil of himself and his son Samuel, who was then less than five years of age. Both were painted in full military uniform, the boy wearing an elaborate headdress. In the picture Jarvis is shown seated while Samuel stands beside him, one tiny, gloved hand thrust under his father's arm, the other holding a miniature rifle with bayonet affixed. In the light of Jarvis's limited means as a Loyalist pensioner, and the financial demands of his growing family, it is difficult to see how he could have justified the luxury of this portrait as well as two others he commissioned at the same time, one of himself alone and another of his wife Hannah and their two daughters. Perhaps the answer is to be found in the fact that one of the paintings has been attributed in recent years to the Reverend Matthew William Peters, a member of the prestigious Royal Academy.[8] If Matthew Peters was an English relative of the Reverend

William Jarvis (1756-1817), secretary and registrar of Upper Canada, with his son, the first Samuel Peters Jarvis, who died of diphtheria at Niagara in 1792 at the age of five. The portrait was painted in England and is thought to have been the work of the Reverend Matthew William Peters, R.A. —Private Collection

Samuel Peters, as seems probable, he might well have painted the portraits for William at little or no cost, as a memento of Jarvis's sojourn in England.

Hannah Owen Jarvis (1763-1845), wife of William Jarvis, with their daughters Maria Lavinia, born in 1778, and Augusta, born in 1790. The portrait was painted in England just before the Jarvis family set out for Canada in 1792.— Private Collection

The final Order-in-Council creating the Provinces of Upper and Lower Canada was passed at the Court of St. James's on August 21, 1791. A few days before, on August 15, Peter Russell was in an expansive mood as he reflected upon his improving fortunes. The long and empty years in England were about to end, and he would soon embark with his sister, Elizabeth, for British North America to fill a lucrative post. He wrote to her that day from his lodgings in London to keep her informed of developments:

8

Mr Samuel Peters, the intended bishop, is a cheerful man, has an agreeable wife and family and his daughter and Son in Law Mr & Mrs Jarvis are good natured and pleasing people. Mr Jarvis is to be Secretary of the Province and Clerk of the Council. This however I have from report but I shall know more of them tomorrow as I supp with them tonight.[9]

Russell's assumption that the Reverend Samuel Peters was to be the intended bishop turned out to be without foundation. While Simcoe favoured the appointment and Peters wanted it, Pitt's government refused to co-operate. No Anglican bishop was in fact to be appointed in Upper Canada until the Reverend Dr. John Strachan was named bishop of Toronto in 1839.

With the formalities of legislation completed, the Simcoes, having arranged for a friend to look after their four oldest daughters at *Wolford*, prepared to set out for Canada. As befitted his vice-regal role, Simcoe was the first of the three men to leave England. Before embarking from Weymouth, however, he and Mrs. Simcoe, their youngest daughter Sophia, and their four-month-old son Francis, had to spend nine days at the south-coast port waiting for the ship to be provisioned and the weather to clear. There, on several occasions, they met the King and Queen. Mrs. Simcoe was particularly pleased when the King enquired warmly about the arrangements that had been made to ensure her comfort on the passage.

They finally sailed on the *Triton*, a frigate of twenty-eight guns, on September 11, 1791, and reached Sable Island, off the Canadian east coast, on October 28. The *Triton* dropped anchor there briefly just as a dense fog-bank rolled in and enveloped the ship. Before leaving England, the Simcoes had heard a number of disquieting opinions about the timing of their passage: they were told that because of the lateness of the season they might find that the pilot that would be needed as they entered the Gulf of St. Lawrence would have been withdrawn, and that the St. Lawrence River in any event might be so blocked with ice that they would be forced to divert their course to Barbados. Colonel Simcoe, however, remained serenely confident throughout the voyage and was vindicated when a pilot was picked up without difficulty and the passage up the river was completed uneventfully. The family finally arrived at Quebec during the early morning hours of November 11, after a voyage that had consumed forty-six days, and the *Triton* dropped anchor in the river to await the arrival of daylight.

Mrs. Simcoe did not obtain her first view of Quebec until she rose and peered through her cabin window at 7 A.M. She was not impressed. The grey and cheerless Lower Town was covered with snow, and she decided to remain on the ship for the rest of the day. She described her arrival in her diary:

> I was not disposed to leave the ship to enter so dismal looking a Town as Quebec appeared through the mist, sleet & rain, but at 6 o'clock Lt. Talbot went ashore with me, & Genl. Clarke's covered Carriole (a small Post Chaise on Runners instead of Wheels) was ready to carry me to the Inn in the Upper Town to which we ascended an immensely steep hill through streets very ill built. The Snow was not deep enough to enable the Carriole to run smoothly so that I was terribly shaken & formed a very unpleasant idea of the Town to which I was come & the dismal appearance of the Old-fashioned inn I arrived at . . . was not prepossessing.

First impressions are important, but often misleading. Such was the case with Mrs. Simcoe's "unpleasant idea of the Town" which she formed in dreary weather after a long sea voyage and following a jolting carriole ride. In a few days she had changed her mind and became enchanted with the customs and the natural beauty of the place.

It was not until late in the following spring, while the Simcoes were still at Quebec, that Peter and Elizabeth Russell and some of the other government officials joined them. Mrs. Simcoe noted tersely in her diary on June 2, 1792, that "Mr. Osgoode, Chief Justice of U. Canada, Mr. Russell, the Receiver-General, & Mr. White, the Attorney-General, arrived from England. Mr. Russell had his Sister with him."

William Jarvis had yet to put in an appearance, but Colonel Simcoe decided to proceed to Upper Canada without his provincial secretary in the expectation that Jarvis would catch up with the official party as it wended its way up the St. Lawrence. Accordingly, they left Quebec at six o'clock in the morning of June 8 after walking through the St. Louis Gate and descending on foot to the wharf. Colonel and Mrs. Simcoe embarked with their two aides in a large bateau fitted with a colourful awning; another bateau carried the two children with their nurse, and a third the servants and baggage.

Meanwhile, as Simcoe's flotilla drew away from Quebec, William Jarvis was impatiently whiling away the time on board the transport *Henniker* as it tacked up the broad St. Lawrence, still about three days' sailing distance from Quebec. The voyage from Gravesend had been long and arduous for him and his family. In the end it took a full sixty days to complete, as compared to Simcoe's Atlantic crossing of forty-six days the previous autumn.

Just before sailing from England on April 12, Jarvis had been in a jubilant mood. He wrote a lengthy letter to his older brother Munson, in which he happily described the events preceding his departure and, perhaps with greater warmth, the lucrative employment opportunities that awaited him in Upper Canada. Munson Jarvis, a merchant, had settled in St. John, New Brunswick, in 1783 along with a number of other Loyalists. Like William, he had served with Simcoe's Queen's Rangers during the Revolutionary War. The main passages of William's letter, which was dated March 31, 1792, are worth noting:

I am in possession of my sign manual from His Majesty, constituting me Secretary and Register of the Province of Upper Canada with the power of appointing my deputies, and in every respect a very full warrant. I am also much flattered to be able to inform you that the Grand Lodge of England have, within these very few days, appointed Prince Edward, who is now in Canada, Grand Master of Ancient Masons in Lower Canada, and Wm. Jarvis, Secretary and Register of Upper Canada, Grand Master of Ancient Masons in that Province. However trivial it may appear to you who are not a Mason, yet I assure you it is one of the most honorable appointments that they could have conferred. The Duke of Athole is the G. M. of Ancient Masons in England.

Lord Dorchester, with his private Secretary, and the Secretary of the Province called on us yesterday and found us in the utmost confusion, with half a dozen porters, etc., in the house, packing up. However His Lordship would come in and sit down in a small room which was reserved from the general bustle, then took Mr. Peters home with them to dine. Mrs. Jarvis leaves England in great spirits. I am ordered my passage on board the transports with the regiment and do duty without pay for the passage only. Government have been so tardy in dispatching the Loyalists to Upper Canada that I shall be obliged to comply with the order, before mentioned, from the War Office. The ship I am allotted to is the Henniker, Captain Winter, a transport with the 2nd Rangers on board.

I am told that, at this moment, there is not a single grant of land in U. C. but the lands are held by letters of occupation and that the grants are all to be made out by me after my arrival, at which the Secretary of L. C. is not well pleased, as the letters of occupation have been issued by him for some years without fee or reward, and by the division of the Province of Canada all the emoluments fall to my portion; there is, at this moment, from 12 to 20,000 persons holding lands on letters of license in Upper Canada at a guinea only each, is a pretty thing to begin with.[10]

As is evident from Jarvis's letter, the *Henniker* had been requisitioned as a troopship to transport the reorganized Queen's Rangers to America, where they were to be employed in building roads and military installations in Upper Canada. Captain David Shank, who commanded the Rangers in Simcoe's absence, was on board, of course, along with Major E.B. Littlehales, Simcoe's military secretary.

Their ship reached Quebec on June 11, but paused only briefly since its final destination lay further up the river, near Sorel, a few miles below Montreal. For this reason, only Jarvis, Shank, and Littlehales were allowed to go ashore at Quebec. In the short time that was available to them, they managed to pay their respects to Prince Edward (Duke of Kent), the commander-in-chief and later Queen Victoria's father, and to Sir Alured Clarke, the lieutenant-governor of Lower Canada. The success of their fleeting visit, however, was marred by a lapse on the part of Jarvis who dallied too long in the town and as a consequence missed the boat—an occurrence that augury-watchers may have perceived as foretelling the course of his future career in Upper Canada. In a reference to the incident, Jarvis explained in a letter, "Before I could reach the wharf I was sent for and stopped by so many people that the ship was under weigh before I could get on board."[11] He did, however, manage to overtake the *Henniker*, and was safely aboard when it reached Sorel the next day.

The relief of the passengers was intense as they escaped the clutter and below-deck stench of the ship. Characteristically, William Jarvis was deeply affected by the ecstatic reactions of his children as they flew along the shore like birds released from a cage. He described the scene in a letter to his father-in-law:

> Their little hearts rejoiced at the approach of land and when they found themselves safe landed they were perfectly mad. Little Maria took hold of my hand and said, "Now Papa I would be glad if you would show me my grandpapa and uncle, I want to see them very much." Poor little soul, the affection that her countenance betrayed was too much to withstand. Sam ran off into the meadows instantly and had twenty tumbles in the grass which was nearly up to his chin, before we could catch him. Augusta's joy was by no means the least of the family.[12]

Illustrating a typical English diversion at the seaside, this original pencil drawing is pasted into an old Jarvis family ledger in the Baldwin Room of the Metropolitan Toronto Library. It undoubtedly depicts the three children of William and Hannah Jarvis, possibly at Gravesend as they awaited their passage to Canada in April 1792. The first Samuel Peters Jarvis occupies the saddle while his sisters Maria Lavinia and Augusta (foreground) are seated in the donkey's panniers.

William and Hannah Jarvis and their three children remained in Sorel for ten days as they awaited the arrival of a bateau from Montreal

13

to carry them on the next leg of their journey. They stayed with the Doty family, with whom the Simcoes had paused for "some refreshment" a few days before. Mrs. Simcoe had noted in her diary that Mr. Doty was a clergyman whose wife came from New York and that the house was the cleanest and neatest she had ever seen.

As compared to their Atlantic crossing, the trip to Montreal was like a picnic excursion for the Jarvis family. It was their first experience with a bateau. The children were enchanted with the songs the French Canadians who manned the boat sang as they dipped their oars rhythmically into the water. In the same setting a few days earlier, Mrs. Simcoe had murmured appreciatively that the scene was so calm and pleasant "as almost to persuade me it is worth while to cross the Atlantic for the pleasure of voyaging on this delightful Lake-like River, the setting sun reflecting the deepest shades from the shore & throwing rich tints on the water." William Jarvis probably felt the same.

Certainly, the reception he and his family received in Montreal, where they stayed for several days with John Gray, was further consolation for the hardships they had suffered during their marathon crossing on the *Henniker*. Gray was then emerging as an influential merchant in Montreal, and in 1817 was to become the first president of the Bank of Montreal. "His generosity and hospitality," Jarvis enthused, "exceeds anything I have ever met with; his whole house at our disposal and flowing with milk and cream and strawberries for my lambs."

Resuming their journey, the Jarvis family left Lachine at the end of June and reached Kingston, their destination, on July 7—at least, they thought they had reached their destination. Jarvis had earlier formed the impression that Mrs. Simcoe was to spend the winter in Kingston, and he had concluded that his family would do the same. Shortly after his arrival, however, he found to his chagrin that Simcoe intended to push on to Niagara and establish the provisional capital there in time for the opening of the first legislature in September.

But first the formalities of establishing the new government of Upper Canada had to be completed. With the most impressive ceremony that could be mustered in the little town of fifty houses, only one of stone, Simcoe was sworn in as lieutenant-governor in St. George's Church on Sunday, July 8. The following day, now properly installed in his own office, Simcoe formally appointed the members of his Executive Council. Those that were present, William Osgoode, Peter Russell, and James Baby, took their oaths of office followed by Littlehales as clerk and William Jarvis as secretary of the council.

A flurry of proclamations then ensued which taxed Jarvis severely. "I have been very busy since my arrival here writing Proclamations," he complained to Dr. Peters on July 15. "It has been my ill luck to be obliged to copy so many in manuscript; the one at this moment in hand contains 11 sheets of foolscap. Tomorrow they go to Montreal for the press, yet I have had to prepare 8 copies in manuscript." He had earlier been rebuked by Simcoe for not having brought a screw press out from England to enable him to affix the Great Seal of the Province to the documents his office was responsible for preparing, and now he had discovered that his supply of other needed materials was running dangerously low as well. In the same letter, therefore, he implored his father-in-law "to send out fifty skins of parchment also fifty weight of Beeswax. There is no more," he added ruefully, "to be had here or in Lower Canada."

Resigned to leaving Kingston, which he described as a comfortable place, the harassed secretary of the new province set out by ship for Niagara, across Lake Ontario, on August 15 in order to find a place to live. En route, he nearly perished in a violent storm. "I verily believed," he exclaimed later, "I had been preserved on the Atlantic to be buried on this Lake." A couple of weeks earlier, on her first voyage to Niagara with Governor Simcoe, Mrs. Simcoe had raised serious doubts as to the capabilities of the *Onondaga*'s crew; her opinion must have been shared by Jarvis. "We sailed with a light wind," she noted in her diary. "A calm soon succeeded & we anchored 7 miles from Kingston. The men who navigate the Ships on this Lake have little nautical knowledge & never keep a log book. This afternoon we were nearly aground."

After a search of ten days in Niagara, Jarvis finally found a dwelling for his "wife and lambs." It was a miserable log hut containing three rooms, two of which he described as being indifferent. He had to pay £140 for the house which included a half-acre of land. He found little consolation in the fact that Governor Simcoe had described Navy Hall, his intended residence at Niagara, as "an old hovel," and had refused to move into it, nor in the fact that Peter Russell and his sister Elizabeth had found it necessary to buy a cabin with only two dank and dismal rooms for which the receiver-general had laid out £60. Before leaving Niagara, which Simcoe had now renamed Newark, Jarvis managed to buy a supply of logs and engage a carpenter who agreed to add a "decent room" along with another garret as quickly as possible.

On his return to Kingston, William Jarvis didn't attempt to conceal from Dr. Peters the gloomy view he held of his imminent move across the lake. "Col. Simcoe is at present very unwell at Niagara," he related, "and if he has a good shake with the ague I think it will be justice for his meanness in dragging us from this comfortable place, to a spot on the globe that appears to me as if it had been deserted in consequence of a plague. Neither age or youth are exempt from fever and ague in Niagara." And with chilling prescience he added, "How will it go with my poor souls."

A few weeks later, on October 10, while William and Hannah were still settling themselves into their Newark house, young Samuel became ill. The carpenter was still dawdling about the place, but with any luck he would finish his work and depart by mid-November, just before the winter storms would sweep across the lake and isolate the community. It had been a typical autumn day: clouds of wood-smoke had curled and hung over the town, the sounds of the place, children playing, dogs barking, all seemed intensified by the crisp air, and the roads and paths were strewn with leaves of a variegated brilliance the Jarvis children had never seen before. William had taken Samuel out with him for part of the day, and their tour around the town had been a welcome diversion for them both.

After they returned home, Samuel complained of feeling ill and was immediately put to bed. In a few days his condition worsened and finally became critical. Dr. James Macaulay, the regimental surgeon of the Queen's Rangers, and another doctor were called in, but neither could save the boy. He died on October 19, a victim of what today would have been diagnosed as diphtheria.

The child's burial service was conducted by the Reverend John Stuart, the rector of St. George's Church, Kingston, who happened to be in Newark at the time, and by the Reverend Robert Addison, the garrison chaplain. It is probable that the small, crude coffin was placed in Butler's Burying Ground, on the outskirts of the town, since no other cemetery existed in Newark at that time.*

In the aftermath of Samuel's death, Hannah Jarvis stood like a rock at the centre of her stricken family. "Poor Bill cannot write you more than on business," she said of her husband a few days later, "his heart is almost broken." While she herself was expecting the birth of another child almost hourly, she stoically related to her father the circumstances surrounding Samuel's death:

---

* According to tradition, the child was later reinterred in the Dickson family plot in the cemetery of St. Mark's Church, Niagara, after it was opened in 1804. The small stone marking the grave was said to bear only the initials "S.P.J."

It has been a sickly season out here, and a deadly one to children, so much so that there is scarcely a child left in the fort the other side of the river and numbers have died here. Maria is ill but Augusta is well and a lovely babe.[13]

William's grief was inconsolable. He had been utterly devoted to his only son and eldest child. Before leaving Kingston, he had proudly described him as being "like a young 'Mohawk,' very tall and straight and saucy," and as they were settling into Newark a few weeks later, he had assured his father-in-law that "my dear babes are in rude health and grown quite out of your knowledge." For many years, Samuel's death that autumn was to hang like a pall over the Jarvis family.

CHAPTER TWO

Nehkik

When William and Hannah Jarvis left England in April 1792, three servants accompanied them. They had been recruited to help look after the children during the long sea voyage, attend to the baggage and dining arrangements on board ship and, when they reached Upper Canada, to assist in setting up and running the Jarvis household.

Despite the Atlantic gales that buffeted the *Henniker* for most of the crossing, Richard, the manservant, proved himself reliable and competent. Miss Adlem, however, through no fault of her own, was continuously stricken with seasickness and, as Jarvis understated it, was unable "to stir about much" in her role of lady's companion. Fanny, the kitchen servant, on the other hand, though a good sailor, was restrained by her prickly temperament and peevish, egalitarian notions from deferring to her mistress on any important issue. Jarvis described her as a "perfect Devil incarnate," adding that she was worse than no servant at all. Throughout the crossing, as William and Hannah lay in their cabin immobilized by seasickness, Fanny refused to help. She told the ailing couple that as soon as they were prepared to treat her like a lady, "then she would treat her mistress as such." Before the voyage ended at Sorel, however, Fanny had fallen in love. Her passion had been kindled at night under the romantic skies of the St. Lawrence, and its hapless object was Sergeant Bausneap of the Queen's Rangers. As soon as the Jarvis family had reached Kingston, she left them abruptly, without a word, and accompanied the bemused sergeant to Niagara where she persuaded him to marry her. "Fanny has left me and gone to the dogs," Hannah Jarvis complained to her father with understandable bitterness, but it was left to William to write the final chapter of her faithless saga: "Fanny married to a sergeant Bausneap of the Queen's Rangers (about one month since.) The day before yesterday she provoked him to shoot himself through the heart

18

with a soldier's musket at Niagara." Far from abandoning herself to remorse over the affair, Fanny rallied quickly and obtained a new position with "a Mr. Hamilton" in Newark.

While Richard had favourably impressed his employers with his conduct throughout the difficult crossing, as soon as the Jarvis family reached Newark it became painfully obvious that he, too, was unfit for domestic service. Writing in the period of gloom that surrounded Samuel's death, Hannah Jarvis related to her father that "rum dear rum is his idol . . . he has turned out a drunkard and so very insolent that I think Mr. Jarvis must, in his own defence, part with him." Mr. Jarvis put it more bluntly: "He is a perfect sot," he wrote, adding darkly, "he thinks nothing of kicking the servant maids; with a number of things equally distressing if not worse." In the light of what Hannah had to say about one of her maids, it is doubtful that they were intimidated by Richard's odd behaviour. "I have a Scotch girl from the Highlands," she related, "Nasty, Sulky, Ill Tempered Creture (*sic*)." She then cited an incident in which the enraged girl had flown at another servant with a pair of tongs and nearly killed her.[1]

As for the languid Miss Adlem, who had been too sick to be of much help on the *Henniker*, the cause of her defection from the troubled Jarvis family rested on more serene and conventional grounds. Infected perhaps by republican sentiments that had wafted across the Niagara River from the United States, Miss Adlem's manner towards her employers grew increasingly condescending. Inevitably, when the time came for her to leave, William described her departure with relief: "Miss A. is to be married in a few days to a young Scotchman, a good match for her, it will be a great relief to us. She has grown such an unmerciful fine lady that she does not spend a day in the week at home and really needs an interpreter, she has grown so affected."

By mid-November, William Jarvis's carpenter had finally finished his work around the house, and Hannah was able to move into a spacious, new room in time for the birth of her second son. In a rambling letter that was written on November 18, 1792, William informed his father-in-law in England of the momentous event:

On the 15th inst., your daughter was put to bed of a fine and promising child, it is a son; both mother and child are unusually well. Mrs. Jarvis has not the least fever and a pretty good appetite, tho' too cautious to take anything except a cup of tea or gruel. . . . She is very comfortably placed in a large room in the new part of my house which with unremitted

perseverance I got ready for her reception. . . . She is in the green bed that
you used to lay in, and the large Turkey carpet under her; the bed stands in
the middle of the room to prevent the possibility if there should be any
damp in the walls from leaving any effect; I have been thus particular to
relieve your natural anxiety.[2]

In the same letter he returned for a moment to the melancholy
subject of Samuel's death as a result of which, he reminded Dr. Peters,
he had "lost the pride and ambition of my heart." And following the
then-common practice in a family of naming an infant for a deceased
brother or sister, he went on, "I intend the infant shall bear up the
name of his brother." A week after the birth of the second Samuel
Peters Jarvis, he wrote again to his father-in-law, and in an unguarded
aside commented, "I have not the same feeling for him that I had for his
brother."

Two days after Sam's arrival, Governor Simcoe had called at the
Jarvis house and invited William to come and stay with him at Navy
Hall until Hannah was up and around again. As a result of the
governor's visit, William was able to report to Dr. Peters that while the
location of the capital of the province had not yet been finally settled, it
was his expectation that Toronto would be chosen.

It was not until the following May 1793, however, that Simcoe's
schedule allowed him to visit Toronto for the first time. The previous
February he had left Newark by sleigh for Detroit, proceeding first to
the Mohawk Village on the Grand River, where he joined forces with
Captain Joseph Brant, who had then conducted him on to Detroit.
Simcoe was impressed with the country around the present London,
Ontario, and when he returned to Newark on March 10, Mrs. Simcoe
noted that "he is confirmed in his opinion that the forks of the Thames
is the most proper scite (sic) for the Capital of the Country, to be called
New London on a fine dry plain without underwood but abounding in
good Oak Trees."

When he set out for Toronto on May 2, therefore, Simcoe's main
interest was in examining the site as a potentially useful and defensible
naval station, not as a location for the provincial capital. Later,
however, the idea of London as the capital was allowed to wither and
die in the face of criticism from the governor general, Lord Dorchester,
who felt that Simcoe's preference was visionary and impractical; the
site on the Thames River, he felt, was too remote from communication
with the vital St. Lawrence River, which tied the economic and
military life of the new province to the old centres of Montreal and
Quebec.

Simcoe and the seven officers who accompanied him on his reconnaissance of Toronto made the trip in bateaux, following the shoreline of Lake Ontario by way of Burlington, which was then called the head of the lake. The governor normally preferred to travel by bateau because that mode of transportation, though much slower than a direct crossing of the lake in a sailing vessel, enabled him to display the vice-regal flag and maintain contact with the scores of Loyalists who had taken up their allotments along the shore of the lake. At Forty Mile Creek, for example, now the town of Grimsby, over a hundred Loyalists had already established a flourishing settlement before Simcoe had arrived at Niagara. The name "Forty Mile Creek," which indicated the measured distance from the mouth of the Niagara River, recalls the traditional route taken by the early Loyalists after 1783 when they poured across the Niagara frontier and made their way to the mouths of various numbered creeks that provided sheltered inlets for unloading and water power for their mills. Thus, the venerable Servos family of Loyalist fame was always identified as living at Four Mile Creek, and Great Sail, the Indian chief whom Mrs. Simcoe later sketched, was described as living with his wife and ten children at Eighteen Mile Creek. Just as the Iroquois in their light canoes followed the shoreline around the lake when their chiefs launched war parties against the Hurons to the north, so did the British bateaux hug the shore in order to avoid risking the open water where squalls and storms could develop without warning. Mrs. Simcoe, attesting to this when overtaken by a sudden storm on Lake Ontario, related, "It was extremely calm when we set out but on our return we were almost seasick the water was so rough. A little breeze on this Lake raises the waves in the most sudden manner."

After spending a week at Toronto familiarizing himself with the terrain, Simcoe returned to Newark on May 13. He spoke enthusiastically of Toronto's natural harbour and "a fine spot near it covered with large Oak" which he thought ideal for a townsite. While he was absent, however, word had reached Newark that Britain was now at war with France. Consequently, Simcoe decided to withdraw the Queen's Rangers from their unhealthy huts at Queenston, on the Niagara River, and relocate them at Toronto where they would not only be at a more comfortable distance from the United States, which still had strong ties with France, but would also be more usefully employed in laying out and fortifying the proposed town. To this end, on July 19 he sent Captain Aeneas Shaw and a hundred men of the Queen's Rangers in bateaux to Toronto. A few days later a further detachment of the

Rangers was despatched in schooners from the Niagara River.

Captain Shaw, a rugged Scotsman, had served with Simcoe in the Queen's Rangers during the Revolutionary War, and in 1792 had plodded overland on snowshoes from New Brunswick to join his commanding officer in Quebec. Shaw, who was now a member of the Executive and Legislative Councils of Upper Canada, had as his first priority the establishment of a tented camp for the Rangers in the area of the present Fort York, opposite Simcoe's "Gibraltar Point" which guarded the narrow entrance to the Toronto Bay. The knowledge that the governor, his wife, and children would be following in a week's time to establish their own summer quarters beside his encampment added an unwanted note of urgency to the captain's preparations.

With a fair wind rising and the band playing, the governor and his family boarded the *Mississaga* at Newark late in the evening of July 29, 1793. "It was dark," Mrs. Simcoe noted in her diary, "so I went to bed & slept until 8 o'clock the next Morning when I found myself in the Harbour of Toronto." Ironically, the first person she was to see in the destined capital of the province that Pitt had created as a bastion of British institutions was not a Loyalist but a French fur trader, Jean Baptiste Rousseau. He lived near the mouth of the Humber River and, there being no other pilot available, had guided the *Mississaga* safely into the Toronto Bay. Mrs. Simcoe's experience, in a paradoxical sense, was not unlike that which had befallen the young Chateaubriand when he had arrived in America for a visit two years earlier. On reaching Chesapeake Bay he had gone ashore with a party in the ship's launch to obtain some fresh supplies. A young black girl held a farmyard gate open for him and he had responded gallantly by giving her his silk handkerchief. "It was a slave," he related later, "who welcomed me to the land of Liberty."[3]

The Simcoes spent their evenings on board the *Mississaga* until their new quarters were ready to receive them. Mrs. Simcoe helped choose the location for the canvas houses which were erected on rising ground just east of Captain Shaw's camp with a meandering creek in between. The governor and his wife tested the amenities of the bivouac by spending the night of August 4 on shore, and the following day their children, Sophia and Francis, were released from the ship and allowed to join them in their oddly picturesque house.

Mrs. Simcoe soon developed a great enthusiasm for Toronto: she galloped her horse happily across the sands of the peninsula (now the Toronto Island); from a small boat on the bay she examined the water and found it "beautifully clear and transparent"; she strolled around the proposed townsite at the eastern end of the bay and socialized with a group of Ojibway Indians who had travelled from Lake Huron to pay their respects to the governor. She judged them to be "extremely handsome" and possessed of a "superior air." They were attired in scarlet leggings and colourful broadcloth blankets, and wore a profusion of broaches and armbands of brilliant silver. In mid-August, having heard that there was "a fever" at Niagara, she quickly concluded that Toronto was healthier, and that it would be better to spend the winter there.

The governor shared his wife's enthusiasm for Toronto, at least for its location if not its name. In fact, on August 24 he changed it to York. He had just received word of the Duke of York's victory in Holland over the French Revolutionary Army, and he promptly marked the occasion by proclaiming that Toronto henceforth would be known as York. A royal salute was fired by the cannon, the Queen's Rangers discharged their muskets, and in the harbour the guns of the *Mississaga* and *Onondaga* responded with a resonant salvo. "It was a damp day," Mrs. Simcoe observed, "& from the heavy atmosphere the Smoke from the Ships' Guns ran along the water with a singular appearance." Canise, one of the Ojibway visitors whom Mrs. Simcoe had admired, took Francis Simcoe in his arms, and was impressed when the child was amused and not frightened by the sound of the guns.

Governor Simcoe next arranged for the first meeting of his executive council to be held in his improvised council chamber at York early in September. Among other matters, the council was to consider the petitions it had already received for land in the new settlement area and, perhaps more particularly, the allocation of lands that was to be made to Simcoe's officials to compensate them against the day when they would be required to uproot themselves in Newark and resettle themselves in York.

The only members of the Executive Council who were available for the historic meetings, in addition to the governor, were the Honourable Peter Russell, the receiver-general, and the Honourable William Osgoode, the chief justice. Russell was the first member to reach the vice-regal camp, arriving from Newark in the *Mississaga* on August 30. His trip across the lake, as befitted a man who in his career was to accumulate large holdings of land in Upper Canada, was made in record time. An incredulous Mrs. Simcoe duly recorded the details of his astonishing crossing, noting that it had been accomplished in exactly four hours.

The receiver-general, not sharing Mrs. Simcoe's affection for romantic, natural vistas, was dismayed with the conditions under which he found the Simcoes living. He was, however, enthusiastic over the location of the new town at the eastern end of the Toronto Bay. In a letter written to his sister, Elizabeth, shortly after his arrival, he said:

> The Governor & Mrs. Simcoe received me very graciously—but you have no conception of the Misery in which they live—The Canvas house being their only residence—in one room of which they lie & see company—& in the other are the Nurse and Children squalling etc—an open Bower covers us at Dinner—& a tent with a Table and three Chairs serves us for a Council Room. . . . Nothing can be pleasanter than this Beautiful Bason (*sic*)—bounded on one side by a number of low sandy Penninsulas, & on the other by a bluff Bank of 60 feet, from which extends back a thick wood of large forest Trees. The Town occupies a flat, about 50 yards from the Water—the Situation I believe healthy, as the ground is perfectly dry.[4]

The council meeting held on September 2 concerned itself with the routine petitions of numerous settlers like Christopher Robinson, the father of the later chief justice of Upper Canada, Sir John Beverley Robinson, but on the following day it concentrated its attention almost exclusively on the provisional land grants that were to be made to the gentlemen of the judiciary, the government, and the military.

All the officials as a matter of course were allotted "Front Town Lots," upon which it was intended that they would build houses, as Peter Russell explained, "46 feet in length & to be built after a uniform Model with Columns facing the water." In addition to these residential lots, the officials received an assortment of hundred-acre park lots in the First Concession from the bay, or 200-acre farm lots in the Second or Third Concessions. The First Concession extended from today's Queen Street to Bloor Street, the Second from Bloor Street to St. Clair Avenue, and the Third from St. Clair Avenue to Eglinton Avenue. Under Simcoe's model-town concept, York was to be sustained by the produce of the farms that his officials were expected to create out of the wildlands of the outlying concessions.

Along these lines, Chief Justice Osgoode received 300 acres, Peter Russell 500 acres, and John White, the attorney-general, one hundred acres. Of the fellow passengers on the *Henniker*, Captain Shank of the Queen's Rangers was awarded 500 acres in the concessions, and Major E. B. Littlehales and William Jarvis each received one hundred acres.

Since the grants that were made by the Executive Council were provisional, being subject to settlement work being performed on the land before a deed from the Crown could be obtained, it was not surprising that some trading of lots occurred between various recipients before the deeds were finally issued. Such was the case with William Jarvis, David William Smith, the acting surveyor-general, and John Small, the clerk of the Executive Council. Before seeking registration of his ownership, David Smith decided to turn over his hundred-acre Park Lot 6 to Jarvis, and Jarvis similarly surrendered the Park Lot 3 he had been allotted to John Small. Small obtained his deed from the Crown in 1801, but Jarvis didn't get around to registering his own deed to Park Lot 6 until 1811. It was on this hundred-acre property, extending from modern Queen Street to Bloor Street, that Toronto's celebrated Jarvis Street was later to be laid out, not certainly under the tranquil conditions that existed when the lot was granted by Simcoe in his embowered "Council Chamber," but urgently, when its later owner, Samuel Peters Jarvis, was in the grip of a personal, financial crisis.

Meanwhile, back in Newark, William Jarvis was busy preparing for a trip to New England he had planned on behalf of his father-in-law, the Reverend Dr. Samuel Peters. The trip was his first to the United States since he participated in the exodus of the Loyalists in 1783. His purpose was to try to settle the tangled affairs of his father-in-law, who was in financial distress in England, and also to try to secure support for his election to the proposed bishopric of Vermont. Before setting out from Newark on December 20, 1793, he wrote a long, reassuring letter to Dr. Peters telling him of the arrangements he had made to ensure that his larder was well stocked and his family fully provided for during his winter-long absence.

His comments offer a vivid insight into the extensive preparations for winter that it was possible for a settler of the official class to make at that time despite the undeveloped state of the country. Of greater significance, however, is the self-revealing enthusiasm with which Jarvis describes how he had developed his house, after a year in Newark, into the most comfortable cottage in the province. For the first time, the picture he drew of his condition was one of happiness and contentment. He had achieved his primary goal. His family was well housed, its cellar full. Often to the detriment of his public office, his own comfort and that of his family were always to be his paramount concern.

After extolling the advantages of his own place in Newark, in the same letter he unconsciously compared his lot to that of the Simcoe family when he mentioned casually that "The Governor is to winter in

Toronto (now York) in his canvas house and two log huts." The virtue implicit in Simcoe's conscientious renunciation of the amenities of Navy Hall, in order to concentrate his energies on establishing York, seemed to have escaped the secretary's notice. While the general tone of Jarvis's letter was unusually cheerful, his mood changed abruptly to one of pathos, as if his ear had caught the distant tolling of some burial bell, when he recalled again the "calamity" and "dreadful agony" that Hannah had suffered in Samuel's tragic death thirteen months before.

Referring first to the arrangements he had made for the coming winter, Jarvis wrote:

> I shall leave my family well provided for, I have a yoke of fatted oxen to come down, 12 small shoats to put into a barrel occasionally which I expect will weigh from 40 to 60 lbs., about 60 head of dung-hill fowl, 16 fine turkeys, and a doz. ducks, 2 breeding sows, a milch cow which had a calf in August, which of course will be able to afford her mistress a good supply of milk through the winter. In the root house I have 400 good head of cabbage, and about 60 bushels of potatoes and a sufficiency of excellent turnips.
>
> My cellar is stored with 3 barrels of wine, 2 of apples (for my darling), and a good stock of butter. My cock-loft contains some of the finest maple sugar I ever beheld, 10,000 lbs. was made in an Indian village near Michellemackinac. We have 150 lb. of it. It was my intention to send you a small keg of it, but I was taken ill. Also plenty of good flour, cheese, coffee, loaf sugar, etc. In my stable I shall have the ponies and a good slay (*sic*); the snugest and warmest cottage in the province. Thus you see I shall have the best of companions abundantly supplied with every comfort in the wilderness, where few have an idea only of lonely existing. In fact I am early provided with every requisite for a long and severe winter which is close on our heels. Your daughter never had so good health or spirits; even, in our deepest calamity she was cheerful, yet the most dreadful agony had possession of her heart; such a share of fortitude I believe never woman possessed before.[5]

At the end of his letter, Jarvis returned to his earlier optimism. "I am in great hopes," he concluded, "I shall succeed in this grim country."

William Jarvis returned to Newark from New England in March 1794, and while he had failed to settle Dr. Peters' affairs, which he admitted were still "in a very deranged state," he was successful in organizing support for his father-in-law's election to the bishopric of Vermont. This set in train the gleeful expectation on the part of

Hannah and William that they would soon be reunited with her father in Upper Canada. "Your residence in Vermont," Jarvis pointed out, "will not be required, I trust, more than six months in the year. The other six months I hope you will devote to your children's comfort." But it was not to be. Despite William's strenuous efforts to resolve the problems that beset his father-in-law, the favourable result of the election, which had taken place before the state of Vermont had formally accepted the Constitution of the United States, was nullified by Dr. Peters' inability to obtain consecration in England and the United States. He was not to return to his native America until 1805 when at the age of seventy he was judged too old to be of further use to the Church.

By the end of the summer, during which the Jarvis family had been afflicted with "the fever and ague," William's interest was suddenly awakened in his son, the second Samuel. "You must expect to see a most lovely boy," he exclaimed to his father-in-law, "very large for his age, auburn hair, very fair and blue eyes, and an uncommon share of vitality, in fact he is all we could wish him to be at his tender age." Word had reached Newark that Francis Simcoe had celebrated his third birthday in York dressed in Indian costume, and following the vice-regal example, Sam's parents immediately outfitted their two-year-old son in full Indian dress: "We have him in Indian dress," the secretary enthused, "and fur cap, or chapeau, Indian leggings and moccasins, and a fine fellow he is." And carrying matters a step further, a band of Mississauga Indians, in a simple ceremony, adopted Sam into their tribe. They gave him the name Nek-Keek.

In the month of January 1795, the Honourable Robert Hamilton, the wealthy Queenston merchant and a member of the Executive Council, set out with his three sons for Scotland where he had arranged for them to be educated. Jarvis took the opportunity to have him deliver to Dr. Peters in England two portraits in watercolour of Sam in his Indian costume which had been recently painted in Newark. In his accompanying letter he observed, "What you will readily trace is his resemblance to the lamb that fell a sacrifice to this inhospitable climate. . . . He is an astonishingly large boy and otherwise a fine boy." Jarvis provided no clue as to the name of the artist. While the portrait must have been hurriedly painted, the fine lettering of the inscription and the general quality of the work raises the strong possibility that it was produced by William von Moll Berczy. In addition to the important role he was to play as a builder and developer in York and Markham, Berczy was an accomplished artist, and a frequent visitor to

Samuel Peters Jarvis.

Nehkik,
A Missasaga by Adoption
Aged two Years.

1794.

One of two sketches in watercolour made of the second Samuel Peters Jarvis in his new Indian costume at Newark. The artist may have been William von Moll Berczy or his wife, Charlotte.—Private Collection

Newark on government business in the summer and fall of 1794. His wife, Charlotte, was also a talented artist, and the sketches of Sam might equally have been the work of her brush.

While Jarvis told his father-in-law that the Indians had given Sam the name Nek-Keek, the artist who lettered the portrait transcribed the word with phonetic accuracy though with a different spelling, Nehkik. William offered no English equivalent for the name, but there can be little doubt that it was simply a variation of the Ojibway word *ningik*, meaning an otter, a small, playful, and elusive animal. The old Indian chief who bestowed the title doubtless felt it was an appropriate name for an active and precocious child like Sam. If the chief had possessed a shaman's gift of clairvoyance, he might also have foreseen the day when Nehkik would occupy the troubled office of chief superintendent of the Department of Indian Affairs.

Oddly enough, the Indian words *Niagara* and *Toronto* are far more troublesome when their original meaning is sought than is Nehkik. Mrs. Simcoe, for example, recorded in her diary that the word *Niagara* signified a "Great House." It was inspired, she said, by the "large Stone House built by the French in the Fort at Niagara." Long before that period, however, the chief village of the Neutrals, who lived between the Iroquois and the Hurons, was located on the site of the present Niagara-on-the-Lake, on the west side of the Niagara River, and it was named Onghiara. Niagara is the modern form of that word, and while different English renderings have been extracted from it, like Mrs. Simcoe's "Great House," or "the thunderer of waters," or simply, "a neck or strait," none can be supported by solid, historical evidence. William Kirby, who is best remembered today as the author of *The Golden Dog*, lived at Niagara-on-the-Lake until his death in 1906. As Lorne Pierce has put it, "He made the history and language of the Indian his own." In his *Annals of Niagara*, which was written after years of study and reflection, he stated flatly that the real meaning of the word "Niagara" was irretrievably lost centuries ago. He explained:

> The Seneca tribe of the Five Nations took possession of the east side of the Niagara River after the destruction of the Neutrals in 1650. They continued the name of Onghiara with a slight change, calling the river Nyahgeah. It was a foreign word to them to which no meaning was attached. They found the word when they came here, and its meaning remains an etymological puzzle. . . . Explanations of its meaning from the Iroquois and other Indian tongues, are freaks of the imagination.[6]

The true meaning of the ancient Indian name *Toronto* is likewise a matter for conjecture and debate. Dr. Percy J. Robinson in his *Toronto During the French Régime* weighed carefully the claims of such popular interpretations of the word as "a place of meeting," "trees in the water," and "a gate or entry," and while he didn't reject any of them with the fervour or finality of William Kirby, he expressed his own preference for a less familiar interpretation:

> Whether the name is Huron or Iroquois, whether it originated in the Georgian Bay and gradually worked its way south, or began at the south and was afterwards applied to all parts of the *passage de Toronto*, historical testimony and the evidence of the majority of the maps favour the theory that the name originated as an appellation of Lake Simcoe.

In support of this theory, he pointed out that the place-name *Toronto* occurs for the first time in any document or map on a large manuscript map now in Paris, France, which was prepared around 1673. On it the name *Toronto*, under the form of *Taronto*, is attached to Lake Simcoe, which is called *Lac de Taronto*. Dr. Robinson reminds us that the Huron name for a strait or pass such as exists between Georgian Bay's Christian Island and the mainland was *Tarontaen*; if the Hurons knew the Narrows at Orillia by the same name, he surmised, "the step to Lac Taronto is a short one." Under his reasoning, then, the name that was originally descriptive of the Lac de Taronto region came gradually to encompass the whole portage enclave that led from the land of the Hurons to the mouth of Toronto's Humber River.[7]

In the same letter to Dr. Peters that accompanied Nehkik's portraits, written in January, 1795, Jarvis made the startling disclosure that he intended building a new house in Newark in the spring. He had decided that his present house, which also contained his office, was now too small. On the face of it, his decision, with all signs pointing towards his early removal to York, appears to have been perverse. Indeed, the year before he had paid a Christopher Danby sixteen shillings to draw a ground plan for him for a house in York. Nothing had occurred since that time to suggest that Governor Simcoe had relented in his intention to relocate the provisional capital in York, although the governor still held to his idea that the permanent capital would later be firmly established in the vicinity of the present London, Ontario.

Simcoe's fuzzy, capital-hopping concept naturally created in the minds of his officials intense feelings of uncertainty, frustration, and resentment. "I understand that all the public offices are to be ordered over to York (alias Toronto) this Autumn," Jarvis wrote to his father-in-law in April 1795, responding to the latest rumour, "if so the Lord have mercy on those who have families to cover from this unfailing frost. My offices may go and so may I, but my family are housed and comfortable, and their removal is optional with me."

By the following November, however, Hannah Jarvis was still far from certain that their next move would be to York: "It was and I believe is still very doubtful where the city will be," she observed. She still kept alive the idea of building in Newark, on an ambitious scale, but clearly the house that was intended to be constructed in the spring of 1795 had not yet been started. She expanded on the theme of their new house in a letter to her father:

> The intended [house] must be something large, and for sale in case of removal. The dimensions 40 x 24 with two wings 36 x 12 which would admit us to have a bedroom for the children and ourselves, the kitchen and office, two sitting-rooms, and a room for a friend occasionally. It was never meant to be finished only as much as necessity required until the seat of Government should be known. The frames, windows, doors, etc., are ready to go up, and have been all summer, but the rumours of York has delayed its use, as in that case it would have been ready to transport . . . to York.[8]

And there the matter rested until early in 1796. Governor Simcoe then announced, perhaps not unexpectedly, that he and his family were returning to England on leave of absence later that year. To dispel the confusion he had created in the minds of his officials as to their removal to York, he instructed Major Littlehales, his military secretary, to forward a circular letter to them, including, of course, Mr. Secretary Jarvis. It read:

> York, 28 Febr. 1796
> I have the honour to signify to you His Excellency, the Lieut. Governor's directions, that immediately upon the conclusion of the ensuing meeting of the Provincial Parliament, you will be pleased to remove your office to York, the present Seat of this Government.[9]

It is to be noted that the vice-regal instruction referred only to the removal of their "office" and did not stipulate that the families of the various officials also be relocated in the new town by the required date. For Hannah Jarvis, the air had been finally cleared. On April 15, 1796, in a tone that wavered between defiance and resignation, she informed her father that "Mr. Jarvis has orders to remove his office to York by the first of June; at any rate if he does, his family will remain here until such time as he has a house to remove them into."

The first of June date had been selected by Simcoe on grounds more political than practical, because on that day, under a treaty made between Great Britain and the United States, Fort Niagara was to be formally handed over to the Americans. As a result, Newark would lie within range of the guns at Fort Niagara, an intolerable position, Simcoe felt, for the provisional capital of the province to find itself in; hence his determination to transfer all the government offices to York as quickly as possible. Henceforth, Newark would be spoken of as lying "on the King's side of the river."

Governor Simcoe's orders, however, could not possibly be complied with. There was simply no accommodation available in York, and because of the acute shortage of masons, carpenters, and materials, any attempt to have a house built there at that time was fraught with problems of nightmarish proportions. The Honourable Peter Russell, for example, reluctantly complied with Simcoe's wishes and bought Christopher Robinson's modest house in York in 1795 when only twelve such houses existed. He paid a hundred guineas for it, and later employed a contractor to make some alterations. The work didn't begin until the fall of 1796, after Simcoe's departure, and was still dragging on through January of the following year when a fire, attributed to the carelessness of the workmen, gutted the building one night and left only the chimneys standing. Russell, choleric with frustration and disappointment, turned next to the architect-builder William von Moll Berczy, and a new start was made on a house for the receiver-general at a location closer to the Toronto Bay, at the northwest corner of today's Front and Princess streets; by the time it was ready to receive Peter and Elizabeth Russell in the fall of 1797, the cost of the structure, which was later to be known as *Russell Abbey*, had soared to over £1,000.

In the light of Peter Russell's experience, William Jarvis could hardly be blamed for ignoring Simcoe's deadline of June 1. Having made his decision to hold to his ground in Newark until he could accommodate himself comfortably in York, Jarvis settled back to await the arrival of winter and its attendant pleasures.

The winter had barely arrived, however, when the Jarvis family was stricken with another disaster: a fire of unexplained origin broke out and largely destroyed their house.

The fire was first detected at eight o'clock on Saturday night, December 3. It spread rapidly through the frame dwelling, but as a result of the strenuous efforts of several strangers, among them some American officers on leave from Fort Niagara who happened to be wandering past the secretary's house at the critical moment, the Jarvis family escaped injury. Most of their furnishings were saved as well, including Jarvis's treasured family portraits that he had brought with him from England. The *Upper Canada Gazette,* which was then printed in Newark, gave prominent coverage to the story in what must have been one of the earliest eye-witness accounts of a personal tragedy to be published by any newspaper in the province:

> About 8 o'clock on Saturday evening last the dwelling house of William Jarvis, Esq. of this town, was discovered to be on fire & which had made such progress as to render all attempts to extinguish it almost abortive; notwithstanding which, the assembling of the people was so speedy, and their exertions so well directed that the province records, the most valuable house furniture and the right wing of the building are saved. The conduct of several, of Miss Vanderliefs in particular, in rescuing two of Mr. Jarvis' children, is spoken of with much applause: and credit in general is due. We are authorized to mention with gratitude the friendly exertions of the officers of the United States garrison, and other strangers who rendered essential service.

Jarvis, of course, was forced to make immediate arrangements for the accommodation of his family elsewhere. In the process, as he sorted out the wreckage of the house that three years before he had proudly called "the snugest and warmest cottage in the province," he noticed that a number of his possessions had disappeared. He was certain that they had not been lost in the conflagration, but that they had been stolen, deliberately and shamelessly carried off in the confusion of the fire and its aftermath. He therefore hit upon the idea of publishing an acknowledgment of his gratitude to those people who had emerged from the darkness to help him, while at the same time, with appropriate delicacy, urging them to return his missing property. His notice appeared in the same issue of the *Gazette* that carried the news of the fire:

Mr. Jarvis takes the earliest opportunity of returning in this public manner his most sincere thanks to the gentlemen and others who so generously exerted themselves in the preservation of his family and property, at the fire on Saturday evening last. He assures every individual that the uncommon solicitude shown on the occasion, has made the most lasting impression on his feelings.

He will thank those whose goodness induced them to carry articles to their houses, to inform [him] where to send for them.

Avid readers of the *Upper Canada Gazette* were to discover in later issues of the paper the surprising nature of the "articles" that the secretary was anxious to recover.

CHAPTER THREE

Caroline Street

William Jarvis was keenly disappointed by the reaction to his advertisement in the *Upper Canada Gazette*. He had simply asked for the return of some missing articles by those "whose goodness induced them" to carry them off to their own homes during the fire that had nearly destroyed his house the previous Saturday night. Faced with a negative response, he decided upon a more direct approach and inserted a new notice in the *Gazette* which not only offered a reward for the return of his property, but also included a clear description of the items he was particularly interested in recovering. His advertisement appeared in the paper a week after he had issued his first, unsuccessful appeal:

FIVE GUINEAS REWARD!
Taken Away
On Saturday evening, the 3d inst. from the subscriber, during the fire, two
BEAVER BLANKETS.
One very large, the other small;—
ALSO
ONE BUFFALO SKIN;
whoever will bring the said blankets to the subscriber, shall receive one guinea reward for each, or give such information that they may be procured on prosecution of the offender or offenders to conviction, shall receive the above reward. But if returned by the offenders without delay, they will be thankfully received, and no questions asked.

Wm. Jarvis

Newark, Dec. 14. [1796]

The secretary continued to run these advertisements each week for the rest of December and well into January. A notice that appeared in the

December 21 issue, however, modified the first advertisement. "In the loss sustained by Mr. Jarvis," it read, "was also a Buffalo Skin, which, if returned with or without the beaver blankets will be thankfully received and no questions asked."

The generous reward of five guineas that was offered must have considerably exceeded the commercial value of the two beaver blankets and the buffalo skin that had been stolen. Beaver were still plentiful throughout the southern wilds of the province, and vast herds of buffalo still roamed the western plains. Three years before, when a delegation of Ojibways from Lake Huron had visited Governor Simcoe in York, they had presented him with a beaver blanket "to make his bed" as they had put it. While a blanket of beaver skins, prized for their durability, may have been considered by the Indians as a gift fit for a King's representative, the skins were by no means so rare as to prevent Jarvis from replacing them easily had he wished. In his amending notice, in which he focused on the missing buffalo skin as the article he was most anxious to recover, here in particular his interest must have been more sentimental than practical. The role of a buffalo skin as a covering for children of that day was illustrated by Thomas Gibbs Ridout in a letter he wrote to his brother, George, from Quebec in 1815. He recalled as children in York how they had gathered around the stove at night while their father, Thomas Ridout, had read to them, and at ten o'clock, by the time their feet were warm, they had been hurried off to bed, "each dragging a Buffalo skin out of the passage to cover over."[1]

While the true significance of the secretary's concern over his loss remains a mystery, the probability is obvious that the stolen articles, especially the buffalo skin, had once belonged to his first son, the cherished Samuel, who had now been dead for over four years.

At least one reader of the *Upper Canada Gazette*, the Honourable Peter Russell, must have viewed with astonishment the secretary's conscientious attempts to recover his animal skins. A plodding, cautious man, Russell had long held the opinion that Jarvis was inefficient and that he shirked his responsibilities of office. Jarvis was, Russell must have concluded, like the lawyer in Chaucer who always "seemed bizier than he was." Now, as the senior government official in Simcoe's absence, and responding to his earlier concerns, Russell was on the point of looking into the whole matter of the secretary's administration. The fire suffered by Jarvis in December, however, and the destruction of his own new dwelling in York in January 1797, forced Russell to postpone his inquiry for the moment.

While Jarvis had been toying with the idea of building a larger house in Newark since 1795, and some preparatory work had been done on it at that time, the partial destruction of his existing house at the outset of winter forced him at once to look elsewhere in Newark for shelter. In the light of his imminent move to York, it wouldn't have made sense for him to have revived his project in Newark when at the same time he was faced with the spectre of building afresh in York. Luckily, his dilemma was resolved just four days after the fire when Alexander McDonell, the sheriff of the Home District, agreed to let him occupy a house McDonell owned in Newark for an annual rental of £30. Since one wing of Jarvis's own house had been spared, along with the provincial records, it was a simple matter for him to have that part of the building patched up for use as an office. While these arrangements at best were makeshift, they allowed the secretary to concentrate his energies on preparing for his unwanted move across the lake.

As the year 1797 progressed, however, Jarvis's preparations were diverted abruptly by the implementation of Russell's plan to launch a full inquiry into the administration of his office. The blow fell during the summer when Russell, acting as administrator of the province, and president of the Executive Council, set up a committee consisting of the new chief justice, John Elmsley, and the surveyor-general, David W. Smith, with full powers to examine into the operations of the secretary and registrar's office. The inquiry was prompted, of course, by the delays that were now being experienced by settlers in obtaining their land patents, and the committee was asked to discover, if it could, the actual number of patents that remained unissued and to make recommendations for speeding up the whole land-granting process.

As Russell's committee set about its task of caulking up the secretary's leaky boat, it is tempting to attribute the confusion that was seen to exist in Jarvis's office to the effects of the fire. In fact, the operation of his office, and questions as to his general competence, had been matters of official concern throughout the preceding year.

Jarvis's functions were divided generally between drawing up proclamations and commissions of appointment, and recording and issuing Crown grants against the payment of fees, of which he received a part. His administration had begun with high promise. In the halcyon days, the most difficult problem he had wrestled with was trying to affix the Great Seal of wax with the wrong kind of press to the documents he was required to prepare. Early in 1793, Hannah Jarvis had reported to her father that "Mr. Jarvis desires me to say that he finds everything very easy in his office. Mr. Osgoode (the Chief Justice) is very kind in sending his assistants." And later that year, Jarvis had stated that "I have made out but three grants since my being in office (except two Indian grants)." However, by the following March 1794, things had picked up a little, though not much: "Official business in this Province goes on but very slowly," Jarvis then related, "only 52 deeds have been made out."

The winds of change started to gust ominously in December 1794, when Jarvis admitted that the attorney-general had been instructed by the council to make out the deeds, although he assured his father-in-law that the fees he enjoyed from this branch of his government work would not be affected. As registrar of the province, of course, he continued to record the Crown grants and to deliver them to the public against payment of the necessary fees.

By the spring of 1796, William was able to report sanguinely to Dr. Peters that business was increasing rapidly in his office: "I have now about 500 patents," Jarvis declared, "that will be issued between this and May. . . . In the course of the summer I expect to pass more than a thousand grants, etc." It is significant that the secretary mentions only that he is involved in issuing and passing on the patents, not in making them out, a responsibility that now lay with the attorney-general. But a month later, on April 15, Hannah Jarvis wrote a bitter and indignant letter to her father in which she described new restraints that were being imposed upon her husband just as the volume of business in his hands was at last reaching a lucrative level. She related that the Executive Council, naming specifically Governor Simcoe, Captain Aeneas Shaw, and Receiver-General Peter Russell, had now decreed that Attorney-General John White would be entitled henceforth to collect half the fees that had previously been enjoyed by Jarvis to compensate White for the work involved in preparing the land grants in his own office. Next, Jarvis, who had always understood that only he had the power to appoint his deputies, was told that the council had taken the matter out of his hands and appointed registrars for each provincial district "even in the town of Newark," Hannah added acidly. In the same turn of the council's wheel, Thomas Ridout found himself named registrar for the County of York, with the responsibility of opening an office in the proposed provincial capital.

Hannah Jarvis ended her April 15 recital of woe on an ominous note. "It is now circulating," she wrote, "that the Secretary is an American and the King has given him all *the monies, which is the reason that the grants are spread* and all the stones at headquarters are turned upside down to rout him out of office."[2] It will be noted that Hannah's letter was written three months before Governor Simcoe left the province. Since Jarvis owed his position to the influence of Simcoe, it can only be concluded that the governor's earlier confidence in Jarvis had waned, and for that reason he had concurred in the council's decision to reduce Jarvis's responsibilities.

When Hannah Jarvis alleged that a sinister cabal was working to drive her husband from office, she had understandably closed her eyes to his possible shortcomings as an administrator. It is the most natural of all human defects to blame others for our own failures—Montaigne reminds us that "Nobody suffers for long except by his own fault"— and William and Hannah easily persuaded themselves that the council's decisions were mainly motivated by the malice and self-interest of Russell and Shaw. Moreover, William was equally convinced that it was the council that should be blamed for the confusion and delay that was now frustrating the provincial land-granting system; it arose, he believed, as a direct result of the council's earlier decision to have the deeds drawn up in the attorney-general's office rather than in his own. The motive for this change, he suspected, was not to increase efficiency, but to line the attorney-general's pocket with a new source of income.

Having learned that the house Berczy had been building for them was now ready, Peter Russell and his sister left Newark and landed at York on December 3, 1797. As they came ashore a violent storm swept the bay, making it extremely difficult to land their baggage safely and carry it through the driving snow to their new house on Front Street, a short distance away.

A few days later, Peter Russell wrote to Governor Simcoe in England to tell him of his arrival in the provincial capital and to bring him up to date on developments within the town. He mentioned with satisfaction that both Attorney-General White and Surveyor-General Smith had succeeded in settling themselves in York. On the subject of William Jarvis, however, his comments were less encouraging. "But Mr. Jarvis," Russell grumbled, "having not made the smallest effort for the removal of his Office remains still at Niagara and most probably means to do so until your Excellency's arrival." While Jarvis was dallying fretfully at Newark, Russell was pressing forward vigorously with various building projects in the new capital. As Russell reported to Simcoe:

The Two wings to the Government House are raised with Brick & Completely covered in. The South One, being in the greatest forwardness

I have directed to be fitted up for a temporary Court House for the Kings Bench in the ensuing Term, and I hope they may both be in a condition to receive the Two Houses of Parliament in June next, I have not yet given directions for proceeding with the remainder of your Excellency's plan for the Government House, being alarmed at the magnitude of the expence.[3]

The two brick wings referred to by Russell stood near the foot of Berkeley Street and were built by the Queen's Rangers. Conceived by Simcoe, they were to form part of the eventual residence for the lieutenant-governor, but in the meantime were designed to accommodate the legislature and the courts, and to provide a centre for religious services.

Shortly after Russell wrote his letter to Simcoe, William Jarvis visited York and noted that the new government buildings were rapidly taking shape and that Thomas Ridout was planning to open his new registry office for the County of York in January. In the face of these developments, he decided to speed up his own arrangements for the removal of his family and office to York. The site he chose for his new house contained two lots which were located at the southeast corner of Caroline and Duke streets—today's Sherbourne and Adelaide streets—which placed him in the centre of Simcoe's little town, comfortably distant from both the mouth of the Don River, which in the summer turned into a mosquito-infested marsh, and from Toronto Bay, which in the winter became ice-choked. He was, however, still within convenient walking distance of the new government buildings that lay to the southeast.

Peter Russell was quite correct in telling Simcoe in December 1797 that the secretary hadn't made the smallest effort to remove his office from Newark. It wasn't until February 1798 that Jarvis acquired the first of his two lots, Lot 12 at the corner of Caroline and Duke Streets, from John Coons, a former sergeant in Butler's Rangers. One of the earliest settlers in the district, Coons had a farm about six miles up the Don River to which Mrs. Simcoe had rowed one day and noted that it was under a pine-covered hill. His Lot 12 measured 132 feet on Caroline Street and sixty-six feet on Duke Street, and it contained one-fifth of an acre.

A few days later, on February 22, Jarvis wrote to the surveyor-general to ask for his permission to acquire the second lot he needed, Lot 11, from a Samuel Backhouse, and he requested that Backhouse be granted in exchange a comparable lot elsewhere in the town. Lot 11, lying to the east, was the same size as Lot 12, and its northerly boundary of sixty-six feet also fronted on Duke Street. As Jarvis pointed out, "one fifth of an acre is very little indeed to build upon [and] also very dangerous in a *wooden town*." Jarvis was granted permission to acquire the extra lot and thereby increase his holding to two-fifths of an acre. Later, he extended his property farther east along Duke Street by acquiring the adjoining Lot 10, which also comprised one-fifth of an acre. And he rounded out his holdings by acquiring a property across the road from his house almost an acre in size, known as Lot 3, that lay at the northeast corner of Caroline and Duke streets.[4]

The first evidence that Jarvis's new house was finally under way appears in a letter written to him from York by his brother-in-law, William B. Peters, on April 25, 1798. For Jarvis, again it was bad news:

> Your House is at a stand for want of materials, the Kitchen is covered, but nothing more, there are no boards to be had; you will have to send over bricks and lime from the other side for the Chimneys, as there was none of the former made here before July, and the latter at all events cannot be procured here. I can get men to cut the Pickets for 12/ the hundred. It will be best to get a number ready cut as they will come in play one way or another—the sooner you come over the better.[5]

It is generally accepted that William Smith, an English builder and contractor who had helped Governor Simcoe design *Castle Frank*, the Simcoe's summer home on the heights west of the Don River, was the builder of Jarvis's Caroline Street house. The dwelling was placed close to the street line, and had its main entrance on Caroline Street. It was of squared-log construction covered with clapboard and contained two floors and an attic. It had a plastered interior, and is said to have measured thirty by forty-one feet.

In his *Landmarks of Toronto*, John Ross Robertson provides a useful description of the Jarvis house as it was related to him long after the place had been demolished around 1848. The description, which mentions numerous outbuildings, almost certainly refers to a later period than the building year of 1798 since the secretary took nearly ten years to develop his property fully. Robertson wrote:

> It was built directly on the street lines, and the main entrance was through the Sherbourne street—then called Caroline street—door, over which there was an attempt at ornamentation. Quite a long extension ran back along Duke street, and there was an entrance to the house from that street.

This building was the home of Secretary William Jarvis on Caroline Street from 1798 until his death in 1817. The small addition to the right was made after his death, and the entire structure, which occupied the southeast corner of today's Sherbourne and Adelaide streets, was demolished around 1848.—John Ross Robertson, Landmarks of Toronto

Farther along was a fence with a high peaked gate opening from Duke street into the lot where were built capacious barns, outhouses and a root house for the Secretary, who brought with him from Niagara a number of horses, cows, sheep and pigs. About the house were planted fruit trees, among which were many pear trees, for the pear seems to have been an especial favourite with the early settlers. At the rear of the house was a roomy verandah. The building was painted white. At the time of its erection this house was probably the largest building in the town of York. The large room at the corner on the ground floor was converted into an office, the living rooms of the family being at its rear and upstairs. Up stairs above the Secretary's office was the large drawing room where balls and parties were frequently held. It was reached by a handsome flight of winding stairs from the main hall.

In anticipation of his move across the lake, Jarvis offered for sale in the *Upper Canada Gazette* of February 27, 1798, "the dwelling house & Lot containing one acre in the town of Newark, now occupied by the subscriber." The same advertisement offered five horses for sale, "the proprietor having no further use for them." The dwelling house referred to could only have been the original house that had been converted into an office, since on September 5, 1798, Jarvis also terminated the lease to Alexander McDonell's house which he had rented immediately after the fire in December 1796. A later letter to Jarvis from McDonell's office in Newark requesting payment of the rent refers clearly to the sheriff's house as having been "in your possession . . . to the 5th September, 1798."[6] Finally, commencing in May, the secretary's financial papers reveal that he had a carpenter busy crating up his furniture in preparation for the move to York. Included in the work were "two walnut boxes for Mrs. Jarvis dress feathers."

When William and Hannah sailed from the Niagara River in September 1798, they left Newark with poignant regret. Newark had been their home for six years, and after losing their first son there, they had seen their family grow to five sturdy children. (William Munson, described by his father as "the finest boy ever born," had arrived in 1793, and Hannah Owen in 1797.) True, they had suffered myriad difficulties and disappointments, but on the whole these had been typical of most pioneer families and had been largely offset by consolations. William Jarvis, for example, often liked to recall the gala occasion, just two days after Christmas in 1792, when he had been installed as the first grand master of Free Masons in Upper Canada. The ceremony had included a procession with festive music, a stirring sermon by the grand chaplain, the Reverend Robert Addison of Newark, and to cap it all, a hearty, fraternal dinner. Hannah had been the centre of attention one evening early in 1793 when she was called upon by Mrs. Robert Hamilton of Queenston to open a ball in Mrs. Simcoe's absence. While her choice of a stately minuet had been unfortunate, no one in the room choosing to follow her, Hannah's embarrassment had been relieved when the assembly broke spontaneously into a country dance. And in 1794, when tension had arisen with the United States, William had been elated when Simcoe appointed him a deputy lieutenant of the County of York and named him commander of the militia. But now, as they faced the task of settling themselves anew in a pioneer community, this time with the added concern of their children's adjustment, their enthusiasm was at low ebb. For William especially the inquiry into the affairs of his office the previous summer had dashed the high hopes he had once held for his success.

The recommendations of Russell's committee resulted in tighter restraints being imposed upon the operations of the secretary's office. Henceforth, he was to be under the critical surveillance of President and Receiver-General Russell who had now had his worst suspicions confirmed when Jarvis had been unable to account for a large deficiency in the monies that had flowed into his hands through the collection of land grant fees.

Lieutenant Allan MacNab, the father of the later Sir Allan Napier MacNab of *Dundurn*, was employed by William Jarvis around the time of Jarvis's arrival in York, and remained with him until the end of the War of 1812. He later provided a striking picture of the difficulties that beset the secretary in the period following Russell's enquiry. Marion MacRae, in *MacNab of Dundurn*, describes how Lieutenant MacNab, who had been Simcoe's aide-de-camp, was on the point of following Simcoe to a temporary command he had accepted in San Domingo shortly after returning to England. MacNab left Newark, but upon reaching Halifax was informed by Colonel Littlehales on behalf of Simcoe that the "General was obliged to leave the Island suddenly in a dangerous state of health." MacNab's position was critical after he had dragged his young wife and children to Halifax in expectation of obtaining an attractive appointment abroad. Now, with only a modest position available to him in Nova Scotia, he seemed to have no alternative but to respond to Jarvis's brighter promises for his future and return to York. This is what he found:

> Having the offer of a place that would enable me to support my family, I concluded to remain there, but the repeated solicitations of Mr. Secretary Jarvis and the flattering promises he made me of a Permanent Situation by taking charge of his office I could not, in justice to my family, refuse. Relying on those promises and after having spent my last shilling in getting here [York] and at a very late season of the year, my Situation cannot easily be conceived to find all the Secretary's property, real and personal, seized by the Sheriff to cover a large sum of Government money that ex officio fell at different times into his hands that he could not account for and the perquisites of his office, all that he had in the world to

depend upon for carrying on the business of his office, was stopped in the Receiver-General's hands for upwards of five years.[7]

That Jarvis assumed responsibility for housing the MacNab family upon their arrival in York is evident from entries in his journal that record the payment of $100 per annum in rent to William Willcocks "for the House Mrs. NcNabb (*sic*) lives in," commencing October 13, 1798. This arrangement was continued at least throughout the year 1800. Willcocks, a colourful figure in York at that time, was briefly in business as a merchant. Earlier, in June 1798, William Jarvis had purchased from him "screws, lead, brass knobs, etc.," with a value of £57.7.3, for use in the construction of his Caroline Street houses.[8]

Lieutenant MacNab's assessment of the discouraging state of affairs then prevailing in York was confirmed by Jarvis himself when he wrote to Dr. Peters in January, 1799: "I do a great deal of business in my office," he admitted, "but to very little account. I am in reality a man of property without being able to command scarcely a most trifling sum." He added that he never had less than three and most of the time four persons employed in his office, all of whose salaries had to be met from his own income. And in his household, adding to his financial woes, he was also employing four black servants: "I have two negro men and two negro women their wives;" he reported, "the men are good, one of the women is tolerable and the other a devil was brought up in the family of old Mrs. Harrison in Boston."[9]

In the same letter, he referred to his new place on Caroline Street as "a tolerable house" with "house-room in abundance," and he also mentioned that he had a one-hundred-acre lot adjoining the town on which he was developing a small farm. It was located on his Park Lot 6 through which today's Jarvis Street was later to be laid out. The task of clearing the virgin land dragged on for years, however. Even in September 1803, when Jarvis attributed a value to the Crown-granted property of £300, he noted that he had so far improved only twenty acres. While the farm was by no means remote from his Caroline Street house (today the walk from Sherbourne and Adelaide streets to Jarvis and Queen streets would consume less than fifteen minutes), the security of the property, as crops matured, was a constant problem. For example, in April 1800, Jarvis ordered eighty apple trees from Queenston at a cost of £12. A month later, before he had even had a chance to plant them, the trees were stolen from the farm. Once again he turned to the *Upper Canada Gazette* and in an indignant notice offered a reward for information leading to the conviction of the miscreants who had "lately entered the improved grounds of the subscriber, and taken therefrom a quantity of fruit trees belonging to him."

The fears Jarvis had nurtured at Newark that his enemies were conspiring to dislodge him from office didn't diminish when he reached York; "I have enemies in all quarters," he remarked to Dr. Peters early in 1799. While he was still in Newark, after commenting upon the powerful interests that were attempting to unseat him, he had ended with a fine, bravura passage, "to die game, I am determined at all events."

It was, perhaps, in such a spirit of defiance that he decided to offer himself as a candidate for Durham, Simcoe and the East Riding of York in the first election held in the town of York for the provincial Parliament. His election address was published in a broadside dated July 14, 1800, which was displayed throughout the town, and it also appeared a few days later in the *Upper Canada Gazette*. His message lacked neither originality nor candour. In effect, making a political virtue out of inactivity, he explained that he had abstained from door-to-door canvassing out of concern for the feelings of his constituents, nor had he vigorously pressed his claims to their support, preferring instead to allow the constitutional process to run its serene and certain course. In part, this is what he said:

> ... I think it a duty which I owe to my Fellow-subjects to state explicitly, that it is now, as it ever has been, fully my Intention to Offer Myself a Candidate at the approaching Election; it is true I have not solicited the Suffrages of my Fellow-subjects *from door to door*, such conduct, I am confident, you would think ill-became a Man who, ardently wishes, shortly to be in the Character of your Representative; I have not been urgent in the pursuit of so distinguished a preference, deeming it the most Constitutional way for you to exercise your own Discretion and Judgement in the Choice of a Person to represent you in the next Provincial Parliament.[10]

The election turned out to be anything but serene, and the secretary's low-profile campaign, predictably, ended in failure. Voting started on July 24, and the polls closed that day at 2 P.M. They reopened the next day at 10 A.M., and an early count showed the standings to be: Judge Henry Allcock, 30; Samuel Heron, 30; John Small, 21; William Jarvis, 17. As the day developed, as one observer put it, "Mr. Jarvis appeared discouraged, and told some of his friends that they were at liberty to vote for Mr. Alcock." Later, a riot broke out, and Magistrate William Willcocks who was actively supporting Judge Allcock, who then held a majority, read the Riot Act forcing the remaining voters to disperse. The faction supporting Allcock declared him the winner. As a result of a later petition, however, Judge Allcock was disqualified, and the proceedings were pronounced void. In a re-run of the election, Jarvis didn't stand again, and Angus McDonell was elected with a comfortable majority over John Small. McDonell was a brother of Sheriff Alexander McDonell, who had rented Jarvis his Newark house after the fire. Angus, who later served as treasurer of the Law Society of Upper Canada, was among those drowned in 1804 when the vessel *Speedy* was lost in a storm on Lake Ontario. His friend Robert Isaac Dey Gray, the solicitor-general, died with him.

The following February 1801, still perhaps reflecting upon the defiant philosophy he had evolved for himself at Newark, Jarvis one day roused the townsmen of York from their winter somnolence and led a fox hunt on the frozen surface of the Toronto Bay. By now, the secretary must have become a great favourite of the *Upper Canada Gazette*, not only as a faithful subscriber, but also as a determined and dependable advertiser; as a consequence, the paper gave him generous coverage:

HOICKS! HOICKS! HOICKS!

On Thursday last, William Jarvis, Esq; entertained the inhabitants of this town with a diversion new in itself to many; and in some of its circumstances to all. About noon he caused a fox of full growth to be unbagged, near the center of the fine sheet of ice which now covers the Bay, and when at a suitable distance, turned loose the hounds upon it.— As previous notice had been circulated, the chace (*sic*) was followed by a number of gentlemen on horseback, and a concourse of the beau monde of both sexes in carioles and sleighs.—Poor Reynard was probably the first of his species cavalcaded in this manner to his fate.—A light coat of snow covered the surface of the shining plain, and contributed much to steadiness in driving and confidence in riding. After the death of the unfortunate poulterer, his remains served as a dragg, to prolong for several hours the sport. . . .

Just as the Honourable Peter Russell, scanning the pages of the *Upper Canada Gazette* in December 1796, must have followed with scepticism and amusement the secretary's attempts to recover his stolen animal skins, so the new lieutenant-governor of Upper Canada, the Honourable Peter Hunter, though absent from the province in Quebec, must have pondered critically the report of his secretary's winter diversion. He could only have concluded grimly that Jarvis was again neglecting his office and that matters would have to be set right, once and for all, upon his return to York in the spring.

Governor Hunter, a Scottish professional soldier and fifty-three-year-old bachelor, had first arrived in York for a brief ceremonial visit in August 1799. In addition to his appointment as lieutenant-governor of Upper Canada, he had also been named commander-in-chief of all military forces stationed in British North America. In that capacity, he had to spend considerable time in Quebec, where the British forces were largely concentrated. For this reason, he maintained a private bateau in Kingston which was elaborately equipped for his comfort. He regarded his military role in Canada as paramount and left much of the civil administration of Upper Canada to his officials. When he was in residence in York, he occupied a one-storey house that was built especially for him on the site of the present Fort York. A stern disciplinarian, he demanded from the outset a high standard of efficiency in the operation of all government offices. In such an atmosphere, it was inevitable that the provincial secretary's office would fall under his criticism. Hunter became particularly concerned with the delay in issuing land patents, and as an observer of the period has put it, William Jarvis "constantly annoyed him by his habitual procrastination and neglect of duty and was repeatedly rebuked and warned of impending dismissal."[11]

In one instance, illustrative of Hunter's reaction to Jarvis's "habitual procrastination," a number of Quakers, led by Timothy Rogers and Jacob Lund, who had settled in the area of today's Newmarket, complained to Governor Hunter of the long delay they had experienced in trying to obtain their land patents. The governor at once ordered the surveyor-general, the clerk of the executive council, the clerk of the Crown, and William Jarvis, secretary and registrar, to assemble in his office, together with the disgruntled Quakers, at noon the next day.

The governor opened the meeting by stating to his officials, "These gentlemen complain that they cannot get their patents." After an icy interrogation, Hunter soon discovered that the order for the patents had been outstanding for over a year. The blame was finally perceived to lie with the hapless secretary, who, in an attempt to excuse himself, pleaded that the pressure of business in his office had prevented him from completing the work. "Sir!" the governor stormed, "if they are not forthcoming, every one of them, and placed in the hands of these gentlemen here in my presence at noon on Thursday next [it was now Tuesday], by George!, I'll un-Jarvis* you!"

By the fall of 1801, two years after the governor had first appeared in York, William Jarvis's morale had crumbled to its lowest point since he had arrived in Canada. "Self-preservation," he exclaimed in a letter written in November of that year, "has been the great struggle with me for more than two years last past, but the struggle seems at length to be at an end." Hannah Jarvis, in an accompanying letter, grimly set forth the details of the painful relationship that had now developed between the governor and her husband, and its destructive effect upon him:

[Jarvis] is ordered by the Gov. P. H. to have in readiness as many grants as possible for his signature on his arrival as he winters in Lower Canada, to accomplish which he has ordered the Surveyor-General, and Council Officer and his own Clerk to make out 48 each by the winter during his absence, and three soldiers to write in the Secretary's office. The Secretary has to find fuel for the office, clerks are all at the Secretary's expense also, and for fear that he should gain a sixpence by purchasing stationery at a cheaper rate he has confined him to Lower Canada, where everything is inferior and dearer by one-third than in New York, and next ordered the Receiver-General to furnish the Secretary with parchment, wax, etc., to be stopped out of the profit arising from the grants.

He ordered him to furnish immediately the office with 3,000 sheets of parchment, wax, etc., and to make prompt payment for the same or he would suspend him in the failing thereof within such a time. The Secretary endeavoured to remonstrate with him the impossibility of complying with the order, by saying the office was greatly in his debt, to which in a great passion he politely but indirectly, for he did not think proper to do it directly, dammed him and told him he did not inquire about the office, that he must do as he was bid, or take the consequences. He lived two miles from the town where the Secretary has been obliged to go, from two to four times a day, in the heat of the most sultry weather we had during the Summer, when a written answer would have answered every purpose. Up from four in the morning to ten at night and frequently called out of his bed for some trifling thing or other. The

---

* The Governor's pun, not immediately intelligible to the modern ear, was a play on the word *jarvey*, which was derived from the personal name Jarvis, and signified the driver of a hackney coach. Hunter was simply threatening to *unseat* Jarvis.

Secretary has come home crying like a child from the treatment he met with and dare not open his lips, those who saw the manner he was treated advised him to command himself and be silent; as words were what was sought for, that some hold might be had against him.[12]

In the face of the governor's merciless demands and criticism, it was to the secretary's credit that he clung tenaciously to his office and, by continuing to involve himself in the life of the town, managed to preserve not only his sanity, but his public credibility as well. At the time he was engaged in his great struggle for self-preservation, as he had called it, he sat on a committee, with William Allan and James Playter, which was given responsibility for supervising the building of an improved road to connect the town with Yonge Street; he was also active as a magistrate, and when the lieutenant-governor presented York with a fire engine, he was among the subscribers who underwrote the cost of constructing a building to house it.

And, in 1805, desiring a convenient school in his neighbourhood, he donated for a year the use of the house he had built on Lot 3, on the north side of Duke Street, just across the road from his own place. Under the arrangement, in which he joined forces with his neighbour Thomas Ridout, Allan MacNab, James Macaulay and William Chewett, a schoolmaster was employed to instruct their children, and it was stipulated that the number of pupils would not exceed twenty-five. The schoolmaster, Alexander William Carson, agreed to provide instruction for one year, commencing May 1, in the "art" of spelling, reading, writing and arithmetic. He was required to attend his school five and a half days a week, from eight to twelve in the morning, and from two to five in the afternoon. For his efforts, he was paid £3.15.0 monthly with free board and lodging, "Liquors excepted."[13] Jarvis, naturally, was excused payment of his children's fees since he was providing free use of the building that housed the schoolmaster and his pupils.

Later in 1805, York was stunned when it received word of Governor Hunter's sudden death in Quebec, on August 21. He was preparing to return to Upper Canada when he suffered an attack of gout in his stomach, and died a few days later at the age of fifty-nine.

Shortly after the news reached York, as Jarvis was preparing to retire one night, he heard a commotion in the dirt road that lay beside his house. As a magistrate sworn to uphold the King's peace, he felt it his duty to investigate. Strapping on a heavy sword, he strode from the house into the darkness and immediately found himself surrounded by a noisy, belligerent group of carousers who were doubtless returning from a nearby tavern. Jarvis was a big man and in the fracas that followed he probably owed his life as much to his commanding physical stature as to the fact that he was better armed than his assailants. The outcome of the brawl was vividly described by Hannah Jarvis in a letter she wrote to her father a few days later:

> Mr. Jarvis is sick, having gone out to suppress a Mob, four men fell upon him and cut his head very bad—and bruised him so much that he is not able to lift his hand to his head or open his left eye—it happened at midnight—he took his Broad sword with him which saved his life—he cut one man's hand off a little below the Fingers, saving the fore Finger & thumb, disarmed another, the others ran away—but have since been taken & thrown into Gaol one who endeavoured to escape is shackled with 50 lb of Iron.[14]

Hannah Jarvis must have regretted that Governor Hunter's death had occurred just before William had won distinction for himself in the eyes of York as a result of his heroics that bizarre September night. Undoubtedly, the governor would have been impressed.

CHAPTER FOUR

The Residue of Peace

The school William Jarvis helped to organize lasted only a year. Like others in York at the time, it was replaced by the Home District Grammar School, which opened under government auspices on June 1, 1807. The rector of York, the Reverend George Okill Stuart, was appointed headmaster, and the first classes were held in his house at the corner of King and George streets. Further west along King Street, at Church Street, the rector a few months before had presided at the dedication of the new St. James' Church. After surmounting delays that would have tested the mettle of Job, the church, which had been built in a clearing in the woods, had finally opened its doors just in time for the Easter services. As York's first formal place of worship, St. James' was the object of considerable comment. Anne Powell, the wife of Judge William Dummer Powell and a severe arbiter of the town's social life, gave the edifice, especially her accommodation in it, an encouraging nod of approval: "We are got into our new Church," she informed her brother following the Easter Sunday service, "it is a good building, & we have decidedly the best Pew in it."

The first student recorded on the rolls of the new school was John Ridout, aged eight, who ten years later was to lose his life in a controversial duel with his neighbour, Samuel Peters Jarvis. John was joined later in the month by his sister, Mary, aged ten. Two of William Jarvis's daughters were also enrolled in June, Hannah Owen, who was the same age as Mary Ridout, and Ann-Elizabeth, who had been born in 1801 in the Jarvis house on Caroline Street. During July, three more Jarvis children turned up, William Munson, Maria Lavinia, and Augusta. In fact, the only Jarvis child who wasn't enrolled in Mr. Stuart's school at its opening was Samuel Peters Jarvis. Now aged fifteen, he had instead been sent by his father to the grammar school in distant Cornwall that the Reverend John Strachan had opened in his parish church.

The Ridout children lived on the north side of Duke (Adelaide) Street, across the road from the Jarvis property, where their father, Thomas Ridout, had built a rambling, one-storey house shortly after he had obtained the land by Crown grant in 1798. His two-acre property lay immediately east of Jarvis's schoolhouse lot. To the south, looking down Princess Street, it afforded a clear view of the Toronto Bay. In later years, the Reverend Dr. Henry Scadding recalled the Ridout house as having been "a good specimen of the old type of early Upper Canadian family residence of a superior class; combining the qualities of snugness and comfort in the rigours of winter and the heats of summer."

Sam Jarvis was not the only neighbourhood boy in attendance at John Strachan's celebrated school that year: both George Ridout, aged sixteen, and Thomas Gibbs Ridout, aged fifteen, sons of Thomas Ridout, had also sailed down the St. Lawrence River to avail themselves of Strachan's demanding instruction. We may be sure that Sam, as their neighbour and friend, would have sometimes accompanied them on their long journey by bateaux to and from Cornwall.

In November 1807, Hannah Jarvis reported to her father, who was now in New York, "Samuel is down at Mr. Strachan's." She added proudly that "if report can be relied on he is likely to be a favourite with his master." Perhaps the report she had received came from the Ridouts; Thomas Gibbs Ridout, writing to his father earlier that fall, had commented, "Sam Jarvis learns his lessons well, and he and Stanton are almost always head of their class."[1]

The following year, however, Hannah's optimism must have been mildly shaken when word reached York that Sam had been involved with some of his school friends in a vicious fight with some local Indians. At the time of the incident, Colonel Stephen Jarvis, a cousin of William's, had stopped off at Cornwall on his way from New Brunswick to visit York. While he was there he decided to introduce himself to Sam and pay his respects to Mr. Strachan. In his *Reminiscences of a Loyalist* written many years later, the Colonel recalled a highlight of his visit:

> I forgot to mention that at Cornwall I met with Samuel Peters Jarvis, a son of my relation, Mr. Secretary Jarvis. He was then at school at Cornwall, and with some others had been engaged in a fray with some Indians. They had nearly killed one of them and the magistrates of Cornwall were making an examination of the matter when I passed through the town.[2]

While the cause of the battle and the result of the magistrates' examination are unknown, it is likely that Strachan succeeded in persuading the magistrates to leave the matter in his hands. It is ironic that Sam, who had been adopted by the Mississaugas and given the affectionate name of Nehkik, should have allowed himself to be drawn into a bitter brawl with a group of neighbouring Indians, doubtless youths like himself, and have it end in so bloody a dénouement. Characteristically, the Indians never sought a quarrel with the early settlers, unless provoked. Mrs. Simcoe attested to this fact after she had closely observed a large band of Mississaugas in Kingston when she was staying there in 1792: "They never quarrel with White People," she asserted, "unless insulted by them." It is difficult to avoid the suspicion that the Cornwall incident was more likely provoked by Strachan's hot-headed students than it was by the Indians who stood to gain nothing from such an encounter.

Later in 1808, on Boxing Day, William Jarvis sat down morosely in his office to consider his financial position. He had been under pressure for over a year from Quetton St. George, one of the town's leading merchants, to settle his account. Indeed, the previous January his credit had been cut off. "It would be unjust in me," William had written at that time, "to ask a farther credit at your store, more especially since you have stopped it at this critical moment when every day, I have reason to expect to have it in my power to give ample satisfaction to your demands."[3] While St. George restored his credit a short time later, he still kept the secretary under constant pressure, even offering to accept some of his undeveloped real estate in payment of his account. There is an element of pathos in Jarvis's reaction to that particular proposal. In a letter written in April, 1808, he replied:

> When you made your proposals to me the other day, I thought at that time to have been enabled to give you an answer before this time; but as I have not as yet received an answer myself cannot at present give you that kind of answer that I could wish—However I am for the present very averse to convey what wild lands I have left, or even to give a Bond in Judgments and I am equally averse to your not being perfectly received in every shilling that I am indebted to you.[4]

And the following month, threatened now with legal action, Jarvis wrote:

> In answer I have to observe that at present I have it not in my power to make you a proposal that I think will be not only satisfactory to you but

highly gratifying to my own feelings. If it is your ultimate determination
to put my note and account into the hands of an attorney either the Atty
General or the Solr General will be equally satisfactory to me. I am
persuaded that you have no wish to injure me whatever. At the same time
I think I can say as an honest man that you run no risque in deferring such
a measure for a short time.[5]

It was, therefore, against the background of his indebtedness to St.
George, whose big, bustling store on King Street was crucial to the
needs of Jarvis and his family, that the secretary had paused to assess
his current position. As a government official, he received a salary of
£300 a year. That income, of course, was augmented by his propor-
tionate share of the fees his office collected in issuing Crown grants to
new settlers. But that was an irregular and unpredictable source of
revenue which he consistently overestimated and overspent. As a
result, to the end of his life, Jarvis lived continuously beyond his
means.

In a signed statement, Jarvis listed his debts as amounting to £1,786, of
which St. George's unpaid account loomed largest at £800. The last
item on the list, "In arrears to office clerks—£150," must have caused
him and his clerks particular distress since he had been unable to settle
even those small claims in time for Christmas.[6]

In 1803, Jarvis had calculated the total value of his real and personal
property, including his wild lands, as being £2,399.4.0. By 1808, as a
result of capital improvements to his house and farm, and perhaps
some modest appreciation in value, that figure had probably increased
to £3,000. In order to eliminate his indebtedness he would have had to
sell everything he had so far accumulated in Upper Canada except his
Caroline Street house and its furnishings.

Notwithstanding his chronic financial embarrassments, by 1812
William Jarvis had good reason to be more satisfied with his life in
York than at any time since his arrival there fourteen years before. He
had survived his tormentors, those people who had sought to erode the
perquisites of his office, and had threatened his tenure as well. It is said
that whenever Talleyrand met with a temporary set-back in his plans,
counselling patience he would observe gravely, "Let time do its work."
For Jarvis, time had now done its work. John White, the attorney-
general who had been awarded part of Jarvis's fees, had been killed in a
duel with John Small. Peter Russell, who as president of the Executive
Council had once directed a damaging inquiry into Jarvis's office, had
died at *Russell Abbey*. And after the demise of Governor Hunter, who

was Jarvis's most relentless tormentor, his successors, Alexander Grant and Francis Gore, had mercifully refrained from meddling in the affairs of Jarvis's office.

On the domestic side, William and Hannah had been delighted when in August 1811 at St. James' Church the Reverend George Okill Stuart had officiated at the marriage of their eldest daughter, Maria Lavinia, to George Hamilton of Queenston. He was a son of the influential Queenston merchant, the Honourable Robert Hamilton, and the city of Hamilton, Ontario, was later to be named for him. When Hannah informed her father of her daughter's marriage, she commented with evident relief that George was "a very good young man, and in cosy circumstances—she has everything necessary to make her happy."

All in all, as the storm clouds of the War of 1812 were building in the southern sky, Jarvis should have been content with his lot in life. But he wasn't. As luck (a condition with which he was only faintly familiar) would have it, he became seriously ill in February with a crippling attack of gout. With her usual directness, Hannah described his plight in a letter to her father, "Mr. Jarvis is again attacked with the gout, in the head, stomach, feet, hands—for ten day (sic) he has not been able to move himself in bed without help."

As Jarvis lay incapacitated in his house on Caroline Street, the life of the town swirled around him. Major-General Sir Isaac Brock, who had been appointed provisional lieutenant-governor the previous autumn, was giving urgent attention to strengthening the defences of the province for a war that now seemed inevitable. To Hannah Jarvis, General Brock was a distinct improvement over his predecessor, Francis Gore. She thought Brock appeared "as if he had a Mind of his own."

Although the Americans did not declare war against Great Britain until June 18, 1812, the militia of York had been called out in May, and active training had begun on a drill-field near the site of the present Fort York. Amidst the beat of drums and the rattle of muskets, the ladies of York met regularly to work on a flag they were making for the 3rd Regiment of York Militia. (The flag survives today in the archives of St. James' Cathedral, Toronto.) Dr. John Strachan, who had arrived from Cornwall with his wife and family late in June to assume the rectorship of York and the chaplaincy of the garrison, provided a succinct motto for their colours, "Deeds Speak." While the ladies were plying their needles, it became fashionable for the young bloods of the town to drop in for a few minutes to observe the progress of the work, especially after General Brock had created a stir one day by visiting the ladies unexpectedly. Among the regular visitors were D'Arcy Boulton, Jr., and his brother Henry, Samuel Peters Jarvis, and John Beverley Robinson, who entertained the ladies by reading aloud from an epic work.

Sam Jarvis was now in his twentieth year, his Cornwall school days behind him. Impatient for the excitement of military life, he was awaiting his lieutenant's commission and an early posting to the militia.

Meanwhile, Sam's neighbour John Ridout, who was only thirteen, had already enlisted in the navy and was serving as a midshipman on the *Royal George* as it patrolled the Canadian shores of Lake Ontario. On June 25, 1812, George Ridout wrote to his brother Thomas Gibbs Ridout who was in Quebec and described their young brother's service:

> I know not whether Father has told you that John is a Midshipman on Board the Royal George on this lake with pay altogether equal to about 150. dollars for the first year—with an increase of pay every succeeding year—John is quite contented & indeed delighted with it—he dresses in uniform and is quite snugly rigged off. He entered on Board the 24th. of May—draws provisions &ca among other things nearly a Barrel of Rum a year which he will sell as York is to be head Quarters for the Navy. John will remain with us next Winter, when he will avail himself of the opportunity to go to Mr Strachan's school, who is hourly expected here as the wind is fair. . . .

In a hurried post scriptum written two days later, Ridout added,

> 27. June
> Since I wrote an Express has come here announcing to us that *War is declared*—every one is on motion Genl. Brock went off to Niagara last night dispatches to the Indians who are all in readiness—I do not know what we will do with our large family, the Militia is ordered out—I must now go. Adieu G. R.[7]

Six months later, when Thomas Gibbs Ridout had returned to York, he had a wholly unexpected opportunity to observe at first hand John's aplomb under fire when the *Royal George* actually engaged some American vessels:

> The excellent musket your Father presented me with I take the greatest

57

care of. It has not seen any actual service further than an affair between the Royal George & American fleet, in which I happened to be present by going on board to see my brother John who is a midshipman & behaved himself very well on that day. I continued cruizing on the Lake 10 days, when we returned to Port.[8]

Sam Jarvis obtained his commission on June 30 in Captain Stephen Heward's Flank Company in the 3rd Regiment of York Militia. Shortly later, however, he was transferred to a rifle company under the command of Captain Peter Robinson that was attached to the North York Militia. Robinson was the older brother of Sam's friend, John Beverley Robinson. After the American General William Hull had crossed the Detroit River and invaded Upper Canada from Fort Detroit in July, the North York unit was made part of the whirlwind expedition that General Brock organized and led against Hull's advancing army.

It had always been Brock's view that in the event of war with the United States, the co-operation of the Indians would be critical to the defence of Canada. To assure himself of their support, he recognized the need for early and decisive victories against the Americans, in short campaigns with limited objectives. To this end, at the outbreak of the war, he had immediately ordered the officer commanding a small British post near the American station at Michilimackinac to capture that position. The American commander, unaware that hostilities had begun, was taken by surprise. Learning that the largest element in the British attacking force consisted of several bands of Indians, he quickly surrendered. General Hull, who also had a paranoid fear of the British Indians, later related, "after the surrender of Michilimackinac, almost every tribe and nation of Indians . . . joined in open hostility, under the British standard against the Army I commanded. . . . The surrender of Michilimackinac opened the northern hive of Indians, and they were swarming down in every direction."[9]

Hull's fear of the Indians, together with the American naval weakness on Lake Erie, had enabled Brock to transport his force with impunity and had led Hull to withdraw hurriedly to his fortifications at Detroit. His retreat was completed on August 11. Four days later, at sundown, Brock began a deafening cannonade of the American positions from the Canadian side of the river. His force, half the size of the American defenders, consisted of 300 regulars, 400 militiamen and 600 Indians under the Shawnee chief Tecumseh. His cannonade over, Brock next despatched a formal demand to General Hull for the surrender of the fort, warning him that in the event of an assault he might find it difficult to control Tecumseh's implacable "hive of Indians." The following day the British landed at dawn on the American shore, but before they could reach the fort, Hull capitulated. Brock's ultimatum, playing upon the American general's known dread of the Indians, had proved a master-stroke. As a result of Hull's surrender, the British reaped a rich harvest of war equipment: for the next few days, Captain Peter Robinson and Lieutenant Sam Jarvis were busy issuing new American muskets to their militiamen.

Their work at Detroit finished, Brock led his expedition back to the Niagara frontier where he was certain the next American attack would be launched. He deployed 1,500 soldiers, together with about 250 Indians, along the Niagara River, and established his own head-quarters at Fort George, close to Newark, where he expected the first American blow would fall. In the early hours of October 13, however, a large force under General Van Rensselaer swarmed ashore farther up the river, near the village of Queenston, and soon established a bridgehead after driving back a British detachment of 350 men. The British were supported by guns at Vrooman's Point below Queenston as well as by a battery in position high on the Niagara escarpment. The sound of the heavy firing upstream could be heard clearly at Fort George. In fact, it was the sound of the guns that awakened Brock. Ordering all available troops to follow him, he galloped out of the fort and up the winding river road to Queenston, where he quickly rallied and reorganized his small band of defenders. His first concern was to recapture the battery on the high ground the Americans had just overrun. Placing himself at the head of a few regulars and militiamen and pointing the way with his sword, he started up the side of the escarpment. As he struggled to maintain his footing in the wet grass, his elaborate uniform made him an obvious target for an American marksman concealed in the bushes above. Minutes later he fell mortally wounded, a bullet near his heart.

Major-General Roger Sheaffe, who succeeded Brock, gathered the balance of the British forces together as they converged on Queenston from their outposts. They then made their way up the heights from the west and attacked the Americans from a woods on top of the escarpment. Their ammunition low, their losses heavy, and no reinforcements in sight, the Americans' resistance collapsed. After their surrender, the British counted 958 prisoners, among them a brigadier and five lieutenant-colonels—and once again, the Canadian militia benefited from the arsenal of American arms that fell into its hands.

For Lieutenant Sam Jarvis, the memorable victory at Queenston Heights was the highlight of his service during the War of 1812. While he had been present at the capture of Fort Detroit, his role there had been largely that of a spectator, and though he was to take part later in successful engagements at Stoney Creek and Lundy's Lane, they were never to hold for him the poignant memories of Queenston Heights. Though only twenty years of age at the time, he had been given the responsibility of carrying General Brock's battle plan to General Sheaffe. At the combined funeral for Brock and his provincial aide Lieutenant-Colonel John Macdonell, who had fallen shortly after Brock, Sam and Lieutenant George Ridout were among Macdonell's pallbearers. Both Brock and Macdonell were buried in an earthwork battery at Fort George, and throughout the impressive funeral, as a mark of respect for the British commander, the Americans across the Niagara River maintained a steady fire from their minute guns.

In April 1813, the Americans retaliated by invading York. On the 27th of that month, a force of 1,700 men, transported across Lake Ontario in fourteen ships, landed west of the present Exhibition grounds. Pushing back a small body of British defenders, they moved quickly towards the town. En route, as they were fighting their way through the garrison area, the defenders blew up the grand magazine; the resulting losses to the Americans were severe and included General Zebulon Pike, who died a few days later on a ship in the bay. The magnet that had drawn the Americans to York was the frigate, the *Sir Isaac Brock*, which was being rushed to completion on its stocks at the corner of modern-day Bay and Front streets. The invaders realized that once it was launched and joined the fleet at Kingston, naval supremacy would pass decisively to the British. While the Americans had hoped to capture the frigate intact, their main objective was achieved when General Sheaffe set fire to York's proud ship as he withdrew his outnumbered British regulars to Kingston. By the time the Americans reached the stocks, only a wall of smoke and flame remained.

During the four-day occupation, the barracks and government buildings were also destroyed. Only the vigorous intervention of Dr. John Strachan saved York from catastrophe. Under the terms he extracted from the American commanders, General Henry Dearborn and Commodore Isaac Chauncey, all government stores were surrendered, but the security of private property was guaranteed, and the militia was paroled and allowed to remain in York.

On Caroline Street, the Jarvis family was by no means unaffected by the American assault and occupation of the capital. While William

60

Jarvis, enfeebled by recurring attacks of gout, could do little more than observe events from his house, his youngest son, William Munson, now aged nineteen, had taken his place in the militia just before the American landing. He had been critically ill with pleurisy the previous month, and his mother had despaired of his life. Jarvis's anxiety was intense, therefore, when he had heard the distant explosion of the magazine. From a second-storey window he had watched a black funnel of smoke as it hovered in the western sky above the *Sir Isaac Brock*. Soon after, to the east and much closer to his house, his despair had deepened when he observed another flame-streaked cloud rising from the blazing government buildings. Later that day, young William who had suffered a minor wound in the early hours of the attack, returned to Caroline Street for a further period of convalescence.

William Munson's patriotic exertions, however, were largely nullified by the treasonable conduct of his uncle, William B. Peters. Years earlier, Peters had followed his sister Hannah and William Jarvis to Upper Canada from England and had served as an ensign in the Queen's Rangers. After the regiment was disbanded in 1802, Peters qualified himself in York as a lawyer and became a protégé of William Jarvis. At the time of the American invasion Peters was thirty-nine, married, and had a small family. Always a shadowy figure in the life of the town, he was notoriously sympathetic to the Americans, and was seen to welcome their arrival openly and warmly. Worse, along with other malcontents in the town, he was suspected of having provided the Americans in advance with critically important information concerning the state of construction of the *Sir Isaac Brock*, the condition of the town's defences, and the disposition of its troops.

The Peters episode must have been painfully embarrassing to William and Hannah Jarvis, especially after General Sheaffe ordered Peters' arrest and imprisonment on July 13, 1813. Clearly, the order had not been enforced by the time the Americans staged another nuisance raid on York on July 31, because Peters was again seen unabashedly in the company of the Americans, actively assisting them in their mission. Colonel William Allan, commanding officer of the 3rd Regiment, York Militia, vividly described the second visit of the Americans and the help they received from local sympathizers like William B. Peters:

> It is not a New thing for me to tell you that not a Single transaction has
> been done by any individual but what was made known to [the

61

Americans]. They broke open my Store because they were informed it contained Flour belonging to Govt. they took everything that was in it broke open several Trunks and gave away all their Contents to any person who would take them they burnt a large Quantity of Hemp and other things took all my Flour away. This was owing to their being informed that I was in the Constant habit of using & sending information to our Army and Aiding the forwarding of troops &c altho I am returning for a day or two—I cannot remain wh any Safety—the Number of enemys & Spys are beyond all conception they are allowed to remain and have been all this season altho' well known—without a Military Establishment & Power & that severely exerted—there is no posability of living in Safety at all—They have destroyed all the Barracks Provisions Store Wood Yard— & Blockhouses on Gibralter Point—After they had embarked all their troops they land wh their Boats loaded wh Men to execute some further information they got.—There was several of the Inhabitants constantly wh them who are notoriously known to be as great Enemys as are in the County to wh a Mr. John Young Mercht. Mr. Stebbins a Tavern-keeper Mr. Gilbert Blacksmith *Mr. Peters a Lawyer who receives half Pay & a Pension besides*, a notorious man.[10]

Public feeling having turned bitterly against him, Peters disappeared from the province and made his way to the southern United States. He died there four years later.

Though the tide of war ebbed and flowed along the Niagara frontier during the remaining months of 1813 and throughout 1814, York was not directly threatened again. When word of peace finally reached the town in February 1815, the rejoicing of the inhabitants soon yielded to the realization that the capital's economy had been artificially stimulated by the war. The building of the *Sir Isaac Brock* and the abnormal demand for military supplies had transformed York into a thriving centre throughout the long Niagara campaign. Without these sustaining influences, business activity slowed, confidence waned, and the town fell into a depression.

For successful merchants like Joseph Cawthra and William Allan, who had laid the foundations of two of York's early fortunes during the war, the dark months of 1815 imposed little more than a temporary interruption on their business activities. For others, like William Jarvis, who depended largely for their existence on a steady flow of settlers taking up land, paying fees, building houses and roads, the economic slowdown was painful. In fact, in a move that was later to cause difficulty between him and Lieutenant Allan MacNab, Jarvis "coolly dismissed" MacNab from his office on the grounds that there was insufficient work to warrant keeping him. Even for the secretary, retrenchment was the order of the day.

During September 1815, Francis Gore returned to Upper Canada to resume his duties as lieutenant-governor after a four-year absence. He was welcomed enthusiastically by the inhabitants of York, who were probably grateful for the opportunity to stage a ceremony as a distraction from their gloomy concerns. Ignorant of the fact that Gore was about to disclose the calamitous news that Lord Bathurst, secretary of state for war and the colonies, had instructed him to remove the seat of government from York to Kingston, the delegation presented him with a rousing address. Gore must have winced when their spokesman ended on this rapturous note:

> We rejoice that the blessings of peace are to be dispensed by one who is so well acquainted with the wants and feelings of the colony, and we flatter ourselves that York, recovering from a state of war (during which she has been twice in the power of the enemy), will not only forget her disasters, but rise to greater prosperity under your Excellency's auspicious administration.[11]

The lieutenant-governor was acutely aware that York had recently been "twice in the power of the enemy" because that was precisely the reason the colonial secretary had given when he informed Gore of his decision to move the capital to Kingston: while York had been overrun twice by the Americans during the war, Kingston had never been threatened.

As soon as Francis Gore had exploded his bombshell, the Reverend Dr. John Strachan was predictably the first to fire off a letter denouncing the decision. Around the first of October he wrote to Sir George Murray who had served as a provisional governor in Upper Canada earlier in 1815. Murray immediately forwarded Strachan's well-argued letter to Lord Bathurst. Next, the officers of government prepared a memorial, or petition, which was addressed to Lord Bathurst and signed by twenty-three office-holders in York. Among them were Chief Justice Thomas Scott, Judge William Dummer Powell, who is believed to have drafted the petition, Attorney-General D'Arcy Boulton, Sr., Secretary and Registrar William Jarvis, Surveyor-General Thomas Ridout, and John Small, Clerk of the Executive Council.

Basically, the petition argued that residential property in Kingston was already costly and scarce as a result of its economy having been stimulated by the construction of a big, new dockyard, and an influx of government officials could only exacerbate an already critical housing shortage. Moreover, the men of York could expect little demand for their properties if the capital was moved to Kingston, and they would all be faced with ruinous losses.

Having had their say, the men of York could only sit back and await further word from England. The mood of the town as it faced the hard winter months of 1815-1816, was probably expressed better than anybody by Strachan in his letter to Sir George Murray: "After struggling through a war to which from the then defenceless state of the town they were particularly exposed," he had stated solemnly, "they are filled with despondency to find that peace instead of comfort puts the seal to their ruin."

CHAPTER FIVE

A Meeting at Elmsley's Farm

It was not until late in the spring of 1816 that the inhabitants of York received the momentous news that the decision to remove the seat of government to Kingston had been rescinded. Lord Bathurst, the colonial secretary, had finally relented and informed Francis Gore that "in view of the inconvenience and expense involved," his earlier instructions were now revoked. "Despatches have been received by His Excellency the Lieutenant Governor," the *Upper Canada Gazette* trumpeted on June 12, "notifying His Royal Highness the Prince Regent's pleasure that the Seat of Government should be permanently established at this place."

As the good news circulated that day, the town awoke slowly as if from a deep and dreamless sleep. The pace of life then quickened. Groups of people, who the day before wouldn't have even acknowledged each other, formed in the streets to exchange greetings and gossip. The proprietors of the York Hotel and Mansion House on King Street struggled to cope with the demands of the merrymakers who thronged their premises. Around the town the lights burned late in the houses of the officials as they congratulated and assured each other, over glasses brimming with Madeira and French claret, that they had never held the slightest doubt as to the outcome of their masterly petition to Lord Bathurst.

Some years earlier, the Reverend John Stuart, rector of St. George's Church, Kingston, had foretold a gloomy future for the struggling capital. In an unwise departure from biblical prophecy, and reflecting the antipathy of both Kingston and Niagara for the pretensions of York, the rector had said, "York never was intended by nature for a metropolis; and nothing but the caprice and obstinacy of Genl Simcoe raised it to that Dignity. . . . I know of no Trade now existing, or to be expected in any future Period, to support it or enrich it." Now, in 1816, having shed its war-induced slough of despond, York was about to

65

embark upon a period of vigorous growth. With the factor of confidence securely in place, the *sine qua non* of prosperity, the men of York could at last dream their dreams and make their plans.

Dr. Strachan, the most influential man in York, pointed the way. He purchased two front town lots at the northwest corner of today's Front and York streets and commissioned a builder to design a substantial house of brick construction which would cost him £5,000 before it was finally finished in 1818.[1] To the northwest of Strachan's place, D'Arcy Boulton, Jr., was also developing the idea of building a solid, brick house on his father's park lot of a hundred acres. When completed in 1818, one of the earliest brick dwellings in York, it would become celebrated as *The Grange*. And Dr. William Warren Baldwin, who with his family was now living with the spinster Elizabeth Russell at *Russell Abbey*, was busy sketching plans for the two-and-a-half storey frame house he would start building in 1817 on his father-in-law's former farm lot on the crest of the Davenport Hill overlooking York. He would name his place *Spadina*.[2]

But York's lusty rebirth was by no means limited to the fact that several prominent men suddenly decided to build new houses for themselves. By 1817, for example, one observer noted that there had been a great influx of people that summer from the United States:

> The country is improving very fast, there are no fewer than 9 saw and 3 grist mills within 5 miles from where I live and more building. The Town of York increases in size very fast and they are now building 3 wharves which will extend a long way into the lake for the convenience of vessels loading and unloading.

As exuberant York, with a population of only 700, launched its expansion, Samuel Peters Jarvis reflected ruefully upon the clouded outlook for his own career. He was now twenty-three, and having qualified himself as a lawyer the summer before, was filling a minor legal position in a government office in York. He had also maintained his interest in the army and had recently obtained a captaincy in the 2nd York Militia. Above all, however, his most urgent goal was to succeed his ailing father as secretary and registrar of the province. He had set his heart on it. He felt he had qualified himself for it. He had powerful friends in York, men like Dr. Strachan, his old headmaster, and William Dummer Powell, now chief justice; they could be counted upon to lend their support to such a succession, if only he could persuade his father to agree to it now—and step down.

As Sam intensified his pressure, William Jarvis's position became intolerable. His health was failing rapidly; he was still heavily in debt, and his creditors were giving him no rest. Dr. Baldwin, on behalf of his client Quetton St. George, was proceeding against him with a legal action, and his former clerk, Lieutenant Allan MacNab, had retained Henry J. Boulton as his lawyer in a pending action to recover unpaid wages amounting to a staggering £1,800. If Jarvis yielded to Sam's urging and resigned from his office, his official pension would barely sustain him, let alone permit him to head off his lawsuits. Clearly, it was now only through liquidation of his real estate holdings, augmented by his regular income, that he could hope to placate all his creditors. The only practical solution in sight, therefore, was for him to turn all his real estate over to Sam upon the condition that Sam would make such sales or exchanges as were necessary to settle his father's indebtedness. After that, William would be able to withdraw with dignity from his office. It was to this arrangement that Sam finally agreed.

As the first step, a deed was prepared under which William Jarvis transferred his entire real estate holdings to Sam. The document was dated October 8, 1816, and was witnessed by the attorney-general, D'Arcy Boulton, Sr. Significantly, the deed included the condition that "the said Samuel hath taken upon himself the payment of several large Incumbrances upon the Lands Tenements and Hereditments herein-after mentioned." Of necessity, the deed was a ponderous document and described in detail the fourteen parcels that were being transferred.

The first properties mentioned were all located within the town of York. They included William's residential property on Caroline Street (Lots 10, 11 and 12), Lot 3 on the north side of Duke Street which he had once lent for use as a school, two lots of one acre each on the west side of George Street, two lots, each of nine-tenths of an acre, on the north side of Duchess Street, and three acres on Hospital (Richmond) Street.

Outside the town, in the township of York and in the First Concession from the Bay, the first property mentioned was William's farm, the hundred-acre Park Lot 6 on Lot (Queen) Street where a few years later Sam would build his house *Hazelburn*. Finally, 800 acres of township "wildlands" were also included in the transaction. They consisted of Lots 18, 19, 21, and 22 in the Second Concession west of Yonge Street. Each lot comprised 200 acres and extended from today's Bathurst Street to Dufferin Street, north of Sheppard Avenue.

All in all, Sam was confident that with the careful liquidation of such properties as might be required, he could reduce his father's debts to manageable proportions, if not extinguish them entirely. However, it was not until the following April 1817 that Sam started to dismantle his father's land holdings. The first parcel to be sacrificed was one-half of the 800 acres of township "wildlands" in today's Bathurst and Dufferin streets district. The transaction was negotiated by Dr. Baldwin for Quetton St. George. He accepted Lots 18 and 19 "containing together 400 acres of Land—as payment in full of Mr. St. George's judgement against William Jarvis Esq." The agreed value of the parcel was £420, which would have represented St. George's then outstanding claim with legal costs added. Manifestly, Sam extracted an advantageous settlement on that occasion because in 1834 Dr. Baldwin, acting as executor and trustee of the St. George estate, sold the same lots for only £262.10.0, an inexplicable loss of £157.10.0 after St. George had held the property for seventeen years.

In order to complete the transaction with Dr. Baldwin, it was necessary for Sam to register the deed he had received from his father the previous October. This he did on April 11, 1817. The arrangement he had made with his father, therefore, by the simple act of registration, instantly became a matter of public knowledge. To a lawyer like George Ridout, who was fully aware of William Jarvis's confused affairs, the transaction between Sam and his father might easily have been interpreted as a device to enable William Jarvis to elude his creditors. His debts had been contracted in his own name. His creditors could only sue him, and if successful, their last resort, if he was unable to settle, would be against his real estate. But Jarvis had now effectively placed his real estate beyond their reach. The condition in the deed that Sam had "taken upon himself the payment of several large In-cumbrances upon the Lands" was simply an undertaking to his father, not to his father's creditors.

Dr. Baldwin's success in concluding St. George's litigation became instantly known and naturally encouraged other lawyers to move quickly against the failing secretary. Like a colony of bees, they swarmed around the Jarvis house on Caroline Street. At the end of June, for example, Henry J. Boulton, acting for Lieutenant Allan MacNab, commenced his proceedings in the Court of King's Bench with his claim for £1,800,[3] and early in July, George Ridout was busy conducting another action against the secretary.

In the course of his proceedings, Ridout needed to have Sam Jarvis confirm that he had witnessed his father's signature to a document. John Ridout, now an eighteen-year-old law student serving under articles to his brother George, undertook to ask Sam to visit the Crown office in order to sign the necessary papers. After calling several times, young Ridout finally succeeded in finding Sam in the secretary's office in the Jarvis house across the road from where the Ridouts lived. It was Saturday, July 5, 1817.

It wasn't a good day for Sam Jarvis. In fact, at that critical period of his life, Sam was having very few good days as he tried to unravel the tangled skein of his improvident father's affairs. Like arrows directed at him in the dark, new claims were assailing him from every direction. If he succeeded in straightening out the mess that now encompassed him, perhaps one day he would become provincial secretary. It was the only hope that sustained him. Sam, however, already feared that his father's rapidly deteriorating health, together with his customary procrastination, would prevent him from fulfilling his promise and turning his office over to his son.

Such was the situation in which John Ridout found a darkly brooding Sam Jarvis on that Saturday. Their conversation was brief, their meeting short. Sam took violent exception to whatever was said and, in the presence of his father's clerks, threw Ridout out of the office.

Much has been written about the bad blood that existed between the Jarvis and Ridout families at that time. The animosity, it is said, began when Sam's sister and one of the Ridout girls attended school together in Quebec. While they were there, an allegation was made by the Ridouts that Sam had reneged on a promise to pay certain expenses that had been incurred on his sister's behalf by Thomas G. Ridout, who was also in Quebec at the time. This charge was vigorously denied by Sam, and in 1816 the prospect of a duel had loomed between George Ridout and Sam Jarvis. Dr. Strachan quickly intervened and the matter was dropped. While the incident did little to help the relations between the families, it is an exaggeration to suggest that the episode was the reason for John Ridout's ejection from the secretary's office or for the dire events that followed. In fact, the school incident was merely a symptom of the fundamental incompatibility that had grown and hardened between the two neighbours. Thomas G. Ridout, who was later to become cashier (general manager) of the Bank of Upper Canada, made a significant reference to the gap that had widened between the families in a letter he wrote to his brother George in 1816. Referring to the element in York that was soon to become famous as the Family Compact, in which Sam Jarvis already enjoyed full spiritual membership, he wrote, "They do everything in their power to crush our house for they perceive we are getting to be a powerful tribe & of independent principles."[4] It was a prophetic statement because the Ridouts later

69

were to march under the banner of political reform with the crusading Baldwins, while Sam Jarvis, throughout his career a conspicuous beneficiary of the *status quo*, dallied with the Powells, the Boultons, and the Robinsons.

No one knows what John Ridout said in the secretary's office that provoked Sam so sorely. Perhaps with affected innocence he asked him about the recent transfer of his father's property. Perhaps it was simply the nature of the request that outraged Sam. While Ridout had unwittingly wandered into a bear's den, we may be sure he didn't back off when the conversation became heated. For his part, Sam was in no mood to be harassed by an officious young law student who had the audacity to seek his cooperation in advancing a suit that was entirely opposed to his interests. Impulsive and combative by nature, it was not out of character for him to express his hostility towards Ridout by an outright assault.

The following Wednesday, still brooding over his ignominious exit from the secretary's office, John Ridout encountered Sam Jarvis on King Street. Sam was strolling along the road arm in arm with an old school friend George Markland. Ridout, intent upon gaining revenge for the humiliation he had suffered in front of the clerks in the secretary's office, immediately attacked Sam. A crowd gathered, but the fight was soon broken up by Colonel James Fitzgibbon and a Mr. Robert Kerr. Some years later Fitzgibbon recalled that he had marched Ridout off to George Ridout's law office where he described the circumstances to George. He recalled having said, "I had just found his brother in an affray with Mr. Saml. Jarvis in the public streets, and that I had by force separated them and brought his brother to him, to which Mr. Ridout answered, saying, '*Upon my word Sir, I am very sorry you did!*'" Fitzgibbon provided this written statement in 1828, at the request of Sam Jarvis; it was supposed to prove that George viewed his brother with contempt.[5] Accepting Fitzgibbon's remarkable ability to recall with exactitude a conversation that had occurred eleven years before, George's alleged response to Fitzgibbon might equally have been taken to mean that he was sorry that Fitzgibbon had broken up the fight, especially if John was getting the better of it.

Another aspect of the street brawl was presented by George Markland, also in 1828 at the request of Sam Jarvis. In a written statement he recalled:

We were walking arm and arm in King Street, near Dr. Widmer's, where we saw John Ridout coming towards us—when sufficiently near, he stepped up to you using some threatening language, and struck at you with a large stick, which blow I think was warded off—you then immediately closed with him, and a scuffle ensued, which ended in a separation by the persons around.

The reference to John having attacked Sam with "a large stick" is noteworthy, together with Marklands' recollection that "the blow I think was warded off," because Jarvis apologists in later years were to attach great importance to the notion that Sam's hand had been shattered as a result, notwithstanding that no reference is made to such an injury in the statements Sam later published.

In any event, by the following Friday the die was cast. Aggravated by Ridout's attack on Wednesday, the intense animosity between the two men that had smouldered all week now burst into flame. Seconds were chosen, and a duel was arranged. Sam named twenty-seven-year-old Henry J. Boulton his second. Boulton, a lawyer, had as a youth startled York by affecting the extravagant dress of a Regency dandy. John Ridout chose as his second James E. Small, a fellow law student who was nineteen. James's father had killed the attorney-general, John White, in a duel in 1800. In choosing James, perhaps Ridout hoped he would have imbibed something of his father's duelling expertise which would now be helpful to him.

It is not entirely clear as to who issued the challenge. James E. Small, in distant 1828, was under the impression that Henry J. Boulton had called at Small's place to deliver the challenge and fix the time and place of their meeting. Sam's version was that Ridout had sent Small to inform him that he understood Boulton intended to call upon him, and that Ridout was ready to meet Sam. Boulton, according to Sam, then visited young Small.

It was arranged between the seconds that the duel would be fought at daybreak the following morning, Saturday, July 12. The site they selected was a field on Elmsley's Farm, a considerable distance from the town.

The Reverend Dr. Henry Scadding, in his *Toronto of Old*, recalled the location clearly, and from his youth remembered the sinister fascination the place held for wayfarers on Yonge Street, north of today's College Street:

Northward, a little beyond where Grosvenor Street leads into what was Elmsley Villa, and is now Knox College, was a solitary green field with a screen of lofty trees on three of its sides. In its midst was a Dutch barn, or hay-barrack, with a movable top. The sward on the northern side of the building was ever eyed by the passer-by with a degree of awe.

Dr. Scadding's description enables us to establish accurately the location of the duelling site. He placed it "northward, a little beyond where Grosvenor Street leads into . . . Knox College." His book was published in 1873, and at that time Knox College adorned the northwest corner of Grosvenor Street and Stanley Crescent. Much later, Stanley Crescent was absorbed into Bay Street when that street was extended north from College Street. Knox College, therefore, once occupied the northwest corner of modern-day Grosvenor and Bay streets. We are told that the Dutch barn and field were a little north of that point. Since Dr. Scadding recalled having viewed the site from as far away as Yonge Street, it is reasonable to assume that by a little "northward" of Knox College he meant a distance of 150 to 200 feet. That being so, the field with its barn and lofty trees would have occupied the area on the west side of Bay Street where the south section of the Ontario government's new Macdonald Block now stands.

The four men reached Elmsley's Farm an hour before daylight. They were compelled to take shelter in the Dutch barn because a storm was in progress. Flashes of lightning illuminated the macabre scene, thunder rumbled, and the rain drummed dismally on the roof above them. Jarvis left the barn a little before daybreak and was absent, a later report stated, for some time. The three men who remained carried on a forced and nervous conversation.

With the arrival of dawn the rain ended and the four men moved into the field to select the area for the duel. While a distance of twelve paces was first considered, it was reduced at Ridout's request to eight paces because he considered Jarvis the better shot. The eight paces, of course, were taken in opposite directions from a central point so that when the duellists finally turned and faced each other, they would be approximately fifty feet apart. The ground was then measured off, and a space chosen between two stumps, the larger of them being behind Ridout. According to the statement later prepared by Sam, and attested to by James E. Small and Henry J. Boulton, Sam pointed out that the stumps, providing a clearly defined target background, would make it easier for them to sight their pistols quickly and "would be more likely to cause the fire to take effect." As a result, the ground was changed to eliminate the offensive tree stumps.

By explaining in his prepared statement the problem caused by the stumps, Sam Jarvis probably intended to demonstrate his openness,

The house on the right was the original home (built circa 1798) of Thomas Ridout on the north side of Duke Street (now Adelaide Street), a little to the east of today's Sherbourne Street. The sketch was made long after young John Ridout slipped out of this house before daybreak on July 12, 1817, to engage in a duel with Samuel Peters Jarvis in which Ridout was killed instantly.—Metropolitan Toronto Library Board

his fairness, his solicitude. To the critical reader, however, his homily on the duelling landscape also demonstrated that he was the only one present who knew what he was doing. For anyone with a modicum of knowledge of duelling practice to allow himself to be stationed in front of a prominent, stationary object like a tree stump would have been an act of insanity. While Sam may well have relocated the ground out of fairness to both parties, the fact that he alone observed its earlier defects clearly indicates that throughout the affair he was a Gulliver among Lilliputians.

It was also agreed that the count would be given by Ridout's second, James E. Small, and that it would be "one, two, three, fire!" The two combatants took their places and the count was started. Inexplicably, Ridout fired prematurely. The shot missed and he walked casually away. It was later argued by a Ridout apologist that Boulton was the one who gave the count, that it was deliberately muffled and indistinct, and that Ridout therefore mistook the count of "two" for "three," raised his pistol and fired. By firing before the final count, Ridout had committed the blackest sin in the duelling code. His action must have plunged the Lilliputians into a state of utter consternation.[6]

According to the 1828 statement, however, the problem caused by Ridout's *gaffe* was dealt with quickly and efficiently by Messrs. Boulton, Small, and Ridout. They put their heads together, while Sam presumably remained aloof from their anxious deliberations, and decided "that Mr. Jarvis should have his fire." Ridout returned to his place dejectedly, an empty pistol in his hand. Small resumed the count. The statement continued: "Mr. Jarvis, at the word *fire*, did fire, without deliberation, and without raising his arm until the word *fire*." In other words, unlike Ridout, Sam had meticulously followed the rules of the code. "Mr. Ridout partly reeled around," the Jarvis statement went on, "but did not fall—all parties ran up to him—Mr. Jarvis threw his Pistol on the ground and said, 'My God, what have I done.' Mr. Ridout shook hands with all parties, and freely forgave Mr. Jarvis, and said, 'if Jarvis had not shot him, he might have shot Jarvis.'—There was a full expression of forgiveness on the one side, and sorrow and regret on the other. After this conversation Mr. Ridout fainted, and the parties supposing he was dead, left the ground."[7]

Later that morning, in response to a fleeting visit, or a message, from James E. Small, George Playter, the deputy sheriff, accompanied by Darius Forrest hurried out to Elmsley's Farm. Forrest, who owned the Mansion House on King Street, drove a carriage. Rounding the barn and peering anxiously through the rain that was again falling, they quickly located Ridout's body in the field. His head lay beside a small pool of blood, his clothing sodden from the downpour. They carried his corpse to the carriage and immediately headed back to town.

As soon as they returned, Thomas Hamilton, the coroner, hastily organized an inquest and Thomas Stoyell was appointed foreman of the coroner's jury. Trained as a doctor in the United States, Stoyell later became a prominent Methodist layman in York. Dr. Christopher Widmer, the town's leading doctor, was summoned to perform the autopsy. His report on the nature of Ridout's fatal wound was incorporated into the findings of the jury which were completed later that day.[8]

In their verdict, the coroner's jury found Samuel Peters Jarvis guilty of the murder of John Ridout, and that both Henry J. Boulton and James E. Small "feloniously were present, abetting, aiding, assisting, and maintaining the said Samuel Peters Jarvis, to kill and slay the said John Ridout."

In other areas, the jury's findings were equally clear and unequivocal. In part, they were as follows:

> . . . the said John Ridout and one Samuel P. Jarvis, did disagree and for some time did quarrel, until at length they the said John Ridout and the said Samuel P. Jarvis did challenge each other to end their dispute by fighting, and that the said Samuel P. Jarvis not having the fear of God before his eyes, but moved and seduced by the instigation of the Devil, on the twelfth day of July, in the year aforesaid, with force and arms, in a field commonly called Elmsley Field, in the Township of York aforesaid, did make an assault, and that the said Samuel P. Jarvis with a certain pistol of the value of 10 shillings, charged with gunpowder, and a leaden bullet, which he then and there held in his right hand, to & against the body of him, the said John Ridout, with the leaden bullet aforesaid, by force of the gunpowder aforesaid, in and upon the right shoulder of him the said John Ridout, one mortal wound penetrating the shoulder, neck, and jugular vein, from thence to the wind pipe of him the said John Ridout, of which mortal wound, he the said John Ridout, then and there instantly died.[9]

The jury's finding that Ridout's death had occurred "instantly" was based on Dr. Widmer's medical opinion. It is difficult to reconcile his conclusion with the later statements of Jarvis, Boulton, and Small that Ridout had survived long enough to shake hands with all parties while exclaiming that it was all fair and generally offering remarks of a generous and forgiving nature. According to Dr. Widmer's diagnosis, Jarvis's bullet tore into Ridout's right shoulder, penetrating his neck and jugular vein, and finally his trachea or windpipe. We may assume that Ridout was right-handed, and hence as he faced Jarvis in his duelling stance it would have been the right side of his body that was exposed to his opponent. If Dr. Widmer's conclusion as to the nature and effect of the wound was correct, as soon as Ridout was struck he would have staggered and fallen, soon passing into shock. As a result of the copious bleeding that would have occurred, his breathing and speech would have been immediately impaired. In the circumstances, Ridout's ability to stand, extend his right arm and shake hands, as well as converse clearly and coherently, is highly questionable.

In 1915, the Honourable William Renwick Riddell, a judge of the Supreme Court of Ontario, published an article, "The Duel in Upper Canada" in the *Canadian Law Times*.[10] In the course of his discussion of several duels, including the Jarvis-Ridout duel, Riddell noted, "There was the 'unwritten law' that if the duel was fair in all respects, the survivor and the seconds should not be convicted. Accordingly ... the Crown Counsel, if the duel was a fair one, never pressed for a conviction; and the jury knew what was expected of them."

Judge Riddell's reiteration of the principle that if a fatal duel was seen to be fair, a conviction would thereby be avoided, finds a disturbing echo in the helpful statements that were attributed to Ridout by the three survivors of the duel at Elmsley's Farm, two of whom were lawyers, one a law student. They all would have been familiar with the not-guilty verdict pronounced by the jury in the earlier Small-White duel in York simply because the proceedings in that fatal instance were assumed to have been fair.

Following the conclusion of the Elmsley Farm duel, the three men had returned immediately to York. In accordance with the customary duty of a second, in all probability James E. Small would have run on ahead to summon aid for his stricken friend. Boulton and Jarvis, therefore, would have been left to walk back to town together. Both men were certain that Jarvis would face criminal prosecution, and there was a strong probability that Boulton and Small would also be prosecuted—as they were some years later. Jarvis and Boulton at the time were aspiring to important government posts, and would naturally have been intensely anxious to protect their character and reputation. While in the eyes of the law the duel had been fair because the rules of the duelling code had been narrowly followed by Jarvis, it could do no harm, they might well have reasoned, to give clearer and more cogent articulation to Ridout's last, mumbled words that he in fact had been capable of doing himself. After all, a jury would be reassured to hear that Ridout had lingered long enough to testify clearly to the absolute fairness of the proceedings that had brought his life to so sudden an end. Lord Melbourne, at a time of government crisis, once remarked to his cabinet, "It doesn't matter what we say, as long as we all say the same thing." Whatever Jarvis and Boulton may have decided to say, their version of the event remained consistent to the end.

Sam Jarvis's friend, Jonas Jones, put his finger on the crucial point of the circumstances of Ridout's death in a letter he wrote to Sam from Brockville on August 8, less than a month after the duel. Jones had attended the Cornwall Grammar School with Sam, and was a practising lawyer whose frequent visits to York placed him in close touch with the life of the town. When he wrote to Sam, he was aware that he was lodged in the York gaol awaiting trial, and his letter, therefore, in its critical passages was guarded, oblique, and in parts virtually incomprehensible. This is what he wrote:

> My dear Sam, I rec'd Boultons & your letter by last Mail. B. was not half particular enough—your caution not to believe the lies in circulation was perfectly unnecessary—anything to your discredit you may be sure I should at once pronounce false—That which most annoyed me was this—It is that Ridout fired before the signal and then exclaimed "Oh! Sam I hope I have not hurt you," that you replied "If you had, I would still have given you this one" and then fired. This must be a confounded [lie], Nor would such a thing if true, be known but from the second who surely would not be such—as to relate it—You appear anxious that I should attend your affairs if possible—But my Dear Sam of what use can I be to you—The only question which will arise will be whither *(sic)* the words of the deceased or Widmer—and with respect to that, it depends upon the impression under which he laboured at the time the words were spoken—if at the time he was in expectation of dyeing *(sic)* immediately, it is Widmer—Much my dear Sam will depend upon the judge I hope the Chief Justice will try the case. I am much afraid the jury will be prejudiced against you That will depend upon the manner and expression of the deceased with respect to his death, when he made the declaration—Do not be too sure of an acquittal.
>
> God bless you
Jonas Jones[11]

Under any reasonable interpretation, the main point Jones was making was that if Dr. Widmer's opinion prevailed as to Ridout's death having occurred instantly the jury would then conclude that anything Ridout might have managed to say would have been little more than a death whisper and therefore could not be accepted as evidence that the proceedings had been entirely fair. On the other hand, if Ridout had had no sense of the imminence of death when he made his "declaration," the shot not having had an immediately fatal effect, the jury might be more inclined to accept the statements attributed to Ridout as being spontaneous, coherent, and true. In his chilling admonition as to not being too sure of an acquittal, Jones was simply reiterating his view (and doubt) that the jury might not give much weight to the statements attributed to Ridout in the face of contrary testimony from the highly respected Dr. Widmer.

Jonas Jones also revealed his intimate understanding of the social life of York when he expressed the hope that the chief justice would try the case. The chief justice at that time was William Dummer Powell, at whose house Sam Jarvis was a frequent guest.

In its findings, the coroner's jury also established the fact that Ridout had been slain by a pistol worth 10 shillings. While the estimate of value was simply a legal convention, we may be certain that it referred to the ordinary flintlock pistol which was then in common use. Judge Riddell in his 1915 article on duels reported that he had personally examined the pistols that had been used in the meeting at Elmsley's Farm. "They are long and heavy, carrying a large bullet," he recounted, "and are most deadly weapons." The cherished pistols the learned judge examined bear the maker's name, "Henry Tatum Jr. 24 Pall Mall London," and today are displayed at Fort York. They carry the following description: "Matching pair of duelling pistols, 19th Century, property of Samuel Peter (*sic*) Jarvis, reported to be used in the last duel in York."

The Fort York authorities have shown commendable caution in bestowing only a qualified attribution on the pistols, labelling them as "reported" to have been used in the duel. The exhibited weapons, in fact, are percussion lock pistols, not flintlock, and could not have been available to the combatants in 1817 since they were not generally produced before 1825. Moreover, while Henry Tatum, Jr. was earlier in business with his father, according to firearm experts, he did not make weapons under his own name at 24 Pall Mall before 1830 at the earliest. While the "deadly weapons," or percussion lock pistols, examined by Judge Riddell are interesting relics of the period, their alleged association with the famous duel is insupportable.[12]

Following the coroner's inquest, Sam Jarvis had surrendered himself to the magistrates and was immediately committed to the York gaol. His application for bail was refused. A few days later, the *Upper Canada Gazette* took official notice of the duel, carefully omitting mention of Sam's name:

> It is our unpleasant duty to notice the fatal termination of a Duel, fought early on Saturday morning last, in the vicinity of this Town; Mr. John Ridout was mortally wounded and expired before he could be conveyed home.

Dr. Baldwin was more explicit about the affair when he wrote to his friend Quetton St. George who was in France. After mentioning the Ridouts he added, "That family are grievously afflicted now by the death of their son in a duel with Saml. Jarvis—Jarvis is in prison; Small, Ridout's friend is gone across the water—& Henry Boulton the second of Jarvis is gone on the circuit as counsel for the Crown—it is a wretched affair altogether—& S Jarvis is not free from censure."[13]

James E. Small had left York immediately after the duel in order to avoid, as he mistakenly thought, certain arrest and imprisonment. Dr. Baldwin's allusion to Small having fled "across the water" referred to the fact that Small had crossed the lake to Niagara and had then travelled to Albany where he was later located and persuaded to return home.

The immediate effect of the duel on the minds and consciences of the inhabitants of York was deep and painful. Even the magistrates, sensing the chastening influence of the tragedy upon the entire community, ordered the withdrawal of all prosecutions before them. And following John Ridout's funeral and interment in the church-yard of St. James' Church, a large stone was cut and raised beside his grave. The stone, now in the porch of the Cathedral, is celebrated mainly because of its reference to Sam Jarvis as "a Blight":

In Memory of John Ridout, son of Thomas Ridout, Surveyor-General. His filial affection, engaging manners, and nobleness of mind gave early promise of future excellence. This promise he gallantly fulfilled by his brave, active and enterprizing conduct which gained the praise of his superiors while serving as midshipman in the Provincial Navy during the late War. At the return of peace he commenced with ardour the study of law, and with the fairest of prospects, but a Blight came, and he was consigned to an early grave on 12th July, 1817, aged 18.

For Sam Jarvis the effects of the next few months while he awaited trial were also deep and painful. The gaol he was lodged in stood on the south side of King Street, east of Yonge Street, where today's Leader Lane, beside the King Edward Hotel, joins King Street. The prison was a large frame structure surrounded by a palisade of menacing, spiked poles. Two iron doors, guarded by a sentry, opened on to King Street. Into this airless, fetid region were herded hardened criminals, lunatics, women, children, debtors, and people simply awaiting trial. Among them, until the following October, Sam Jarvis was to have his unhappy being.

He had ample time to reflect upon the grim chain of events that had reduced him to his present state. At the bottom of it all, he could only have concluded, was his father's perverse incompetence in handling his own financial affairs. On the threshold of a promising career, Sam had suddenly been afflicted with the crushing embarrassment of his father's debts. In contrast, his friends like D'Arcy Boulton, Jr., and Henry Boulton, and even the contemptible Ridouts, George and Thomas Gibbs, all were free to pursue their own careers unencumbered by a father like William, who for most of his term in office had embraced insolvency as a friend and placed his pretensions, like Mr. Bumble, above the practical needs of his family. That man, Sam must have thought with rising bitterness, was like Humpty Dumpty in reverse, a man whom the King's men, far from trying to pick up, had endeavoured without success to pull down. Sam, too, had tried unsuccessfully to dislodge his father from his office to assure his own succession to it.

Mrs. William Dummer Powell, who sometimes burnished her perceptions with invective, was to describe the picture now torturing Sam's mind when she wrote poignantly the following year to her brother to announce her daughter's engagement to Sam:

> Mary has consented to become the Wife of Mr. Jarvis, and I think it is possible the change in her Situation may take place this Autumn: we can have no personal objections to the connecion but truly regret that an unworthy Father has intailed difficulty upon a Son, who would have been perfectly equal to the support of a family:—he is Wm. J. the late Secretary of the Province whose unprincipled conduct threatened ruin to his family: after being called to the Bar, the young man, to render the office respectable and productive, relinquished his professional pursuits and devoted himself to official business: the Father was urged to resign in his Sons favour and by that means secure the reversion: the young man offering to assume all his debts if he would make over his property to him; to the latter he consented, but the delay of resignation rendered it ineffectual; some discussion with a malignant and vile family, caused a fatal duel; the Father died during the Son's confinement and the established rule of our government, not to allow of an immediate succession in a family, gave the Secretaryship to another.[14]

And so it was, during Sam's "confinement" in the King Street gaol, that William Jarvis's illness became critical. As the end drew near,

Sheriff Samuel Ridout, the surveyor-general's oldest son, in a compassionate gesture, arranged with the magistrates for Sam to be released for a few hours in order to visit his father for the last time. He did so on Saturday night, August 9. After his return to gaol, deeply moved by his family's distress (to which his own contribution had not been insignificant), Sam again applied for permission to visit Caroline Street. This time Dr. Strachan intervened. He wrote to Sam clearly and forcefully to explain why his further release from prison was impossible. The rector of York began:

> The paper you signed last night gave security that you would return this Morning and we Guaranteed the Sheriff against risque for giving you this indulgence—but it cannot in my opinion be repeated without danger or indeed with propriety—as it was admitted on all hands to be illegal— Your Friends are anxious in the name of humanity and would do everything they could for you consistent with duty but it would be cruel in them to use any influence they might have with the Sheriff to induce him to act contrary to his Duty. The urgency of the case may perhaps excuse one deviation but I fear a repetition cannot be expected. . . .
>
> The case with you is hard I feel it peculiarly so but you must acquiesce and blame the unhappy cause and not the exertions of your Friends. . . .[15]

William Jarvis died the following Wednesday, August 13. The notice of his death appeared the following day, perfunctorily, in the *Upper Canada Gazette*. "Died Yesterday," it read, "William Jarvis, Esquire, Secretary and Register of the Province.—Funeral will be on Saturday, at 2 o'clock."

The secretary, as grand master of the Free Masons in Upper Canada, was buried with full Masonic honours in the cemetery behind St. James' Church. While Sam languished in the nearby gaol, powerless to help, all the lodges within William Jarvis's former jurisdiction united to defray his burial expenses. The lodge at Grimsby, for example, which was known as Forty Mile Creek when William had first arrived in Newark twenty-five years earlier, voted £1.15.0 towards the cost of his funeral.[16]

"Mrs. J. was in a state of great distraction for the first day," Mrs. Powell reported to her husband the chief justice in reference to Hannah Jarvis, "but attended the funeral and was at church yesterday."

As for Sam, his trial for manslaughter took place in October. Chief Justice Powell presided, and Magistrate William Allan sat with him as an associate judge. Jarvis pleaded not guilty, and after only a few minutes deliberation, the jury upheld his plea. In the last analysis, as a responsible physician, it would have been impossible for Dr. Widmer, who was not present when Ridout died, to swear categorically that Ridout had not made the statements attributed to him, even though the nature of the wound had clearly pointed to his death as having occurred instantly. Notwithstanding that the charge to the jury, as Judge Riddell put it, "was anything but indulgent to the prisoner," the jury concluded quickly that there was no evidence that the duel had been unfair. Perhaps, to use the judge's words again, they "knew what was expected of them."

In the final, painful sequel, Duncan Cameron, who had commanded a company of the York Militia at Queenston Heights, was appointed provincial secretary to succeed William Jarvis, and Sam, his hopes crushed, turned his attention again to the gritty problems of his father's bankrupt estate.

CHAPTER SIX

Nehkik Becomes a Chief

Following the Jarvis-Ridout duel, and Sam Jarvis's acquittal, any uncertainties that may have surrounded Henry J. Boulton's career were resolved decisively in 1818 with his appointment as solicitor-general of Upper Canada. In the same year his father, D'Arcy Boulton, Senior, who had held the office of attorney-general since 1814, was appointed a judge of the provincial court. For Sam Jarvis, 1818 was also a noteworthy year, not because he obtained an important government office, as his Family Compact friends had, but as a result of his marriage to Mary Boyles Powell, the daughter of Chief Justice and Mrs. William Dummer Powell.

Their marriage service was conducted with grave dignity by the Reverend Dr. John Strachan in St. James' Church on King Street on the night of October 1. It was performed under a special licence which eliminated the need to publish the usual banns of marriage in advance of the ceremony. Since it was a private wedding, the number who gathered in the creaking, drafty church was small, and the only groomsman was Sam's younger brother, William Munson Jarvis.

Sam's prospects for advancement in the government service brightened considerably as a result of his alliance with the Powell family. Mrs. Powell wrote to her brother the following day to inform him of the wedding. She noted with warmth the Jarvis family's satisfaction with Sam's marriage, and frankly conceded that in her judgement their enthusiasm was totally justified.

York Oct 2, 1818

My Dearest Brother
Your Neice (*sic*) Mary last evening assumed the certain cares and doubtful comforts of conjugal life, and early this morning left us to proceed to Queenston where Mr. Jarvis has taken an house and finds a fair prospect

of professional success: God grant that their anticipation of happiness and prosperity may be realized, in the honor and probity of my Son-in-Law I have the most perfect confidence, indeed had he not deserved it, such would never have been his relative character: they are to be at Burlington tonight, and remain there two or three days with his Sister Mrs. G. Hamilton whose recent confinement prevented her being present last evening: all the connecions (*sic*) of Mr. J.—appear greatly flattered by the choice he has been permitted to make, and I think I may without vanity say none could have been more creditable to him or more respectable in every point. . . .[1]

Just a few weeks before Sam's marriage, Sir Peregrine Maitland, K.C.B., had arrived in York as the new governor. Maitland was a distinguished British soldier. At the battle of Waterloo three years before he had commanded a brigade of Guards and had later eloped with the Duke of Richmond's daughter, Lady Sarah Lennox. It was the Duchess of Richmond who had given the famous ball in Brussels the night before Waterloo which was immortalized by Lord Byron in *Childe Harold's Pilgrimage*. Both Maitland and Lady Sarah attended that glittering event. When the Duke of Richmond was named governor general of the Canadas in 1818, having relented over his earlier disapproval of his daughter's marriage, he arranged to have his son-in-law appointed lieutenant-governor of Upper Canada to succeed Francis Gore. Both families then happily crossed the Atlantic together and proceeded to their respective appointments.

When parliament was not sitting in York, Sir Peregrine chose to make his principal residence at Stamford, a few miles west of Niagara Falls. Here in a stately park he built an idyllic house for Lady Sarah and himself which he called *Stamford Cottage*. It was conceived as an oasis of tranquility by Maitland, whom Dr. Scadding described as "a tall, grave officer, always in military undress, his countenance ever wearing a mingled expression of sadness and benevolence." The serenity that Sir Peregrine sought in Stamford, however, was rudely shaken in 1824 when William Lyon Mackenzie, an ardent apostle of radical reform, began publishing the *Colonial Advocate* in the village of Queenston, not far from where the Maitlands lived.

Mackenzie, who had immigrated to Upper Canada from Dundee, Scotland, in 1820, had moved to Queenston with his wife in the autumn of 1823 and opened a small, general store. Early the following year, however, having become wholly absorbed in the politics of Upper Canada, he sold his shop, bought a printing press, and set out to gratify his craving for reform. He was then twenty-nine.

As Queenston lay drowsing by the river in the warm, May sunshine, its orchards already coloured in white and pink, the first number of Mackenzie's *Colonial Advocate* rolled ominously from the press. The opening section served notice that the paper would focus on a discussion of "the merits of public men and public measures with a freedom and plainness rather unusual in the greater part of our colonial publications." With that formality behind him, the editor at once turned his attention to the lieutenant-governor:

> We are blessed with a right valiant and most excellent military chieftain as our governor, Major General Sir Peregrine Maitland, to wit a Knight of noble birth and noble connexions, who after spending his earlier days amid the din of war and the turmoil of camps, has gained enough renown in Europe to enable him to enjoy himself, like the country he governs, in inactivity—whose migrations are by water from York to Queenston and from Queenston to York, like the Vicar of Wakefield from the brown bed to the blue, and from the blue bed to the brown—who knows of our wants as he gains a knowledge of the time of day by *report*; in the one case by the report of the Niagara gun; in the other by the *Gazette*.

And without drawing breath, Mackenzie went on to compare Maitland unfavourably with De Witt Clinton, then governor of the State of New York. Next, after making a thinly veiled and uncomplimentary reference to Dr. Strachan, he launched into attacks on John Beverley Robinson, the attorney-general and member for York, as well as Christopher Hagerman, the member for Kingston and L. P. Sherwood, the member for Leeds.

In succeeding weekly issues, Mackenzie continued to air his grievances and gibe at the governor and his provincial government. And in October, when the cornerstone of the first monument to the memory of Sir Isaac Brock was laid atop the Niagara Escarpment at Queenston, where Brock and Macdonell had been reinterred, Mackenzie contrived to have a copy of the first issue of the *Colonial Advocate* deposited in the sacred stone. Sir Peregrine Maitland was absent at the time on an official tour of the province, but as soon as he returned to York and learned of Mackenzie's act of desecration, he ordered the immediate removal of "the dross from the pure stone of the monument." The foundation of the structure by then had climbed to fourteen feet, and the architect had to dismantle part of it in order to extract the offending issue of the *Advocate*. That being done, the corner-stone was resealed and work on the lofty monument resumed.*

* The first monument to Brock was blown up on Good Friday, April 17, 1840. The present monument was completed in 1858.

For at least a year the fiery Mackenzie and combative Sam Jarvis maintained their homes in the quiet and peaceful village of Queenston. They were probably acquainted with each other only as fellow villagers, exchanging a nod occasionally as they passed in the narrow streets. However, in the years that lay ahead in York, the two men, bitterly opposed in their political views and interests, were to come to regard each other with unrelenting hatred.

And it was to York that both men returned late in 1824, Mackenzie to be nearer the seat of government where he could gather fresh news more effectively and at the same time obtain job printing work for his under-utilized press, and Jarvis to enhance his prospects for advancement in the government service.

During his sojourn in Queenston, Sam revived his father's allegation that as provincial secretary he had suffered a cruel injustice at the hands of Lieutenant-Governor Peter Hunter when he had been deprived of the full fees to which he was entitled for the issuance of Crown patents of land. In 1822, Sam finally decided to seek redress of the old wrongs that had been visited upon his father, and sensing that the climate was favourable, addressed a petition for compensation to the governor in council, Sir Peregrine Maitland. In all likelihood, his claim was examined by Dr. Strachan, Sam's former headmaster, and Chief Justice Powell, his father-in-law, as members of the Executive Council. In any event, the council did in fact approve payment of £1,000 to Sam "as part compensation for the Injury suffered by his father."[2]

It is reasonable to assume that this happy windfall was used by Sam to help build a new house for himself in York on the 100-acre park lot his father had transferred to him just before he died. Construction of the dwelling, which Sam was to name *Hazelburn*, was begun in mid-summer of 1824. It was placed well back from Lot (Queen) Street, at the centre of today's Jarvis Street, a little south of its intersection with Shuter Street. The two-storey house was of brick construction and included a spacious verandah which extended across the front or south elevation. It also provided a covering for Sam's main entrance. John Ewart is said to have been the builder of the house which was mainly distinguished for its interior woodwork of solid black walnut. In January 1825, Mrs. William Dummer Powell reported to her brother in New York that Mary and Sam had moved in to their new house. "It is a very pretty dwelling," she observed, adding with characteristic candour, "but unfortunately the Chimneys have been ill constructed and smoke."

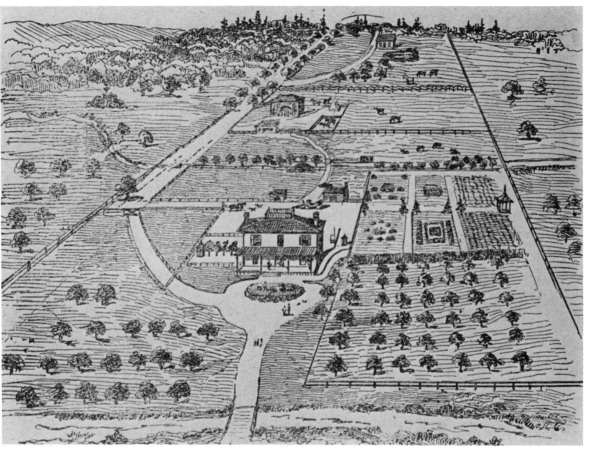

Hazelburn, *the home of Samuel Peters Jarvis. Built in 1824, the house stood at the centre of today's Jarvis Street, slightly south of Shuter Street. It was demolished by Jarvis in 1847 to permit completion of the new Jarvis Street that was being laid out from Queen Street to Bloor Street by the Toronto architect John G. Howard. This view is reproduced from John Ross Robertson's* Landmarks of Toronto.

The main approach to the *Hazelburn* farm was from Lot (Queen) Street, at the head of New Street which led up to the place from Front Street. New Street was later renamed Nelson Street, and finally Jarvis Street. A small creek meandering towards the Don River crossed Sam's property at Lot Street; it was bridged and a driveway laid out that terminated in a graceful circle at Sam's front door. Farther north, beyond today's Gerrard Street, the property remained virtually in its primeval state. At the edge of a swamp, for example, Sam and his

87

friends used to shoot snipe on a warm summer evening after dinner, and in the same area it was not uncommon to see deer ranging through the scrubby growth that lay just south of Bloor Street.

When Sam and Mary moved into *Hazelburn*, their family had already grown to three sons. Mary had lost her first child at its birth in Queenston in September 1819, but Samuel Peters arrived safely the next year, followed by William Dummer Powell in 1821, and George Murray in 1824. Then in York, late on a Sunday evening in October 1825, their first daughter, Ann-Ellen, was born. According to Mrs. Powell, Mary had attended St. James' that morning, walked home up New Street, and had then taken her family to the Powells for dinner in the afternoon. Mary's mother ended her report on the arrival of her new granddaughter by remarking with some feeling, "God grant them means to support their large family."

Mrs. Powell's concern over Sam's prospects, and his ability to provide for his family, was a constantly recurring theme in her correspondence at that time. Just five months after her daughter's marriage, she had observed that "the imprudence of his Father left his Mother and Sister [Ann-Elizabeth] totally dependent upon him." She went on to explain that Hannah Jarvis, Sam's mother, had willingly given up her house on Caroline Street and was dividing her time among her four married children, Maria-Lavinia Hamilton at Burlington, Augusta McCormick at Niagara, Hannah-Owen Hamilton at Queenston, and her son William Munson Jarvis at Hamilton. Ann-Elizabeth apparently lived with Sam and Mary at Queenston until her marriage in 1822 to William Benjamin Robinson, the younger brother of John Beverley Robinson, the attorney-general.

Mrs. Powell also noted in 1819 that the rent from the Jarvis house on Caroline Street "will bring in more than $500 per annum, a comfortable addition to their income, they have difficulties to endure." And when Sam and Mary were settling into *Hazelburn*, looking ahead to her husband's reduced income as a result of his imminent retirement as chief justice of the Court of King's Bench, Mrs. Powell lamented that this was "an untimely circumstance, as it reduces our ability to assist our Daughter Mary in the furnishings [of] her new Home." And finally, in March 1826, she again expressed anxiety over Sam's financial position. "I hope Mr Jarvis will be able to support his growing family," she exclaimed, "either by his own exertions or thro' the influence of those he considers as Friends."[3]

Such was Sam's position in the spring of 1826 when William Lyon Mackenzie, himself under acute financial pressure, began in the pages of the *Colonial Advocate* to intensify his attacks on the privileged position of the oligarchy that dominated the provincial government. He liked to call them the Family Compact. For some years, Sam had held the undemanding sinecure of the clerkship of the Court of Chancery, and more recently he had managed to augment his income by helping out in the provincial secretary's office. His duties there were finally formalized by his appointment in 1827 as deputy secretary, a position the ever-watchful Mackenzie acidly described later as being "a newly invented office."

The creation of such offices, the rewarding of the families and friends of government, was Mackenzie's steady battle cry. In the famous issue of the *Advocate* of May 18, 1826, which largely led to the destruction of his press by a mob the following month, Mackenzie expatiated upon the abuses of the governing faction in York:

> How many of you have fallen into the dreadful gulph of the law, rendered twice as deep as heretofore by the enormous amount of Attorney's fees, Clerk of the Crown's fees, Crier's fees, Constable's fees, Witnesses' fees, Juror's fees, Clerk of Assize and Marshall's fees, Sheriff's fees & Jailer's fees, left by the late corrupt Parliament in the hands of the Judges of the King's Bench, to increase at their pleasure. These Judges are made and unmade at the mere pleasure of the Crown, receive their salaries from a foreign country, have their sons and nephews and relations practising law and depending on it alone (or on the hope of place) for subsistence.

The same issue of the *Advocate*, in which Mackenzie luxuriated in his penchant for colourful invective, referred to the contemporary *Kingston Chronicle* as a "worthless dung heap," the works of J. B. Macaulay, shortly to become chief justice of the Court of Common Pleas and a member of the Executive Council, as being "a common standard for stupidity in Upper Canada," to the mother of John Beverley Robinson as having "kept the cake and beer shop in King Street, York," and obliquely to former Chief Justice Powell as a man who "shook hands with and caressed a murderer," implying, of course, as York could only have concluded, Sam Jarvis.

Sam naturally shared his friends' feelings of revulsion and outrage against the red-wigged editor for the monstrous calumnies he was now heaping upon their heads. But there was another ominous item in the same issue of the *Advocate* that must also have caught Sam's eye, not because it referred to him personally, but because it gave warning of Mackenzie's ability to ferret out confidential government information and use it indiscriminately against the objects of his ridicule and censure. Referring to the attorney-general, who had earlier returned from a trip to England on government business, Mackenzie wrote, "He returned and claimed and obtained £500 sterling of your money for his pains from Sir P. Maitland, whether with your consent or without it as the case may be." As Sam filtered that disturbing item through his mind, he couldn't have helped wondering what Mackenzie might yet have to say about the £1,000 he himself had received from Sir P. Maitland in compensation for the "injury" done to his father over twenty years before, certainly a more tenuous ground for vice-regal indulgence than John Beverley Robinson's recent official visit to England. Moreover, Sam had always regarded Maitland's isolated handout only as "part compensation" for the ancient wrong done his father. Clearly, Sam's lingering hopes for further compensation, perhaps in the form of a senior appointment such as that of provincial secretary, would dissolve like a patch of snow under a hot sun if Mackenzie were allowed to continue to prowl the streets of York in search of further embarrassing information. While all government office-holders were united in bitter denunciation of Mackenzie's brand of journalism, few men in York could have had a more urgent, practical interest in seeing Mackenzie's press eliminated, his shrill voice silenced, than Sam Jarvis.

And so it was, at half-past six on the fine, clear evening of June 8, 1826, a strange entourage was seen winding its way along Front Street towards the offices of the *Colonial Advocate* on Frederick Street. The crowd, consisting of fifteen men directed by Sam Jarvis, some carrying heavy sticks, marched to Mackenzie's premises grimly and purposefully. They made no attempt at concealment. They knew Mackenzie was absent in Lewiston. They entered his office without interference and set about systematically destroying his types and press. Mackenzie's son-in-law, Charles Lindsey, related later:

> Three pages of the paper in type on the composing-stones, with a 'form' of the Journals of the House, were broken up, and the face of the letter battered. Some of the type was then thrown into the bay, to which the printing-office was contiguous; some of it was scattered on the floor of the office; more of it in the yard and in the adjacent garden of Mr. George Munro. The composing-stone was thrown on the floor. A new cast-iron patent lever-press was broken. "Nothing was left standing," said an eye-witness, "not a thing."

The wrecking of Mackenzie's press took only a few minutes. The participants then separated and drifted nonchalantly home along the byways of York to reflect upon their actions and await developments. It is tempting to speculate about Sam Jarvis's return to *Hazelburn* that evening. Perhaps after a late dinner he retired to his front verandah for a few minutes, a glass of claret in his hand. His gaze would have focused on the distant bay at the foot of New Street as he meditated upon his role in the decisive victory his forces had just won. It would hardly have occurred to him to ponder as well the strange conjunction of planets that seemed to impel him to commit impulsive acts of violence in regular nine-year cycles: in 1808 in Cornwall, along with his school friends, he had nearly killed an Indian youth in a brawl; in 1817 there had been the fatal duel with young John Ridout; nine years later, Mackenzie's press lay in ruins, the work largely of his hand. Napoleon once exclaimed after winning a costly battle, "Another such victory and we are ruined!" Sam's victory in York that evening would also prove costly—and illusory.

Public reaction to the press-wrecking incident, if not wholly sympathetic to Mackenzie, was at least strongly critical of the wreckers for taking the law into their own hands. Writing to Mackenzie a few days later, Jesse Ketchum, a tanner by trade, told him that he had sampled the "Public expression" and found it "very Strong in your favour." Robert Stanton, the King's printer and editor of the *Upper Canada Gazette*, observed presciently to a friend, "I fear the zeal of some of our friends has been rather intemperately expressed, . . . the measure was too strong I fear and may be the means of affording the blackguard a sort of triumph at the expense of respectability." And Mrs. William Dummer Powell, who was in New York at the time, informed her husband in England that "a most disgraceful scene has been about at York." She thought Mackenzie's paper "an infamous production and not worth postage," and earnestly hoped that her sons hadn't been involved in the "degrading transaction." Apparently Mary Jarvis hadn't yet told her mother of Sam's role in the affair because Mrs. Powell went on to say, "I hope Mr. J. would not permit his zeal for the Robinson and Boulton families to land him so far from respect to the Laws of the Country, and expose himself to a share in a criminal prosecution. Mary says they are all well but the Gardens are suffering." Mary had written to her mother from York on June 12, four days after the raid on Mackenzie's office.

As matters developed, no criminal prosecution did in fact occur. Instead, seizing the opportunity so fortuitously presented to rescue his paper from its tottering financial position, Mackenzie launched a civil action for extensive damages against the eight wreckers who had been positively identified. Among them was Sam Jarvis. The others were young bloods around town, mostly law students in their late teens or early twenties. They were, Henry Sherwood, nineteen, a son of Judge Sherwood; James King, a law student in Henry J. Boulton's office; Charles Richardson, twenty-one, a law student in John Beverley Robinson's office; John Lyons, a confidential clerk in the lieutenant-governor's office who was called to the Bar in 1826; Charles Baby, twenty, a law student and son of Inspector-General James Baby; Peter MacDougall, a French Canadian merchant in York who was a close friend of the Baby family; and finally, Charles Richardson Heward, nineteen, a son of Colonel Stephen Heward to whose Flank Company in the York Militia Sam Jarvis had been posted at the outbreak of the War of 1812.

Before Mackenzie launched his action for damages, however, J.B. Macaulay, who was acting for the eight wreckers and had himself been maligned by the *Advocate*, sought unsuccessfully on two occasions to settle the matter out of court. Mackenzie had retained as his principal lawyer James E. Small, who had been John Ridout's second, and on July 6, 1826, Macaulay sent Small a final offer of "£300 to end the matter." Without much soul-searching, Mackenzie rejected that offer as well.

The case was then brought to trial before a special jury in York's new court house, and Chief Justice Sir William Campbell of Duke Street presided along with two associate judges. The hearing lasted for two days during which the jury spent thirty-two hours incarcerated "between the sweating walls of a newly plastered room, the air of which was raw and unpleasant." Some of the jurymen were advanced in years, and three of them became ill. One in particular, David Boyer, a German settler from Markham, required urgent medical attention and was bled by a Dr. McCague. Boyer was determined, however, to see the matter through and stated that if necessary he would spend the night on the floor in the cold room, using his greatcoat as a pillow. After endless bickering over an award of damages ranging from £150 to £2,000, the jury finally settled on an amount of £625. Mackenzie was jubilant and later declared, without exaggeration, that he had been rescued from "utter ruin and destruction." The defendants were mortified.

After Macaulay's offer to Mackenzie had been rejected in July, Sam Jarvis took the painful step of mortgaging one of the properties his father had transferred to him just before his death. He doubtless recognized that most of the young men whom he had bound to his chariot wheels for the whirlwind raid on the press wouldn't be able to contribute anything to the damages they would inevitably face, and he approached Dr. Christopher Widmer for a small loan. Widmer, who had performed the autopsy on John Ridout, was agreeable, and on August 19, 1826, Sam signed a mortgage for £200 in the doctor's favour on the security of his father's old Lot 3 on the northeast corner of Caroline and Duke streets, the house the secretary had lent for a private school twenty years before.[4]

When the jury handed down its verdict in October, therefore, Sam was in a position to contribute towards the cost of the damages. Most of the others were not. Accordingly, Colonel James Fitzgibbon took up a subscription in York and elsewhere in the province, and succeeded in raising the balance of the funds that were needed. Referring later to the episode, Sam Jarvis wrote:

> I have on my part to assure the public, that so far from being indemnified by the contributions, which from various motives were made for our relief, the burthen (sic) fell heavily upon such of us as had the means of paying anything: And I affirm, that the share of the verdict which I myself had to defray from no very abundant means, was such that if Mr. M'Kenzie had made as much clear profit by his Press, during the whole time he had employed it in the work of desecration, he would not have found it necessary to leave the work and abandon it to his creditors.[5]

This latter statement, never proven, referred to the allegation made by the wreckers that Mackenzie was absent in Lewiston on the day of the raid because he had absconded from his creditors, not simply because of a business trip.

The result of the attack on Mackenzie's office turned out to have exactly the opposite effect to that intended by the perpetrators. "The press-wreckers were by this time able to gauge the effect of their folly," W. D. LeSeur wrote later in his controversial *William Lyon Mackenzie: A Reinterpretation*:

> They had in effect put their hands in their pockets and the pockets of their friends—for a subscription was taken up on their behalf—the amount of

£625 to equip the *Colonial Advocate* as it had never been equipped before; and had, there is little doubt, rather increased than impaired Mackenzie's popularity. The masses are moved by simple ideas; and the idea that the freedom of the press should not be interfered with is more level with the general comprehension than the idea that the press should abstain from odious personal insinuations and private scandal. That the *Advocate* had indulged in scurrility at the expense of a few individuals, whose favoured position in society naturally exposed them to more or less envy, would not strike a large portion of the community at all a serious offence; but that representatives of the favoured class should violently silence an organ of public opinion, and one aiming specially at popularity, would be regarded almost as an attack on the people themselves. From every practical point of view, therefore, these young men, and most of them law students, had simply, in their impetuosity, wounded the cause they had at heart and given a substantial triumph where certainly it was not deserved. If the die had not been cast before, it was cast now.[6]

The die indeed was cast. In 1828, his financial problems solved, Mackenzie decided to offer himself as a candidate for the county of York in the late-summer elections for the Legislative Assembly. The county was entitled to return two members, and along with Mackenzie, James E. Small, Jesse Ketchum, and William Roe also stood for election. Ketchum headed the polls, Mackenzie was second. Sam Jarvis, who unwittingly had helped launch Mackenzie's political career, must have watched Mackenzie's star rise with disbelief and disgust. And to make matters worse, Sir Peregrine Maitland, who had been staunchly supportive of the Family Compact throughout his ten-year term, was suddenly removed from his office and re-appointed lieutenant-governor of the province of Nova Scotia. Perhaps as a consequence, Sam's career in York came to a complete standstill. William Lyon Mackenzie went on to win election in 1834 as the first mayor of the newly incorporated city of Toronto, as York had been renamed, and it was not until 1837, eleven years after the raid on Mackenzie's press, that Sam was to emerge from the shadows and occupy a high government office.

Following Sir Peregrine Maitland's departure from the province, Sir John Colborne, who was also a distinguished veteran of Waterloo, arrived in York in November 1828, to assume the office of lieutenant-governor. The session of Parliament of 1829, the first under Colborne's administration, is best remembered as the session in which Mackenzie introduced to the House of Assembly his famous thirty-one grievances and resolutions in his unswerving campaign for political reform. Colborne, however, was more interested in improving the system of education in the province and in building good roads and safe bridges as a stimulus to development, than he was in having the House transformed into a forum for noisy, political dissension. While recognizing that Mackenzie's incessant agitation for reform had yielded some useful results, Colborne soon lost confidence in Mackenzie's judgement, and even came to question his loyalty to the Crown. Mackenzie, therefore, remained a piercing thorn in the governor's side throughout his administration, as well as the political enemy of all those who surrounded him. When Colborne left the province in January 1836 and turned over the reigns of government to his hapless successor, Sir Francis Bond Head, the radical reformers were already on a clearly defined collision course with the opposing forces of the deeply entrenched Family Compact.

When Sir Francis was offered the appointment in Upper Canada, he had at first refused it. A former military engineer under Wellington's command, he felt that "nothing could be more uncongenial to his habits, dispositions, and opinions than the station that was offered him." He finally accepted, however, under direct pressure from the colonial secretary, Lord Glenelg.

When he arrived in Toronto, he was amazed to find many of the houses decorated with posters proclaiming him as a "Tried Reformer." With unblushing candour, he later recorded his reaction to his reception:

> As, however, I was no more connected with human politics than the horses that were drawing me, as I had never joined any political party, had never attended a political discussion, and had never even voted at an election or taken any part in one, it was with no little surprise that, as I drove into Toronto, I observed the walls placarded in large letters which designated me as "*SIR FRANCIS HEAD*, a Tried Reformer."[7]

It was not long before Governor Head was in open conflict with Mackenzie and his radical reformers, and in May 1836, he dissolved the House and immediately announced a general election to be held the following month. As a result, Mackenzie and others of his extreme views went down to defeat and the reformers were reduced to an angry, impotent minority in the provincial assembly. While the governor was later severely criticized for the unorthodox role he had played in influencing the outcome of the election by appealing directly to the voters, in November he was congratulated by the colonial secretary and informed that he had been elevated to a baronetcy.

In 1837, flushed with his triumph in the provincial elections, Sir Francis Head, whom C. P. Mulvany was later to describe as "an addle-headed, self-conceited charlatan," appointed Sam Jarvis to the important post of chief superintendent of the Department of Indian Affairs for the province of Upper Canada. At Newark, it will be recalled, when he was two years old, a band of Mississauga Indians had adopted Sam into their tribe and given him the name Nehkik, which signified an otter. Now, in his forty-fifth year, Nehkik was charged by Governor Head with the responsibility, on a temporary basis as his appointment was originally conceived, of supervising the interests and welfare of thousands of Indians whose settlements, under local superintendents and agents, were scattered throughout the province. Nehkik had now become a chief.

Our first, vivid glimpse of Sam in his new office is provided by Mrs. Anna Jameson, a gifted English writer, who visited Manitoulin Island in August 1837. When she arrived, she found numerous tribes of Indians assembled there for the annual distribution of the sovereign's presents, and Sam, in an impressive setting, happily dispensing the Queen's largesse.

Earlier in the summer, Mrs. Jameson had journeyed overland to Detroit, passing through London, Ontario, and she had then proceeded by boat across Lake St. Clair and Lake Huron to Manitoulin Island. When she returned to England in the spring of 1838, her notebooks and sketchbooks full, she published *Winter Studies and Summer Rambles*, a perceptive narrative based upon her year-long experiences and travels in Upper Canada.[8]

Just before Mrs. Jameson had reached Manitoulin Island, her boat had overtaken a large schooner that was becalmed. Her party rowed over to the vessel and hailed a man who was standing in the bow. "What news!" was the cry. Mrs. Jameson recorded the momentous reply:

And the answer was that William the Fourth was dead, and that Queen Victoria reigned in his place! We sat silent looking at each other, and even in that very moment the orb of the sun rose out of the lake, and poured its beams full in our dazzled eyes.

In a setting like this on Manitoulin Island in August 1837, Mrs. Anna Jameson, author of Winter Studies and Summer Rambles, *found Samuel Peters Jarvis dispensing the Queen's annual presents to the assembled Indians soon after his appointment as chief superintendent of the Indian Affairs Department. Painted some years later on Manitoulin Island, this large watercolour by William Armstrong is regarded as one of his finest works.—Private Collection*

Pressing on, Mrs. Jameson and her party finally reached a sheltered bay on Manitoulin Island where the long, sloping shore was covered with wigwams and lodges. A hundred canoes passed them, "darting hither and thither on the waters" and when Mrs. Jameson landed she was received "with much politeness by Mr. Jarvis, the chief superintendent of Indian affairs, and by Major Anderson, the Indian agent."

Mrs. Jameson examined the presents that were being given to the Indians and was unimpressed. She wondered why some of the Indians

The son of Provincial Secretary William Jarvis, Samuel Peters Jarvis (1792-1857), subdivided the old Jarvis hundred-acre Park Lot 6 north of Queen Street in 1845, laid out Jarvis Street from Queen Street to Bloor Street, and gradually sold off the lots adjoining it. He is today remembered mainly as the "surviving principal" of the famous Jarvis-Ridout duel of 1817.—Private Collection

would have travelled as far as 500 miles to receive them, but concluded that an ordinance of the Indian Department required the attendance of every individual who desired to receive a gift. She noted that the men were given three-quarters of a yard of blue cloth, three yards of linen, one blanket, half an ounce of thread, four strong needles, one comb, one awl, one butcher's knife, three pounds of tobacco, three pounds of ball, nine pounds of shot, four pounds of powder, and six flints. The women received a yard and three-quarters of coarse woollen cloth, two and a half yards of printed calico, one blanket, one ounce of thread, four needles, one comb, one awl, and one knife. Even the children were recognized, each receiving a portion of woollen cloth and calico. All these articles were presented to the principal chief of each tribe, and he made the distribution to his own people. Over 3,700 Indians attended the ceremony.

The council then met in a log house where seventy-five chiefs seated themselves on the floor, half of them smoking thoughtfully. Every door and window was filled with pushing and shoving spectators from outside as Sam Jarvis rose solemnly to address the meeting. He stood at the upper end of the log house, flanked by Major Thomas G. Anderson and a bevy of minor officials. Sam's remarks were communicated to the gathering through an interpreter who was known to his tribe as the Blackbird. He enjoyed a considerable reputation as an orator, and his people proudly related that on one occasion he began making a speech at sunrise and didn't finish it until sunset. In the circumstances, Sam's official, tight-lipped address probably didn't tax the Blackbird unduly. When Sam had finished speaking, Mrs. Jameson related, there was a pause, and then a handsome Ottawa chief sprang to his feet. He spoke at length about the future conditions which might govern the presentation of gifts, but matters were left that he and his colleagues would deliberate further on the subject and, like a modern committee, bring in their conclusions the following year. Three other chiefs also spoke, a flag was presented, and at the end of the meeting a few chiefs whose conduct had been particularly meritorious over the past year were presented with medals, silver gorgets, and amulets.

A day or two after the council meeting, Sam learned that a trader from Detroit was lurking in a cove near the entrance to the bay, his boat filled with whiskey and rum. The trader intended intercepting the homeward-bound Indians and relieving them of their blankets and guns in exchange for some whiskey. Mrs. Jameson was impressed when Sam, with a fine cavalier gesture, despatched the Blackbird, who was a Christian teetotaler and therefore could be trusted, with a group of "stout men," to board the trader, dump his cargo into the bay, and tell him that if he wished to lodge a complaint, or apply for restitution, he could do so in Toronto.

Sam Jarvis invited Mrs. Jameson to join his entourage for the return trip across Georgian Bay to Penetanguishene, to Lake Simcoe, thence to Toronto, and this the English traveller was delighted to do. She wrote warmly of the politeness of Mr. Jarvis and his people, adding that "it ended with something more and better—real and zealous kindness."

In a scene that was reminiscent of the departure of Governor Simcoe's canopied flotilla from Quebec City in 1792, Sam's official party pulled away from Manitoulin Island on August 6 amid cheers, musket salutes, and "looking grand and official, with the British flag floating at our stern." The party was transported in two birch bark canoes, each twenty-five feet in length, and Mrs. Jameson shared one of them with Sam, the lieutenant-governor's son, "a lively boy of fourteen or fifteen," old Solomon the interpreter, and seven voyageurs. She snuggled into the bottom of the canoe, her blankets and night-gear serving as a seat, and arranged her other belongings around her: her cloak, umbrella, parasol, notebooks, sketchbooks, a basket containing a bottle of eau de Cologne, "and all those necessary luxuries that might be wanted in a moment."

The second canoe "carried part of Mr. Jarvis's retinue, the heavy baggage, provisions, marquees, guns, etc., and was equipped with eight paddles. The party consisted altogether of twenty-two persons," Mrs. Jameson concluded contentedly, "twenty-one men, and myself the only woman."

It was no mean feat for a woman of her day to travel alone through a vast and unsettled country. Forty-two years of age at the time, she was described as being fair, small, delicately featured. Her friend, Fanny Kemble, the famous English actress, said that she had "a skin of that dazzling whiteness which generally accompanies reddish hair such as hers was." And Nathaniel Hawthorne, the American writer, noted that "she must have been perfectly pretty in her day, a blue or grey-eyed fair-haired beauty."

She was naturally the centre of attention as Sam's flotilla made its way through the rugged, island scenery of Georgian Bay. On one occasion, after bathing in a concealed cove, she returned to find her breakfast placed on a rock, "with my pillow and cloak all nicely arranged, and a bouquet of flowers lying on it." She added, "This was a never-failing *gallanterie*, sometimes from one, sometimes from another, of my numerous *cavaliers*." On another occasion, she was deeply touched when "Mr. Jarvis made me a delicious elastic bed of some boughs, over which was spread a bear-skin, and over that blankets." And another evening, just before they reached Penetanguishene, a heavy storm broke over their bivouac and her tent had to be pitched on high ground. She managed to make a dry bed for herself, and Sam Jarvis brought her some hot madeira. She then rolled herself into a blanket and fell into a deep sleep.

The official party later crossed Lake Simcoe on the steamer, *Peter Robinson*, and from Holland Landing drove down Yonge Street in a coach. Mrs. Jameson was favourably impressed with the condition of the road, and added, "Everything told of prosperity and security: yet all this part of the country was, within a few weeks after, the scene of ill-advised rebellion, of tumult, and murder!" It was into such a setting in Toronto, of mounting alarm and darkening skies, that Sam Jarvis had now returned to play his part in suppressing Mackenzie's rebellion and driving him from the country.

CHAPTER SEVEN

Sam's Street

At noon on December 7, 1837, as William Lyon Mackenzie's insurgents were wrangling among themselves at John Montgomery's tavern on upper Yonge Street, three columns of a hastily assembled loyalist force set out from Toronto to give them battle.

Their plan of attack had been worked out the night before at a tense meeting in Dr. Strachan's library. With Sir Francis Head's approval it had been agreed that Colonel James Fitzgibbon would take charge of the operation. Some weeks earlier, confident of the political tranquility in his own province, the governor had unwisely sanctioned the withdrawal of the British regulars from Upper Canada in order to help Sir John Colborne quell Papineau's uprising in Quebec. Fitzgibbon had been among the first to recognize the folly of Governor Head's decision and to foresee the danger to the security of the government that was posed by Mackenzie's supporters. He knew they were undergoing secret military training on their farms throughout York County, and that their avowed aim was to overthrow the government, by force if necessary. It was not until early in December, however, when word reached Toronto that Mackenzie's men were moving towards their rendezvous at Montgomery's Tavern for an assault on the city, that Governor Head had finally reacted. Only then did he call out the militia.

Colonel Fitzgibbon had briskly sorted out the volunteers as they assembled in Toronto, and he had even paused to help some of the government officials prepare their weapons for battle. His plan of attack called for Colonel Allan MacNab to lead the main loyalist force north on Yonge Street, with Colonel William Chisholm's column advancing on the west side of the road a half mile to the left, and Colonel Sam Jarvis's force similarly moving up the east side of Yonge Street, a half mile to the right. Major Carfrae, of the militia artillery, was appointed to support the operation with two cannon which were to be trundled along with the main column. The governor and his aides were also to ride with Colonel MacNab's detachment, a military band close by.[1]

Curiously enough, although Toronto's population then numbered over 12,000, three days before the march up Yonge Street only 300 militiamen had responded to the governor's frantic call to arms. To his intense relief, they were finally joined by the well-trained "men of Gore," sixty or seventy militiamen led by Colonel MacNab who arrived in a steamer from Hamilton. The appearance of further volunteers from the outlying districts probably boosted the government force to around 700 men, considerably less than the 1,200 trained troops that Mackenzie later alleged had been thrown against him. Meanwhile, at Montgomery's Tavern, just north of today's Eglinton Avenue, the rebel force, discouraged over Mackenzie's indecision and the inadequate arrangements made for their reception, had shrunk to about 400 ill-equipped men.

Clearly, Toronto had not been swept by patriotic fervour. Possibly the city, like the governor, had simply refused to take Mackenzie's uprising seriously, or perhaps, since the province, like the United States, was in the throes of a severe depression, sympathy for the government was at low ebb. In any event, it was into the military vacuum created by the faint-hearted response of Toronto's citizenry that Sam Jarvis had vigorously moved. Invoking the glorious traditions of the past, he obtained Sir Francis Head's approval to raise a new militia unit, with himself at its head, to be called the Queen's Rangers, commemorating the two earlier regiments of that name that had been commanded by Governor Simcoe. Sam was an obvious choice for the command of the new unit. As long ago as 1825 he had attained the rank of lieutenant-colonel in the 2nd Regiment of West York Militia, and had retained that rank when he was later transferred to the 2nd North York Militia. Not only had he maintained an active interest in military affairs since the War of 1812, but his notorious hostility towards Mackenzie also qualified him, in the governor's eyes, for a position of command in the coming campaign.

In addition to Sam, the fledgling Queen's Rangers boasted two majors, ten captains, and ten lieutenants, many of them Sam's friends. A reasonable calculation, based upon the total number thought to have been under Fitzgibbon's command, would suggest that the effective strength of Sam's Rangers was around 150, all ranks.

As soon as Mackenzie learned of the approach of the government forces, he ordered the bulk of his rebels into a small woods that lay a little to the south of the tavern and west of Yonge Street. Another detachment, fewer in number, was deployed in a desolate, open field to the east, in line with Sam Jarvis's advancing column. Around 1 P.M. the loyalist forces reached their objective at today's Eglinton Avenue, and the main attack, led by Colonel Chisholm and Colonel MacNab, was directed by Fitzgibbon against the woods where the government scouts had quickly located Mackenzie's principal force. The engagement lasted less than thirty minutes. After a few raking volleys from the loyalist cannon and muskets, the rebels, including Mackenzie, fled in confusion across the winter fields. The total casualties suffered in the skirmish around the tavern were astonishingly light: on the side of the insurgents, one man was killed and four died later of their wounds; of the government force, no one was killed, and apparently no one was seriously wounded.

For Sam Jarvis, the high drama promised by the occasion had failed to materialize, no stirring epic had been written, the chance of pursuing and capturing Mackenzie as he ran for his life, his short legs pumping hard under the disproportionate weight of his large head and torso, had eluded him. History bestows her favours jealously, and no one was to achieve immortality as a result of the efforts that day at Montgomery's Tavern. As for Sam's outfit, little is known of its contribution to Mackenzie's rout. As one student of the period has put it, "A detailed account of its movements does not, apparently, exist."

Sir Francis Head, having tired of the political pressures imposed upon him in Upper Canada, had already resigned as lieutenant-governor, and his resignation had been accepted by the Colonial Office in November. He hadn't yet received word of their acceptance, however. He naturally regarded the skirmish on upper Yonge Street as a personal triumph, and a fitting finale to his service in Upper Canada. After ordering the burning of Montgomery's Tavern, as a lesson to those who would commit treason, he assembled the military band, turned his horse and led his victorious columns back to Toronto.

Before burning it, the government forces lost no time in searching the tavern for incriminating evidence and were rewarded when they found Mackenzie's abandoned carpetbag which contained the rolls of his supporters. For weeks, their task made easy by Mackenzie's negligence, they swept down upon scores of hapless farmers throughout York County and took them into custody to await trial.

As soon as it was discovered that Mackenzie had fled to Navy Island, on the Canadian side of the Niagara River, where he intended to set up his own provisional government, Sir Francis Head despatched part of the militia to the Niagara frontier. During their brief sojourn there, Colonel Allan MacNab and Captain Andrew Drew, R.N., organized the seizure of the American steamer *Caroline* as she lay one night at her wharf on the American shore. She had been ferrying supplies to Mackenzie's beleaguered party on Navy Island, and Captain Drew's men, in a daring raid, seized her crew and placed them ashore. The *Caroline* was then set afire and cut adrift. The militiamen on the Canadian shore watched with delight as the flaming ship, writhing in the surging current, disappeared over the falls.

After Mackenzie had left his sanctuary on Navy Island to seek refuge in the United States, Sam Jarvis returned from Niagara to Toronto with the Queen's Rangers where they mounted guard over the docks on the bay and patrolled the streets of the capital at night. Finally, by July 1838, the danger to the city had passed, the Queen's Rangers were discharged, and Sam turned his attention again to his duties with the Department of Indian Affairs.

Just as he returned to the office he had fitted up for himself at *Hazelburn*, the Earl of Durham paid a brief visit to Toronto on July 18 and 19 as part of his momentous tour through Upper and Lower Canada. He had arrived in Quebec with appropriate ceremony the previous May to look into the grievances that had erupted into rebellions in both provinces and to formulate his recommendations to the British government "respecting the form and future government" of the Canadas. After he had returned to England and submitted his celebrated *Report*, the Parliament of the United Kingdom enacted the Act of Union in the summer of 1840. Under the Act, which was proclaimed in Canada in 1841, the two old provinces, renamed Canada West and Canada East, were united within a single legislature.

Toronto naturally viewed the emergence of the new United Province with foreboding, especially when Kingston, its ancient rival, was selected as the new capital. One local newspaper prophesied that the depreciation in the city's property values would be fearful once the seat of government had been withdrawn, and its worried inhabitants were not amused when the Kingston *Chronicle and Gazette*, recalling York's capture by the Americans in 1813 and Mackenzie's recent rebellion, jibed gleefully, "We congratulate the citizens of Toronto that the Public Records will now be placed in a situation equally secure from foreign invasion on the one hand and from internal insurrection on the other.''[2]

Whatever Sam Jarvis's initial reaction may have been to these disquieting political developments, by the end of 1842, as the new government, dominated by the Honourable Robert Baldwin as attorney-general of Canada West and the Honourable Louis LaFontaine as attorney-general of Canada East pressed forward with its reforms, he had good reason to view their actions with mounting suspicion and hostility. His concerns arose from the appointment late in 1842 of a three-man commission to investigate the unsatisfactory conditions that were seen to exist in the Department of Indian Affairs. Criticism of the administration of the department was widespread, and growing complaints of its practices by the Indians themselves could no longer be ignored.

The commission of inquiry, which sat in Kingston, threw its meetings open to scores of witnesses for the airing of their grievances. Indian chiefs appeared from their scattered villages to complain bitterly about land transactions that they thought were inimical to their interests. There were complaints of fraud, bribery, religious discrimination, and a lack of concern generally for the welfare of the tribes under Sam's care. At first the charges were directed against the local superintendents of the bands who had settled in the Walpole Island–St. Clair district, and on the Six Nations lands on the Grand River. However, the ventilation of grievances in these localities inevitably cast doubt over the entire department, its administrative practices, and its supervision. As a consequence, the focus of the commission's inquiry quickly shifted to an examination of Sam's performance as its chief superintendent. In a carefully documented paper presented to the Canadian Historical Association in 1976, Douglas Leighton of Huron College summarized the reasons that underlay the commission's decision:

> The commissioners were dissatisfied already with the chief superinten-
> dent's conduct on several grounds. Representatives of different Indian
> bands had expressed their displeasure with Jarvis. Their accusations
> came to a peak with complaints from Lake Simcoe bands of his immoral
> behaviour and blatant favouritism in the distribution of annual presents.
> The commissioners, moreover, had noted certain irregularities in the
> chief superintendent's account books as early as November, 1842. Entries

for warrants issued eighteen months previously had obviously been made only days before the commission had received the accounts for examination. Jarvis had made large withdrawals of funds in advance as requisitions for tribal funds; these were supposed to be signed by the chief and show the purpose and the amount of the money withdrawn, but Jarvis had simply marked them "for the use of the tribe," making it impossible to trace the disposition of these funds. Jarvis' private bank account and his official one, both at the Bank of Upper Canada, indicated some juggling of money back and forth between the two. Jarvis' replies to enquiries concerning these irregularities were "evasive, confused and unsatisfactory."[3]

By the spring of 1843, Sam's position had become untenable. "Every day brings to light some new villany which I have to combat," he wrote bitterly to his wife. "But I trust all the machinations may yet fall to the dust—I have received what I told you I expected of Mr. Anderson [Thomas G. Anderson, the local agent at Manitoulin Island] and have no doubt that I shall have it in my power to bring to him his miserable treachery."[4]

And the following day Sam's son, William Dummer Powell Jarvis, now aged twenty-two, wrote sympathetically to his father from *Hazelburn*. While the reform earthquake that was now rocking the Family Compact had its epicentre in Kingston, William's letter reveals that violent tremors were also being felt in Toronto. After referring to the "Chain of Villany which the *Ministers* are so busy in forging," William continued, alluding to Sheriff William Botsford Jarvis, Sam's cousin who lived at *Rosedale*, "Many are apprehensive that the Sheriff will go next—there is a rigid enquiry going on into the state of his office which he will find difficulty in satisfying."[5] As matters developed, however, unlike Sam, Sheriff Jarvis managed to retain his office, and in fact had sufficient energy left over to try to extricate his harassed cousin from his financial difficulties. In a letter to Sam in Kingston of February 17, 1843, after reporting on some attempted sales of Sam's property elsewhere in the city, the sheriff disclosed that consideration was being given to the sale of at least a part of Sam's hundred-acre *Hazelburn* farm. "It is very desirable that a commencement should be made," the sheriff advised, "and if in time the sales would warrant your pulling your house down—it will be time enough to do it. The barns and stables can be sold on the Lots in which they stand but I would not sell 15 acres to any one person unless that person

107

bind himself to sell again for building purposes, as it would quite cut off the chances of the new Lots coming into the Market."*

And on February 21, the sheriff added an ominous *post scriptum* to a letter that clearly reflected his pessimism over Sam's chances of surviving the government inquiry. "I am trying hard to go to England this Spring," he wrote, "if they turn you out—you had better go, too."[6]

The depth of Sam's concern over the events that had now engulfed him is revealed in a letter, touched with pathos, that he wrote from Kingston to his son William on March 16:

> ... In the meantime I have only to urge upon you all to reduce your expenses as low as possible. My embarrassments are very great and will require every effort and all the energy I possess to overcome them. It is the most critical period I have ever experienced since I entered life & my present position weighs heavily upon me & at times make me feel very miserable.[7]

Later that month, he wrote to Mary in a less despondent tone. He noted that Jennie, one of the *Hazelburn* carriage horses, had succumbed to an attack of glanders, a disease that affected her nostrils and lungs. "It will be a great inconvenience to you," he acknowledged, "for I daresay it will be some time before she is fit for use again."[8] Significantly, he didn't suggest that she be replaced. The ailing Jennie was one of the pair that were used to draw Sir Peregrine and Lady Maitland's old carriage through the muddy, rutted streets of Toronto. Sam had purchased the carriage from the lieutenant-governor when he left the province in 1828. In a reference to Kingston, Sam next reported that

> the Town has been all bustle this morning in the expectation of the arrival of Sir Charles Metcalfe but an express has arrived from him to say he will not be here before tomorrow. A house near the Public Offices has been taken for him; it adjoins that of Mr. Dunn, and the Council have fitted it up for his Excellency's reception. Sir Charles Bagot will therefore remain where he is until he can be removed or return to England.... As to my returning home soon, I fear there is little chance for some time to

---

* In May 1843, perhaps responding to the sheriff's advice, Sam Jarvis sold a parcel of his *Hazelburn* farm to John Ewart, the later father-in-law of Sir Oliver Mowat. Today, the land comprises the block between Carlton and Maitland streets, on the west side of Jarvis Street.

come. If it were left to myself I should not be long absent. My presence is required here to watch the proceedings of that rascally commission, which is now sitting or pretending to, on Indian affairs. They work with closed doors, and therefore it is impossible for me to get any correct information as to the course they are taking, but it will all come out bye and bye.

By July 1843, the commission had given up all hope of winning Sam's co-operation in their inquiry into the irregularities they had discovered in his accounts, and they referred their findings to the governor general, Sir Charles Metcalfe. He in turn quickly delegated the matter to his civil secretary, Captain J. M. Higginson, who for the next four years was to pursue Sam doggedly in an attempt to recover the funds that the government auditors were convinced Sam had appropriated to his own use. From his own frustrating experience, Higginson was soon to discover that Sam had been fittingly named Nehkik by the Mississaugas, the otter being well known for its swift and elusive movements.

With his official position now in jeopardy, together with the heavy burden of caring for a family that included seven children, there can be little doubt that Sam's financial situation was rapidly becoming desperate. While he flatly denied any liability to the Indian Affairs Department for the improper use of its funds, the possibility of a crippling legal claim being launched against him at any moment must have weighed heavily on him. Also, the Bank of Upper Canada must have had serious misgivings as to his financial prospects because on August 1, 1843, Sam mortgaged much of his Toronto and York Township property to the bank as security for advances of £4,300.[9] Significantly, the hundred-acre *Hazelburn* farm was excluded from the mortgage, presumably to enable Sam to deal with it freely if his affairs should worsen to the point where its urgent liquidation was required.

After a fruitless exchange of correspondence with an unyielding Captain Higginson, Sam finally decided to write directly to Governor General Metcalfe in April 1844, to reply to the charges that had been levelled against him. His letter, which consisted of fifty-eight rambling pages, began by attacking the members of the commission for their vendetta against him, which he said was inspired by their own interests. He went on to argue that the difficulties of his department were the result of mismanagement by his predecessor, one William Hepburn. He also accused the commissioners of slanting their questions to the Indian witnesses so as to obtain evidence unfavourable to him, and concluded by observing that if he had been treated in a manner befitting the dignity of his office, the problems complained of would never have arisen. Sam's answers to the specific charges against him, as Leighton has pointed out, were "somewhat more credible."

> The confusion in the Department's accounts could be traced to the shortage of clerical help in his office; his frequent journeys made it impossible for him to look after such matters personally. His explanation for opening the official account in the Bank of Upper Canada was also logical; he had simply wanted to keep confusion to a minimum.

The governor general replied to Sam's lengthy letter on May 8, 1844, and his comments weren't encouraging. In the manner of Sir William Pitt, he said that he was "compelled to admit that your explanations are not thorough and satisfactory," and he went on to say that he was suspending his decision "until your pecuniary transactions with the several tribes are brought to a close by the final adjustment of all monies in your hands being made over to the Receiver General."

A week later, in a circular addressed to the five regional superintendents, Captain Higginson informed them that "it will be your duty henceforth to correspond direct with me on all such subjects as you have been accustomed heretofore to bring under the notice of the Chief Superintendent of Indian Affairs." As Leighton has pointed out, "The reason given for this change was the transfer of the seat of government to Montreal, but the explanation was accepted by few. Samuel Peters Jarvis had been stripped of his official rank in all but name."

And the following September, after the civil secretary had again tried without success to discover the reasons for the discrepancies in Sam's records which Sam seemed unwilling or unable to provide, an exasperated Higginson wrote:

> Unless the orders referred to are forthwith obeyed, and the explanation rendered upon every point which has been brought to your notice, His Excellency will consider it to be his duty, however painful, to remove you from the situation of Chief Superintendent of Indian Affairs; and to adopt such subsequent measures as may appear requisite, to enforce your compliance with the repeated applications that have been made to you.

Sam Jarvis responded to that threat by asking if he could retain an accountant at his own expense to place his books in order. The government agreed, but insisted that it too would hire an accountant for the same purpose, and suggested that the two representatives sign a joint report when they had completed their work. The government accountant later reported that he had found the books in shocking condition, adding "I may say, that under the circumstances, I am not aware of any mode by which it can be accurately ascertained what the total amount of Mr. Jarvis' debits should be." At first he placed the amount somewhere between £4,500 and a little over £9,000, but finally concluded that Sam was in debt to the Department in the crushing amount of £9,733.9s.11d.

To complicate matters further, Sam's accountant produced a figure of £1,086.4s.½d. The government then countered by appointing a third accountant, and both sides agreed that his findings would be accepted as final. Early in May 1845, the new accountant arrived at a debit balance against Sam of £4,132.18s.5d. The government accepted the figure, Sam did not.

In what he must have hoped, mistakenly as it turned out, would be the finale of the long drawn-out affair, the civil secretary wrote to Sam on May 10, 1845, stating the government's final position and suspending him from office. After citing "the unexplained balance against you, amounting to £4,132.18.5 Cy," the letter continued,

> The Governor General will rejoice if this large balance can be in any manner satisfactorily accounted for by you, but until that be accomplished, His Excellency considers it to be his painful duty to suspend you from your Office of Chief Superintendent of Indian Affairs.
>
> The Records of your Department will be deposited in the Indian Branch of the Civil Secretary's Office for which purpose you will be pleased to transmit them to me by an early and safe opportunity.
>
> You are aware that under any circumstances it was not intended to continue your Office on its present footing beyond the 30th of June next, but it was the Governor Generals wish to be able to recommend you to the Secretary of State for an appointment to the Department, which will now be deferred pending the satisfactory adjustment of your accounts within a reasonable period.

In a *post scriptum*, Higginson added, "You are requested to inform the different Tribes under your superintendence that they may for the present communicate direct with my Office until a more permanent arrangement can be determined on."*

---

* This significant document in the history of Jarvis Street is lodged with the S. P. Jarvis Collection, B60, Baldwin Room, Metropolitan Toronto Library.

Sam's appointment, according to the official records, was in fact terminated on June 30, 1845,[10] though the government continued to prod him for several years in an attempt to have him explain or settle his accounts. It was in these painful circumstances, in June 1845, that Sam called on John G. Howard as a surveyor to prepare his *Hazelburn* property for immediate subdivision and sale.

Born in Hertfordshire, England, in 1803, Howard had emigrated to Toronto in 1832 where he began his career as an architect. He later became surveyor for the city and then its engineer. An accomplished artist himself, he helped organize many of the early art exhibitions in the city, and was a prolific contributor to them all. On one occasion, an exhibition with which he was associated suffered a financial loss as a result of the public's inability to attend it because of a cholera epidemic. Howard stepped in and personally covered the deficit. He taught drawing at Upper Canada College on King Street from 1833 to 1857, continuing his labours after he had retired to his *Colborne Lodge* in High Park in 1855. He is best remembered today for his princely gift of that vast park to the city.

Howard was by no means unfamiliar with the *Hazelburn* property. Four years before, he had designed and raised the steeple that soared above the small, frame church that had just been built at the northwest corner of Sam's farm. Bishop Strachan was instrumental in acquiring the land from Sam in 1841 as the site for the first St. Paul's Anglican Church. The property lay on the south side of the Concession Line (Bloor Street) upon which it had a frontage of ninety-nine feet with a depth of 136 feet. When Howard opened up the new Jarvis Street, its west limit lay 132 feet east of the church. The present St. Paul's, for years one of the city's most influential pulpits, still occupies the first parcel of land that Sam Jarvis was to dispose of from his father's Simcoe-granted park lot.

As John G. Howard was launching into his first survey of Sam's property, another Toronto artist, Paul Kane, was setting out on a historic journey through the western wilderness to the Pacific Ocean. In his *Wanderings of an Artist*, Kane recalled, "I left Toronto on the 17th of June 1845, with no companions but my portfolio and box of paints, my gun, and a stock of ammunition, taking the most direct route to Lake Simcoe."[11] He was not to return to Toronto from his wanderings until the fall of 1848. It would be pleasing to think that Sam Jarvis, as head of the Indian Affairs Department, was on hand at the city gates on the memorable occasion of Kane's departure, to wish

John George Howard (1803-1890). This portrait in watercolour was painted in 1848 when Howard was acting as Sam Jarvis's selling agent for the building lots he had earlier surveyed and laid out for Jarvis on both sides of the new Jarvis Street. In August 1850, after working for five years on the subdivision, Howard complained bitterly to Jarvis, "not one shilling in cash have I received from you."—Colborne Lodge, *Toronto Historical Board*

113

The first St. Paul's Anglican Church on the Concession Line (Bloor Street) was completed in 1842 on a small property that Bishop Strachan acquired from Sam Jarvis. The steeple, designed by John G. Howard, was raised under his direction in just six hours. Today St. Paul's Chapel and Church Office occupy this site.—Metropolitan Toronto Library Board

114

him well and speed him on his way, perhaps with some useful letters of introduction. Such was not the case. In fact, by the time the red-bearded artist reached Manitoulin Island, Sam had been succeeded as chief superintendent by Thomas G. Anderson, the local Indian agent who had welcomed Mrs. Anna Jameson to the island eight years before, and whom Sam had recently accused of treachery. Anderson, who was holding the temporary title of provisional visitor of the Indian Affairs Department, received Paul Kane warmly and doubtless took a lively interest in the remarkable sketches and portraits he was making of the Indians at Anderson's station.

From June until August 1845, John G. Howard must have worked tirelessly over his surveys and plans of subdivision in order to enable Sam to publish in the Toronto *Globe* his first announcement of the sale of his *Hazelburn* lots:

SALE OF BUILDING LOTS

THE SUBSCRIBER begs leave to inform the public, that he has recently caused Park Lot Number 6, in the city of Toronto to be subdivided into BUILDING LOTS, which are now offered for Sale.

The proximity of this property to the Market, and to the business part of the city, renders it peculiarly eligible for the residences of private families, of persons engaged in commerce or of mechanics.

An avenue of eighty feet in width has been opened through the centre of the Lot, whereby an uninterrupted prospect is laid open from the Concession Line [Bloor Street] at the rear of the Lot, to the Bay, at the foot of Nelson Street, a distance of more than a mile and a half.

George Street, upon which the Bank of Upper Canada is erected, has likewise been extended through the Lot on the Eastern side of it, and on the West side; Mutual street has been opened sixty feet wide—one half on number six, and the other half on number seven, the property of the Hon. Peter M'Gill.

Plans of this Estate, prepared by John G. Howard, Esq., Architect, may be seen at the office of Mr. Beckman, in Nelson Street, from whom every information relating to the conditions of sale, and terms of payment, may be obtained.

Samuel P. Jarvis.

Toronto, August 19, 1845.

Sam's reference to the opening of an avenue eighty feet in width through the centre of the lot was premature. His house stood in the middle of the proposed new Jarvis Street, just below its intersection with today's Shuter Street, and the new road was not opened completely until the spring of 1847 when Sam's house was finally torn down.

While the sale of his *Hazelburn* property was wholly absorbing Sam's attention during the summer of 1845, his mother's life was moving towards its close. Old Hannah Jarvis had been living at Queenston for several years with her daughter, Hannah Owen, who was married to Alexander Hamilton, the town's postmaster. Alexander's father, the Honourable Robert Hamilton, had been a prominent figure at Niagara when William and Hannah Jarvis had arrived there from England in 1792, over fifty years before.

Until the end of her life, Hannah Jarvis remained a strong-minded, matriarchal figure at the centre of her scattered family. When she was still living in Hamilton, for example, she wrote to her daughter in Queenston about Sam's unused piano and organ at *Hazelburn*: "you should have the Piano and organ," she stated flatly, "if Sam choses to give it up—I think it is only in his way—and I know Mary does not like music—their children cannot make any use of it—for a long time to come." And in September 1842, when she was in her eightieth year, she boarded the steamer *Transit* at Queenston and sailed resolutely across the lake to spend a few days with Sam and Mary at *Hazelburn*. According to her diary, Sam gave two dinner parties for her, "dinner at 7 o'clock," she noted on the first occasion, "half past Ten the House empty." She also rode out with Miss Powell to *Rosedale*, and walked to St. James' from *Hazelburn* where she heard a good sermon. On Monday, September 12, she recorded that Sam had left for Kingston, where, as she was probably unaware, the government commission was just beginning its fateful investigation of his department. On the following Wednesday, she noted, "Fine cool Mrs. and Miss Baldwin called—went riding to College Avenue—through the Town—down past the Don Bridge to the Plank Road." Doubtless on that occasion she drove as well past her old Caroline Street house which Sam had rented to Paul Bishop, a blacksmith. The following day, after rising at 5 A.M., she returned to Queenston. She endured a stormy crossing of the lake, and was still able later in the afternoon to visit Mrs. McMichen, one of her old cronies, where she imparted the latest Toronto gossip and drank tea.

116

With the opening of the Welland Canal in 1829, Queenston's importance as the historic staging centre for the portaging of freight around Niagara Falls en route to and from Lake Erie, diminished sharply. By the end of Hannah's long life, particularly when the navigation season closed, it was as if Time itself had fallen asleep in Queenston. Idyllic as her last days must have seemed in that unhurried and familiar setting where her memories ran deeper than the river itself, Hannah was by no means spared the pangs of financial need. In order to augment her modest income, for some years before her death she busied herself making shirts, nightgowns, and bibs for a wide circle of customers and friends, not only at Niagara, but across the river at Lewiston as well. Her diary of 1842-43 abounds with references to these transactions which kept her usefully occupied, and reduced her dependence upon her family as well. "Finished 11 shirts—got 14 more," she noted on one occasion, and later the same month, "Mr. Ross sent a piece of cotton to be made up." On January 2, 1843, she confided to her diary that she had now turned eighty, "Cloudy—some snow. H.J's birthday—80 years old born in 1763." The following day Mrs. Stayner called and "brought 3 Nightgowns to be made for Louisa." And in February, "Mrs Fitzgerald brought 11 Bibs (& two Dollars) from Mrs O'Ricky to be made."

Sam, however, was still doing his best to support the old lady. When she visited Toronto she had noted that she had "borrowed from Sam $8," and on October 18, 1842, she received "A letter from Samuel P. Jarvis with an order for £14-2-6."

Hannah's end finally came at Queenston on Sunday, September 20, 1845. She was in her eighty-third year. She was buried in the Hamilton family's little cemetery, beside the Niagara River. Later, a stone was raised above her, and it read,

> *Shed not for her the bitter tear,*
> *Nor give the heart to vain regret,*
> *'Tis but the casket that lies here,*
> *The gem that filled it sparkles yet.*[12]

The response to Sam's announcement of the sale of his building lots had been disappointing. Sales were slow, reflecting perhaps the public's awareness of his difficulties and the general expectation that he would soon be forced to reduce his prices. If such a view did exist, it was certainly confirmed by the government's action against Sam early

117

in 1846. As a result of a further audit of the Indian Affairs Department's books, the balance against him was raised to £6,375.6s.11d. Still protesting his innocence, Sam again pleaded for more time to explain the deficiency and clear his name. This time, he enlisted the support of his friend William Cayley, the provincial inspector-general, and one Dickenson, a bookkeeper in Cayley's office. While they could do nothing more than cover the old ground, at least Sam gained valuable time as he intensified his efforts to liquidate *Hazelburn*, his last substantial asset, and raise some cash for a highly uncertain future.

At that critical moment, a miracle occurred. William Cawthra, probably the wealthiest man in Toronto at that time, agreed to lend Sam £4,000 on the security of a mortgage covering the south forty acres of the *Hazelburn* property, extending from Gerrard Street south to Queen Street. It was a development loan, designed to help defray the costs involved in completing the subdivision.

Cawthra's father, Joseph, had laid the foundation of the Cawthra family's fortune when he opened an apothecary shop at the northwest corner of Caroline and King Streets in 1806. William Cawthra was five years old at the time, Sam was in his teens. Since the Cawthra store was at the foot of Caroline Street, Sam must have visited it frequently and would have known William since he was a child. In his adult years, as a man of keen and independent judgement, William Cawthra remained conspicuously aloof from the Family Compact. It was simply in his role as a shrewd investor, therefore, that Cawthra, on July 1, 1846, by a stroke of his pen, provided Sam with the money he needed to finance the final development of his property.

Cawthra's decision to participate in the project didn't pass un-noticed. Realizing that John G. Howard would now be in a position to complete the opening up of Jarvis Street, rolling the broad avenue out like a new carpet stretching from Queen to Bloor Street, investors and prospective housebuilders appeared, and prices started to move up. On December 15, 1845, for example, when Sam's project was first launched, Sheriff William Botsford Jarvis had descended from *Rosedale* to lend his cousin a hand, and perhaps indulge in a little good-humoured speculation. He purchased five lots from Sam at the northeast corner of Jarvis and Gerrard Streets, paying £752 for them. A few days later he mortgaged his new holding to Alexander Burnside for £650. As a result, Sam immediately received a welcome £752, and the sheriff, for only £102 of his own money, obtained an attractive stake in the potential success of the subdivision. On April 17, 1846, however, before Cawthra had made his big development loan, the sheriff prematurely sold two of his five lots to Robert Beckman for £221. The following August 11, in the euphoric aftermath of Cawthra's appearance on the scene, Beckman turned around and sold the same lots for £500 to William Rowsell, a brother of Henry Rowsell who was the city's leading bookseller and stationer.

Following the same pattern, Sam's old school friend Jonas Jones, who had written to him consolingly from Brockville in 1817 when Sam was confined in the York gaol, also purchased for £500 a piece of property on the west side of Jarvis Street at Gerrard Street from Levens Newsom, a carpenter who had paid Sam £104 for it before Cawthra had made his loan.

By the time spring had arrived in 1847, Sam and Mary Jarvis had removed themselves and their family from *Hazelburn*, and demolition of the twenty-three-year-old house had begun. The spacious verandah, where Sam liked to muse at night as he contemplated the bay, was stripped away, the still-bright bricks were knocked down amidst clouds of dust, the joists and interior black walnut panelling were dismantled and sold. Howard's journal shows that he found no trouble in locating willing buyers for the salvaged material. On May 8, 1847, he recorded that he had "Sold Carthu Esq. the old woodwork of the Dwelling House & sheds." He noted in further entries under the same date that he had received "Carthu Capt. cheque on U. C. Bank for old Woodwork—100.0.0" and that he "Paid Saml. P. Jarvis as per cheque on the Bank of U C—100.0.0. Howard's cryptic entries did not of course disclose the use he had found for Sam's old woodwork.

In June 1847, Colonel Arthur Carthew bought five acres of land on today's Lawton Boulevard, overlooking Yonge Street, from Charles Wallace Heath, for whom Heath Street is named. The land was part of Heath's subdivision of his forty-acre estate. Christ Church, Deer Park, now stands on the most southerly lot acquired by Carthew, at the northwest corner of today's Heath Street and Lawton Boulevard. Carthew, with Howard's assistance as architect, built a fine house for himself on his new property, and Sam Jarvis's walnut panelling was fitted carefully into it. In 1850, the Carthew property was purchased by John Fisken, later a co-founder of the Imperial Bank of Canada, who developed the place into a beautiful estate which he called *Lawton Park*. In 1904, the property was acquired by John J. Palmer who renamed it *Huntly Lodge*. The old house, with the *Hazelburn* panelling still in it, remained intact until 1935 when it was finally demolished to make way for the apartment house that now occupies the site.[13]

Meanwhile, also in June 1847, the Jarvis case was still dragging on as Sam and his new supporters, Cayley and Dickenson, sought to fend off the government in its attempts to have Sam settle his accounts. In desperation, the government auditor addressed a long memorandum to the Earl of Elgin, the third governor general to become involved in the affair. He accused Cayley of the unnecessary prolongation of the inquiry. Cayley, in the meantime, was blaming the delay on the complicated methods of accounting that were used at that time by all government departments, an allegation which prompted the government auditor to reply scathingly, "a schoolboy might have kept his Accounts without the slightest difficulty." As Sam's saga with the government approached its fifth year, the tempo of the inquiry slowed to the pace of a game of lawn tennis, played listlessly under a hot summer sun. The stalemate was to continue to the end of Sam's life, the irregularities found in his books neither explained nor settled satisfactorily.

Shortly after the Jarvis house had been torn down, and the way was cleared for Jarvis Street to be extended to its Bloor Street objective, William Cawthra, no doubt encouraged by the summer developments, again entered the picture. On August 18, 1847, Cawthra not only renewed his £4,000 mortgage on the south forty acres, but as part of the transaction, at a discounted price, purchased outright from Sam "eleven acres two roods and three poles" in the northwest section of the park lot. In effect, he acquired the land surrounding the infant St. Paul's Church, which gave him a frontage on today's Bloor Street of 132 feet measured west from Jarvis Street, together with a parcel that extended south along the west side of Jarvis Street to a point below today's Wellesley Street, a distance of 26 chains, or 1,716 feet. It was a momentous purchase in the history of Jarvis Street.[14]

The Cawthras loved land, and it always proved worthy of their devotion. Like Lord Duveen acquiring a lost Titian or a forgotten Rembrandt, they clung to it, savoured it, and only parted with it reluctantly. There was to be a Cawthra presence on upper Jarvis Street for almost a hundred years, throughout the late Victorian period when the district became known as Toronto's Champs Élysées, throughout the Edwardian Era, its age of elegance, and even during its later days of dubious renown, after its glories had faded.

CHAPTER EIGHT

The Death of Sam Jarvis

John Ross Robertson, in his *Landmarks of Toronto*, stated mistakenly that Sam Jarvis's *Hazelburn* house had been demolished in 1848, a year later than had actually been the case, and that this had occurred "at the request of the corporation," implying that the city of Toronto had been anxious to open up Jarvis Street from Queen Street to its dead end at Bloor Street. Sam would have been delighted with such a flattering explanation of the graceless demise of his house. William Cawthra and John G. Howard would have been astonished.

In the original announcement of the sale of his building lots in 1845, Sam had informed the readers of the *Globe* that the plans of his estate could be inspected at Mr. Beckman's office in Nelson Street. Mr. Beckman's efforts to sell the lots were unsuccessful, and a year later, with his financial worries intensifying and his patience at the breaking point, Sam appointed the energetic John G. Howard to act as his exclusive selling agent in place of the unworthy Mr. Beckman. Sam's choice was a good one.

At the same time as Howard was struggling with the problems of *Hazelburn*, he completed the impressive Bank of British North America building at Yonge and Wellington Streets (now demolished), in 1846 he was supervising the construction of the great mental asylum at 999 Queen Street West (now demolished) for which he had won the appointment of architect in an open competition, and in 1847-8 he was responsible for designing and building the House of Industry on Elm Street, the now-threatened Laughlen Lodge and last survivor of his work in downtown Toronto. Howard's reputation as a gifted architect, however, extended beyond the city: in 1843 he enjoyed the distinction of winning an open competition with his designs for the first building to be projected by Queen's University in Kingston. Howard received the coveted prize of £50 for his plans "of chaste Greek Revival detail and an imposing Ionic portico," but the infant university's resources proved insufficient for his ambitious specifications, and the project had to be scrapped.[1] In addition to supervising the construction of St. John's York Mills which he had designed, he was also responsible for the landscaping of the present St. James' Cemetery on Parliament Street, and the classical grounds of Osgoode Hall. "Howard must always rank with the greatest of the 19th Century Toronto architects for his contribution to its early development," Professor Eric Arthur declared in *No Mean City*, ". . . his gift of High Park with its 165 acres and his now historic house place him in the forefront of the city's benefactors."

With Howard securely in charge of his Jarvis Street development, Sam was free to indulge his yearning for travel. Immediately after he had abandoned his house to the wreckers, his travel diaries reveal that he journeyed to Quebec on a fishing trip, from June 8 to August 9, 1847.[2] His companions were William Cayley, who was helping him in his running battle with the government, Captain James McGill Strachan, and a Mr. Todd. Captain Strachan, a keen sportsman and man about town, was Bishop Strachan's son. He occupied a cottage in the shadow of his father's "Palace" on Front Street and, as a consequence perhaps, spoke to history in only a whisper.

By the time Sam had returned from his outing in Quebec, we may be sure that John G. Howard had already completed the critically important negotiations with William Cawthra that assured his continued support of Sam's project. On August 18, nine days after Sam's return, Cawthra not only renewed his £4,000 mortgage on the south section of Sam's property, but, as we have noted, purchased outright over eleven acres on the west side of Jarvis Street, extending from Bloor Street to a point below the later Wellesley Street. With the important Cawthra transaction closed, and the proceeds presumably deposited safely in his account with the Bank of Upper Canada, Sam lost no time in heading for the wilds again. On August 26, he journeyed north to Owen Sound, Manitoulin Island and Sault Ste. Marie, this time with Colonel Casimir Gzowski of Toronto as a member of his party. Sam didn't return to the city until October, and then left again in November for an extended trip to Boston, stopping en route to visit some relatives and friends at Niagara.[3]

From Sam's earliest days as chief superintendent of the Indian Affairs Department until his difficulties arose in 1843, it is not hard to imagine him making the most of his opportunities to fish and hunt as he trekked through his wilderness fiefdom on official visits to his superintendents. Those were the glory days of his incumbency, but even after his downfall in 1845, he somewhat pathetically continued to return year after year to old haunts where he knew the fishing or hunting was especially good. His diaries show him late in the summer hunting for deer, moose, or bear around Penetanguishene or at distant Sault Ste. Marie, shooting snipe in the Holland Marsh in September, ducks at Long Point in November. Through Howard's tireless efforts, the steady flow of cash from his Jarvis Street sales allowed Sam to kick a free leg. After he had paid off Cawthra's mortgage in September 1850, his wanderings became even more frequent and extensive.

Just before the Cawthra mortgage was discharged, however, John G. Howard sat down at his desk one night at *Colborne Lodge* and penned Sam a bitterly critical letter. He began by reviewing his role in Sam's affairs since June 1845, and then gave full rein to the frustrations and disappointments he had endured in his long relationship with the laird of Jarvis Street.

Toronto, August 21, 1850

To S. P. Jarvis Esq.,

Dear Sir;

I was very much surprized at the remarks you made in my office to-day concerning my account. It is five years last June since I surveyed Park Lot No. 6 and staked it out in Lots according to your instructions; I also drew a series of plans which were taken to the Office of W. Beckman; it is now little more than four years since the plans were taken from that Gentleman and put in my possession for the purpose of disposing of the said Lots. I immediately had large handbills printed and employed W. Wakefield on the 7th Nov 1846 to sell the Lots by Auction, but the upset price being too high they would not sell. May 10th 1847 I again had large bills posted and employed W. Wakefield a second time to sell the House and Lots but with little better success, and I have from time to time altered the plans to suit your views. The labour alone for Surveying and Staking out the Lots comes to nearly £100. Advertising and printing to fully as much more which my accounts will prove; I have also superintended the construction of Roads, and drawn your Plans for Dwelling Houses and not one shilling in cash have I received from you on account of the above from the commencement.

The following is a statement of what I have received for the four years service.

Deed for two Lots on Jarvis Street	£200.0
Old fence which surrounds it	2.10.0
Old Brick sold to Gibson	20.11.3
	£231.1.3 (*sic*)

If you consider the £231.1.3 as above a sufficient remuneration for my services you can refuse to give me the Deed for the Lot Last purchased amounting to £200. which together will make £511.1.3. (*sic*)

I wish you distinctly to understand that the Books and papers in my possession are always ready for your inspection, and as soon as convenient I will submit them with the vouchers to the inspection of W. Harrington and W. Wakefield.

I have nothing whatever to do with Mr. Cayley nor will I render my accounts to him.

> I am dear Sir
> Yours Truly
> John G. Howard[4]

It is evident that Howard's letter had little effect upon Sam Jarvis. Indeed, Howard's next letter on the subject of his account, written seven months later, suggests that Sam had ignored the whole matter until the following March. Since Howard's exclusive, five-year selling agreement was due to expire in the summer of 1851—by which time he would have remitted to Sam over £7,000 in cash as a result of his efforts—the patient and perhaps naive architect must have finally come to the chilling realization that if he didn't take action now, his chances of receiving some cash in addition to a couple of lots for his extensive services would be minimal. Accordingly, Howard wrote again to Sam Jarvis, from Toronto, on March 19, 1851.

Dear Sir,

Your letter of the 12th instant did not come to hand until the 17th, in reply to which I beg to state that in referring you to the books in my possession, I never intended it to be a cursory inspecting; I will devote the whole day to you if you wish, and I will also walk over the ground with you and point out all the Lots sold according to Leases made out by me, and Descriptions furnished to you to enable you to make out the Deeds.

I maintain that after you had placed your Estate in my hands for five years/which I am prepared to prove you did/and allowed me to incur very heavy expenses you had no right to dispose of a single Lot without paying me my commission.

I have gone carefully over the Plans and Estimated the quality and value of that portion of your Estate yet unsold, for the information of the Assessors at your requisition, and enclose it to you, a copy of which without the prices I have forwarded to Mr. Trotter.

I have two leases ready for your signature and must request that you will not throw obsticles (*sic*) in my way, of disposing of as much of the remaining property this summer as I can, as you must be well aware that I have been at a great expense on account of the Estate and have always readily concurred in any plans suggested by you which you considered might be to your advantage, regardless of the trouble and expense to myself, I have also at the advice of my friends postponed my intended visit to England this summer in order that I may do my utmost in disposing of Lots until the term has expired.

My friendly feelings toward you and yours are unaltered, whatever you may think to the contrary, and I feel satisfied that if you will spend an hour or two with me in going over the Books, we shall be able to settle the matter amicably without referring it to any legal Tribunal, altho' should it come to that, the evidence that I can bring forward will be sufficient to give me a verdict for all I claim.

> I am dear Sir
> Yours Truly
> John G. Howard[5]

According to Howard's estimate, as referred to in his letter, the unsold lots on Jarvis Street amounted to twenty acres and were worth £14,150, based upon the proposed asking prices.

During the time that Howard was grumbling about his overdue account, to add to Sam Jarvis's discomfiture, William Lyon Mackenzie, like a spectre from the past, returned to Toronto from the United States with his wife and family. After an absence of thirteen years, thanks to a general amnesty having been declared, Mackenzie had suddenly re-emerged in the city as a prominent and colourful figure. He had even presented himself to the electors of Haldimand in a by-election in the spring of 1851 and, his personal magnetism still formidable, had easily vanquished his three opponents including George Brown of the *Globe*. Mackenzie gratefully took his seat as an independent reformer in the May session of the legislature which was then meeting in Quebec.

On occasion, Sam must have glimpsed Mackenzie walking through the streets of Toronto, conversing amiably with his friends, and it is not difficult to imagine the sombre thoughts that filled his mind. When Mackenzie had fled the province in 1837 with a price on his head, Sam had just begun his term as chief superintendent of the Indian Affairs Department. Now at the age of fifty-eight, after having been hounded and buffeted for years by an unrelenting government inquiry, he was without office. Long a symbol, if not an ornament, of the Family Compact, he had suffered the fate of becoming its most conspicuous casualty. In the new scheme of society that was emerging in Toronto, it was Mackenzie who was at home, Sam Jarvis was the stranger. W. D. LeSueur described the changed milieu at the time of Mackenzie's return:

> The place that had known the "family compact" knew it no more; the power of Downing Street was broken; the French Canadians were almost ardent in the support of the new régime, of which they plainly saw the profitable side; ministers rose and fell at the bidding of the parliamentary majority; the politicians were revelling in the so-called "patronage of the crown"; the governor general might still wield a social, or even, if, like Lord Elgin, he was a very able man, a certain intellectual influence; but in all matters of provincial, as distinct from imperial, interests, his executive council was supreme.[6]

In 1856, when the city directory showed him living on the north side of Bloor Street in Yorkville, Sam Jarvis decided to broaden the scope of his travels and visit England and Ireland. While his property sales on Jarvis Street were now largely completed, having been stimulated by the opening in 1850 of the St. Lawrence Hall at King and Nelson streets, and the rebuilding of Bishop Strachan's St. James' Cathedral on a more lavish scale after the Great King Street Fire of 1849, there was still considerable vacant land on Jarvis Street, particularly in its upper section. These tracts were being held by men like William Cawthra for later development. But Sam's fortunes had improved sufficiently to enable him not only to journey in style to England, but also, during his absence, to pay off the old mortgage for £4,300 that had been held by the Bank of Upper Canada on most of his property since the clouded days of 1843.

Sam sailed from New York for Liverpool in April 1856. He spent some time in London sightseeing and again met Sir John and Lady Colborne, now Lord and Lady Seaton. He visited the Lake District, Bath, Epsom, and Ascot, and then journeyed to Dublin where the highlight of his stay was an impressive dinner with the Lord Lieutenant of Ireland.[7] The main reason for his trip abroad, however, was the opportunity it gave him to see two of his married children again. His oldest son and namesake, Captain Samuel Peters Jarvis, now thirty-six, had chosen a military career and Sam was intensely proud of him. He had married Renée Wilson in 1850, and they were living at Sandhurst at the time of Sam's visit. Sam also journeyed to Carlisle in the north of England to see his daughter Emily and her husband, Sydney B. Farrell, who was an officer with the Royal Engineers, and whom she had married in 1854. All in all, for Sam it was a satisfying and timely trip.

He returned to Toronto in the fall, and his diary for the early months of 1857 contains only a few, spasmodic entries. It is evident that his health deteriorated rapidly after his return. He died on Sunday, September 6, in his sixty-fifth year. His funeral took place at 3 P.M. the following Tuesday "from his late residence on Wellington Street," according to the Toronto *Globe*. A black carriage, gleaming with fresh lacquer and drawn by black horses, bore Sam silently up Parliament Street to St. James' Cemetery. There, in the shaded gently rolling grounds that John G. Howard had laid out years before, Sam ended his uneasy pilgrimage.

Sam Jarvis's old enemy, William Lyon Mackenzie had been publishing a weekly newspaper in Toronto since 1853. It was originally entitled *Mackenzie's Message*, but later was called the *Toronto Weekly Message*. As in the days of the *Colonial Advocate*, the editorial tone of the *Message* was sharply critical of the workings of government and of most of the country's public men. It is scarcely surprising, therefore, that Mackenzie, like an old raven croaking from a withered tree, found it impossible to resist the temptation, while he was noting Sam's demise, of commenting caustically upon the highlights of his career.

Died, last Sunday morning, 6th Sept., in Toronto in the 65th year of his age, SAMUEL PETERS JARVIS, Esq, late Chief Superintendant of Indian Affairs, and eldest son of Wm. Jarvis Esq, who was Secretary of Upper Canada, under Governor Gore, the bitter persecutor of Sheriff Wilcox, and the steady patron of Sir Alan McNab. Jarvis was formerly deputy

Secretary, and he embezzled many thousand dollars of the money of the poor Indians which he was paid to protect. Of course the government winked at all this. In 1826, he headed the riot which ended in the total destruction of W. L. Mackenzie's printing Establishment and it is probable he died very rich for he had much property.

Mackenzie's statement that the government had "winked" at Sam's alleged exploitation of the "poor Indians" could only have referred to the governments that were in power from 1837 to 1841, during Sam's early years of office. The inquiry launched in 1842 by the new reform government, it will be recalled, after discovering the earlier irregularities, sought to unravel them, and when it couldn't, dismissed Sam in 1845. If some of his readers found Mackenzie's comments distasteful and inappropriate to an obituary notice, they appear to have forgiven him quickly. The following year, after he had resigned his seat in the legislature because of failing health, his admirers took up a collection on his behalf, easily raising over £1,200. Part of the fund was used to purchase a house for him in Bond Street where he died in 1861. It has survived and is maintained today as a living museum by the Toronto Historical Board.

Mackenzie's demagogic allusion to Sam as probably having "died very rich" is open to more serious question. By the time Sam had paid off the substantial Cawthra and Bank of Upper Canada mortgages, and used the proceeds of the sale of his Jarvis Street lots and other properties to sustain himself and his family for the twelve years he was out of office, to say nothing of the cost of his restless wanderings, it is more likely that his estate was extremely small. Moreover, his churlish neglect of John G. Howard's account, and his reluctance or inability to settle his long dispute with the government by at least offering to pay the minimal £1,086 his own auditor had found to be rightfully owing, are not the actions of a "very rich" man. Finally, the evidence provided by Sam's will also tends to confirm that Mackenzie's statement was greatly exaggerated.

Sam made his last will and testament on April 7, 1853. It was a simple document, its terms straightforward. After leaving his youngest son, Charles Frederick, who was then aged nineteen, his 200-acre lot in Tay Township in the county of Simcoe, which Sam had probably received as a militia grant for his services in the War of 1812, he went on to provide that his wife, Mary Boyles, was to receive the balance of his estate. She was given the power "to dispose by Gift or Sale" of any part of his estate to their children, subject to a significant condition:

Provided always that before any such Sale or Gift be made by her to any of my said children . . . my Executors shall sell or lease such portions of my real estate as will yield and produce unto my said wife when added to the rents and profits of her own real estate (a portion of which real Estate is now under lease) a clear income of Six hundred pounds per annum and so soon as that amount of income is permanently secured to her I hereby authorise and empower her to divide and convey the residue of my said real Estate . . . among my children.[8]

On the face of it, Sam's provision for his wife could hardly be described as liberal. His stipulation that after taking into account her own private income, his estate was then to provide the balance necessary to assure her £600 a year, leaves the question unanswered as to the amount of her own means, and, therefore, the precise liability of his estate. Her father, Chief Justice William Dummer Powell, was a man of considerable property, and it is reasonable to assume that her inheritance from him would have been such as to place Sam's estate under little strain in fulfilling the condition he imposed. All in all, it was a finely honed provision dealing with a small-scale benefit, and as such scarcely confirmed Mackenzie's idea of his wealth.

The only other beneficiary mentioned by name in Sam's will was his oldest son:

And whereas I have heretofore allowed my eldest son Samuel Peters Jarvis at present a Captain in the Eighty Second Regiment of Foot the sum of one hundred pounds Sterling per annum, over and above the sums I have advanced for the purchase of his Commissions. It is my Will and desire that the aforesaid allowance of one hundred pounds Sterling per annum should be continued to him and that my executors should with the consent and approbation of my said Wife Mary Boyles make such provision for the punctual payment half yearly of the aforesaid allowance as in her and their judgment may be most advisable.

Mary Boyles Jarvis was appointed executrix of Sam's will by the Court of Probate on September 30, 1857, and the two other executors named in the will, William Cayley and Philip Vankoughnet,* were given "the right hereafter to come and administer [the estate] according

* Philip Vankoughnet (1790-1873) represented Stormont and Dundas in the legislative assembly from 1820 to 1828 and in 1836 was appointed to the Legislative Council. His son was a later chancellor.

to law." Oddly enough, Cayley and Vankoughnet renounced their executorship in April 1858, leaving Sam's widow solely in charge of the estate. Several possible explanations may be advanced for their withdrawal: in the first place, both were busy men in public office, and the estate, being neither complex nor large, hardly warranted their involvement; second, their appointment was made by Sam in 1853 when he may have thought Cayley and Vankoughnet might be useful in dealing with the government if it should revive its claim and move against his estate. By 1858 when they renounced, both men may have satisfied themselves in advance that the government didn't intend to take further action. Third, at the time of his death, in addition to Captain Jarvis, Sam left three sons, all of age, living in Toronto. In resigning, Cayley and Vankoughnet might equally have concluded that they were capable of helping their mother in the administration of their father's estate, making their roles unnecessary. Whatever the reason, Captain Samuel Peters Jarvis would now be wholly dependent upon his mother's good intentions for the maintenance of his allowance of £100, an eventuality that Sam had not foreseen nor, as it turned out, did the captain welcome. In later years, it is said, he sued his mother as a result of his dissatisfaction with her handling of his father's estate.

If this was so, his action must have arisen more from personal pique than financial hardship since his military career was an unqualified success: he retired from the service in 1881 with the rank of major-general. During the Indian Mutiny, after the Lucknow campaign, he received the brevet rank of major and was later appointed adjutant of the Staff College at Sandhurst, England. As a full colonel in Canada, he commanded a battalion in the Riel insurrection of 1870, and then became commandant of the Northwest Territories with his head-quarters at Fort Garry. Finally, in 1880, we find him on special service in South Africa where he held the post of commandant-general of the Colonial Force at the Cape. He died in 1905, leaving no children. Like the hero of a G.A. Henty novel, he was an outstanding Victorian soldier who moved with equal success from one Imperial station to another.

In reflecting upon Sam Jarvis's turbulent and generally unsuccessful career in Upper Canada, it is hard to avoid the feeling that if Sam's father, William Jarvis, had launched him into a military career, as was the case with Sam's oldest son, the course of Sam's life would have been markedly more productive. Like his father, Sam bungled the one chance he had to fill a senior position, and watched his star sink into a sea of embarrassment caused by the discovery of irregularities in his accounts. On the other hand, Sam's steadfast commitment to the militia, starting with the War of 1812 when he was only twenty, provided a strong thread of continuity throughout his troubled life. When he bought his son his commissions, paid him a regular allowance, visited him in England, and provided for his allowance to be continued after his death, it was as if Sam had grasped the elusive ideal upon which his own life should have been based. His determined support of his son's career, in fact, was the only spark from his unyielding anvil that fell upon dry ground, burst into flame, and illumined the night.

CHAPTER NINE

Toronto's Champs Élysées

Romance came late to William Cawthra. He remained a bachelor until he was forty-eight years old when he finally married Sarah Ellen Crowther. She was a sister of James Crowther, a prominent Toronto lawyer, who had represented Cawthra in 1847 when he had purchased his tract of land on upper Jarvis Street. It is probable that William Cawthra had delayed assuming "the certain cares and doubtful comforts of conjugal life," as Mrs. William Dummer Powell had once described the married state, while he was so deeply involved in his father's flourishing firm.

When Joseph Cawthra died in 1842, he left his youngest son William "the bulk of his wealth," in recognition of his great contribution to the success of the Cawthra business. From its modest beginnings as an apothecary shop, the concern had expanded to become the principal importer of groceries in the province, supplying most of the leading merchants throughout the country. It is said that when the East India company held its tea sales at Quebec and Montreal, the Cawthra interests were generally the heaviest buyers. In the year following his father's death, William discontinued the family business and devoted his time to the management of his own considerable fortune. He converted his office on Front Street in the old Town of York into a private house, and continued to live there with his mother, Mary Cawthra, until her death in 1847 at the age of eighty-seven.

Shortly after his marriage to Sarah Crowther, Cawthra decided to build a fine house for himself and his wife. The site he chose, however, was not on his extensive holdings on upper Jarvis Street, but instead at the northeast corner of King and Bay streets. His choice was hardly surprising because at that time Jarvis Street was largely unbuilt from Carlton Street north to Bloor Street, and it wouldn't have made sense for him to place the kind of house he had in mind in a dark and desolate

William Cawthra (1801-1880). One of the wealthiest men in Toronto at the time, Cawthra loaned Sam Jarvis £4,000 in 1846 to help finance his faltering Jarvis Street subdivision. The following year Cawthra purchased outright over eleven acres of the subdivision. His holding extended south from Bloor Street, on the west side of Jarvis Street, to a point below Wellesley Street. Much of the land was retained by the Cawthras for many years.—Metropolitan Toronto Library Board

133

This photograph of Cawthra House *was taken around 1867. Located on the northeast corner of King and Bay streets, the house was built by William Cawthra (Joseph Sheard, architect) in 1852. Four years after Cawthra had died here in 1880, his widow moved to a new house she had built at the southwest corner of Jarvis and Isabella streets, on part of the lands her husband had bought from Sam Jarvis in 1847.* Cawthra House *was demolished in 1947.—Metropolitan Toronto Library Board*

region of the city that was served by only a dirt road. Moreover, he personally preferred the bustle and stir of life in downtown Toronto to the rural solitude of upper Jarvis Street. With Joseph Sheard as architect, Cawthra's mansion, which was to be called *Cawthra House*, gradually took shape. When it was completed in 1853, and William and Sarah Cawthra had moved into it, John G. Howard, no mean architect himself, described the place as "the most beautifully proportioned house in Toronto." Long regarded as one of the best examples of

Greek revival architecture in the city, the old landmark was finally swept away in 1947 to make way for the new head office building of the Bank of Nova Scotia.

William Cawthra occupied *Cawthra House* until his death in 1880. He died on Tuesday, October 26 of that year, and the Toronto *Globe* the next day carried a report of his final hours:

> Yesterday morning shortly after nine o'clock, Mr. William Cawthra breathed his last at his residence on the corner of King and Bay Streets. Death was somewhat sudden, as on Sunday last he was in comparatively good health. Some years ago Mr. Cawthra became afflicted with cataract in the eyes, for which he was operated on last week. He bore the painful process manfully taking neither chloroform nor any other drug, and to all appearance up to Monday was doing well; but the shock had been too great for the system, and he gradually sank, expiring peacefully, surrounded by his wife and friends, some of whom he recognized up to the last moment.

William Cawthra died without children and without a will. Speaking later of him, the Reverend Dr. Henry Scadding told the York Pioneers' Association:

> Inheriting from his father great wealth, won in the early days of this country by legitimate commercial enterprise and care, he with reason regarded the possession as a serious trust to be conscientiously managed; and I will simply say I do not remember ever hearing of a single instance in all his multifarious financial dealings with a very large circle of his fellow men in every class and grade, a single instance of an act or deed of his not characterized by the strictest honour and the most thoughtful consideration.

Dr. Scadding went on to recall William Cawthra's support of a number of charitable institutions in the city, in particular the House of Industry on Elm Street which John G. Howard had designed and built when he and Cawthra were first associated in laying out Jarvis Street. Offering a picture of practical sainthood, with Cawthra regularly emerging from his stately *Cawthra House* to busy himself with the relief of the poor, Dr. Scadding reminded his listeners, "While his physical powers permitted, he was actively engaged, as many of you will remember, in the work of the House of Industry, taking his regular turn as one of the district visitors and personally engaging in the necessary investigations."

While in 1852 Sam Jarvis must have been disappointed in Cawthra's decision to build his new house on King Street, rather than on Jarvis Street, he must have found some consolation in the fact that his kinsman, the newly appointed sheriff of the County of York, Frederick William Jarvis, purchased two parcels of land in 1856 and 1857 on Jarvis Street, at the southeast corner of today's Wellesley Street, as the site for his proposed new house. (Wellesley Street was not extended through Jarvis Street until 1870.) Jarvis Collegiate Institute now occupies that property.

Sheriff Frederick Jarvis was the eldest son of Frederick Starr Jarvis, sometime Gentleman Usher of the Black Rod in the provincial Parliament, and he was born in Oakville in 1818. In 1849 he moved to Toronto to serve as deputy sheriff to his uncle, Sheriff William Botsford Jarvis of *Rosedale*. The succession assured, his uncle retired from the office he had filled since 1827, and Frederick William Jarvis succeeded him in 1856. The new sheriff didn't buy his properties from Sam Jarvis, however, but rather from two intervening owners, Henry Eccles and John A. Cull. Altogether his frontage on the east side of Jarvis Street, extending south from Wellesley Street, amounted to 292 feet. We may assume that his house was under construction throughout the summer of 1857 and that Sam Jarvis, therefore, who died in September of that year, didn't live to see the first Jarvis residence to be completed on Jarvis Street after his own departure from the property ten years before. The sheriff's new house was certainly in place by 1858 because in that year he obtained a mortgage loan for £5,000 on the property from Sir George Simpson of Lachine, Quebec, the great governor of the Hudson's Bay Company.

Oddly enough, in March 1857, before he had completed the purchase of the Wellesley Street corner, Sheriff Frederick Jarvis bought from Philip Vankoughnet another property on the east side of Jarvis Street, just below Carlton Street, with a frontage of over 260 feet. Vankoughnet, it will be recalled, was a friend of Sam Jarvis's and was named a co-executor of his estate. The sheriff held on to this additional property until 1870 when he sold it for $8,256 to the trustees of the Toronto Grammar School.

The trustees had searched for some time for a new site for their school, and when the building was opened for classes in 1871, as the Toronto Collegiate Institute, they were justifiably proud that their school, after many changes in location, had at last found a fitting and permanent home. The Collegiate Institute was a lineal descendant of

The Toronto Collegiate Institute, as it appeared at its opening in 1871. Located on the west side of Jarvis Street just below Carlton Street, it was renamed Jarvis Street Collegiate Institute when the new Parkdale Collegiate opened in West Toronto in 1890. This school, which had been considerably enlarged, moved to its present site at the corner of Jarvis and Wellesley streets in 1924. The old building was later demolished.—Toronto Board of Education Records and Archives Centre

the old Home District Grammar School that the Reverend George Okill Stuart had launched in York in 1807. John Ridout, it will be remembered, was the first student to be enrolled there, and young William Cawthra later joined him in Stuart's crowded classroom. In 1890, with the opening of a collegiate in West Toronto, Parkdale Collegiate, the school was forced to take the name Jarvis Street Collegiate Institute, since it could no longer be called *the* Toronto Collegiate Institute. It was to remain in its Carlton Street locale, at 361 Jarvis Street, until 1924 when deterioration of the old building and

The Jarvis Street Lacrosse Grounds as they appeared to an artist in 1876. Occupying land owned by William Cawthra, the grounds extended at that time from Wellesley Street north to Gloucester Street, on the west side of Jarvis Street. They were also used in the 1870's by the students of the new collegiate institute for special athletic events.—Metropolitan Toronto Library Board

severe overcrowding compelled it to move again to its present location at Wellesley Street.[1]

Sheriff Jarvis's two-storey house at the Wellesley Street corner was of plain design, square in shape and served on at least two sides by covered, ground-floor verandahs. He called the place *Woodlawn*. Here the sheriff lived for a span of nearly thirty years during which he witnessed the full flowering of Jarvis Street, including the completion of many of its great houses north of Wellesley Street.

For the first twenty years of his occupation of *Woodlawn,* however, Jarvis Street revealed few of the qualities for which it was later to become distinguished. Largely because William Cawthra controlled the vacant land on the west side of the street, from Wellesley to Bloor Street, the upper section of Jarvis Street was slow to develop. And on the east side as well, the sheriff had few neighbours. Until the seventies, in its semi-rural setting, *Woodlawn* seemed remote from the life of the city that flowed around the City Hall on Front Street and its neighbour, the popular St. Lawrence Hall.

As late as 1869, one wayfarer testified to the terrible condition of the street:

> Many streets had their creeks in 1869. I first made the acquaintance of the Jarvis Street one on a dark night. Walking up the east side, the sidewalk suddenly ended a short distance above Carlton Street. Seeking a better footing I crossed to the west side, and found myself wading through a creek. Though shallow at that spot, lower down it had cut a very deep gorge, and the residents had to build a bridge across at each house. It entered the sewer at Carlton Street.[2]

In the same section of Jarvis Street, just below Carlton Street, a student at the new collegiate later recalled, "The lot to the north of the school was usually full of water in wet weather, and certainly would not have been tolerated by the present Medical Health officer. It was not long, however, before a building started, and the present handsome edifice of St. Andrew's was built." Today the edifice is known as St. Andrew's Latvian Lutheran Church.[3]

Later in the seventies, to the sheriff's delight, Jarvis Street was paved with asphalt. It created a sensation. A new era had dawned in Toronto. So great was the excitement that plans were made to celebrate the event with "four days of solid enjoyment." An enthusiastic witness later described the occasion:

> The whole street from Queen to Bloor was strung with flags and lights, and there were probably a dozen bands at the different corners discoursing sweet music to the thousands who paraded up and down the wonderful pavement, for at that time it was thought to be very wonderful, after the mud roads we had had to put up with. The other three days might have gone on all right, too, but unfortunately, it rained good and hard the first night, and the Chinese lanterns and bunting were simply ruined, and the spell was broken.[4]

Of all men living on Jarvis Street, Sheriff Jarvis must have desired most to have his end come, when come it must, at *Woodlawn*. Instead, on an April evening in 1887, he died suddenly in an unfamiliar house on Church Street. The Toronto papers carried a full report of the sheriff's death. They related that he had left his office in the court house on Adelaide Street East at three o'clock on Saturday afternoon, April 16. While his cab was advancing up Church Street on its way to *Woodlawn* he became ill. He tapped on the glass and asked the cabman to slow the horse down, which he did, but a few minutes later, tapping again, the sheriff gasped that he could go no further, that he needed immediate medical attention. The cab then stopped in front of the house of one James H. Rogers on Church Street just below Gerrard. The sheriff, in a fainting condition, was assisted into the place by the anxious cabman and a startled Mrs. Rogers. Dr. Burritt, the sheriff's physician, was summoned urgently, and Jarvis's wife and children also arrived from *Woodlawn*. After diagnosing the ailment as having arisen from an existing heart condition, the doctor administered some medicine and left. It was his opinion that the sheriff would be well enough to be moved to *Woodlawn* the next morning, but that he would have to spend the night where he was, in Mr. Roger's bed. Rogers was a hatter and furrier with a shop at the corner of King and Church Streets. When he had to excuse himself at 6 P.M. to go about his business, the sheriff roused himself, shook hands, thanked him for his trouble and apologized for the inconvenience he had caused the Rogers family. Later in the evening, around 9.30, the sheriff's condition suddenly worsened. "About 10 o'clock," the *Globe* reported, before a doctor could reach his bedside, "Mr. Jarvis raised himself up in bed and then fell back dead."

The following year, in July 1888, Thomas Long, a wealthy Toronto merchant, bought *Woodlawn* from the sheriff's estate for $25,000. Curiously enough, when Long purchased *Woodlawn*, the Canada Life Assurance Company was holding a mortgage on it for $20,000, the equivalent of the £5,000 mortgage Sir George Simpson had held on the sheriff's property thirty years before.[5] Thomas Long later retained Edward J. Lennox, whose reputation as a leading architect was already established, to renovate the house, and after a series of alterations, the Jarvis house was barely recognizable. The architect transformed it into an elegant mansion in the Greek revival style. He removed the old ground-floor verandahs and added a soaring two-storey portico to the front elevation. It was this house and property that Thomas Long's executors sold in 1921 to the Board of Education for $100,000. In order

This ornamental iron gate and fence once adorned part of the site now occupied by Jarvis Collegiate Institute. Some sections of the fence have been preserved and can still be seen at the north and south ends of the school grounds.—James Collection—City of Toronto Archives

to complete their land assembly for the present Jarvis Collegiate, the board also paid $60,000 in 1921 for the property adjoining *Woodlawn*.

Although Sam Jarvis's widow, Mary Boyles Jarvis, was nearly a year older than her husband, she survived him by almost twenty-seven years. Like Sheriff Frederick Jarvis, she lived to see Jarvis Street paved, new churches raise their spires above the broad boulevard, and handsome houses spring from the farmlands of *Hazelburn*. Unlike the sheriff, however, her vantage ground was not on Jarvis Street, but on Isabella Street, a few doors east of Yonge Street. For some years she and her unmarried daughter, Caroline, lived together in a small house at 16 Isabella Street. Caroline, according to the city directory, worked as a "copyist" at Osgoode Hall. When she died peacefully on April 3, 1884, Mary Boyles Jarvis had reached her ninety-fourth year.

Thomas Long, an Irishman prominent in the early development of Colling-
wood, and later with extensive interests in Toronto, purchased this house, now
part of the site occupied by Jarvis Collegiate Institute, in 1888 and had architect
Edward J. Lennox add the two-storey portico and make other substantial
alterations. Hart Massey was Long's approving neighbour on the opposite side
of Wellesley Street. The Long estate sold the property in 1921 to the Board of
Education for $100,000.—City of Toronto Archives

In 1884, as Mary Boyles Jarvis's life was nearing its end, Mrs.
William Cawthra was preparing to move into a Victorian mansion she
had just built farther east on Isabella Street, at the southwest corner of
its intersection with Jarvis Street. Designed by William G. Storm, a
leading Toronto architect, the house was constructed of brick and cut
stone and it had an elevation of three storeys.[6] Its handsome main
entrance, adorned by a porte-cochère also of stone, was served by a

semi-circular driveway that swept in from Jarvis Street. A coach house and stables at the rear of the property were reached by a narrower driveway that entered the service area from Isabella Street.

Mrs. Cawthra's decision to build on part of the eleven-acre property her late husband had acquired from Sam Jarvis was influenced by a number of considerations. In the first place, she had occupied *Cawthra House* at the corner of King and Bay streets for thirty years. She now found herself engulfed in a burgeoning business and financial community that had flowed steadily west along King Street from its earliest beginnings in the old Town of York. Her elegant house had suddenly become an anachronism. Of equal importance in her decision, however, was the fact that her brother James Crowther was already living on the property that lay immediately south of the site she had selected on Jarvis Street.

In 1865, Crowther had purchased for $2,200 a parcel of land from William Cawthra at the northwest corner of Gloucester Street. It had a frontage on the west side of Jarvis Street that extended north for 120 feet.* Disdaining the solitude of upper Jarvis Street at that time, he built himself a house on the property which he occupied the following year. The limited extent of the development of the Cawthra-owned lands on the west side of Jarvis Street until 1884 is strikingly illustrated by Goad's Atlas of the City of Toronto of that year: the vacant land stretching north from Wellesley Street to Gloucester Street is designated as the "Old Lacrosse Grounds" and from that point the Crowther and Cawthra properties occupy the entire block north from Gloucester to Isabella Street, a frontage on the recently paved Jarvis Street of over 300 feet.

The lacrosse grounds were used for a number of years by agreement with William Cawthra as a playing field by the students of the new Toronto Collegiate Institute, south of Carlton Street. In the early seventies, a junior teacher at the school, Sam Hughes, was also an ardent member of the championship Toronto Lacrosse Team. Because of his involvement in the sport, he was able to obtain the use of the grounds for his school. As General Sir Sam Hughes, he was to become a controversial figure of World War I.[7]

---

* In 1856, the mayor and city of Toronto purchased from William Cawthra two strips of land across his property so that Isabella and Gloucester Streets could be extended from Church Street to Jarvis Street. The city paid £600 and £1,050 respectively for the road allowances. There is no evidence that the city made similar payments to Sam Jarvis when he earlier opened Jarvis Street, indicating its lack of involvement in his private project.

A photographic view looking north on Jarvis Street close to Bloor Street, taken in the 1890's. The photographer has made the most of the distinctive sidewalk areas.—Toronto Old and New

By the time James Crowther had established himself on Jarvis Street, St. Paul's Church on Bloor Street, at the head of Jarvis Street, had become a flourishing congregation which still drew most of its members from the town of Yorkville lying to the north of Bloor Street. The church had finally outgrown the frame building that had housed it since 1842, and the old structure had been moved on rollers to the Potters' Field, on the north side of Bloor Street close to its present intersection with Bay Street, where it was used as a mission church for

144

A flowering chestnut tree and a gas light frame this view of St. Paul's Anglican Church on Bloor Street, at the head of Jarvis Street, in 1891.—Toronto Old and New

many years. The new, or second, St. Paul's that replaced it was described in a Toronto newspaper as "one of the architectural gems of Toronto" when it opened its doors for worship in December 1861. More recently, Professor Eric Arthur has referred to it as "a charming little Gothic church that would be a matter of pride in any English village."[8] (Dwarfed by the great new St. Paul's that was completed just to the east of it in 1913 as Jarvis Street was reaching its social zenith, the "little Gothic church," after undergoing a number of alterations since

145

it was originally opened, is described today by a sign at its door that reads, "St. Paul's Chapel and Church Office.")

In May 1870, James Crowther's daughter, Sarah Ellen Cawthra Crowther, was married to William Mulock, a Toronto lawyer. He was later to become the Honourable Sir William Mulock, K.C.M.G., chief justice of Ontario. Sarah, who was living with her mother and father in the new Crowther house on Jarvis Street, had been named for her aunt, Mrs. William Cawthra. As a wedding present, William Cawthra presented the couple with a deed to a piece of land on the south side of Isabella Street, immediately to the west of the property that Mrs. Cawthra later chose as the site for her new residence. Cawthra, however, had another reason for marking the occasion with a gift of property: young Mulock's mother, Mary, was the only daughter of John and Ann Cawthra of Newmarket, Ontario. John was a brother of William Cawthra. John Cawthra's daughter Mary had married Dr. Thomas Homan Mulock in 1838, and their son William was born in Bond Head on January 19, 1843. He attended the Newmarket Grammar School and University College, Toronto, from where he graduated with a B.A. degree in 1863 as well as winning the gold medal in Modern Languages. Mulock was called to the Ontario Bar in 1868, and obtained an M.A. degree the year after his marriage to Sarah Crowther.

Surprisingly, William Mulock and his wife are shown in the city directory of 1871-2 as living at 51 Isabella Street, some distance west of the property that William Cawthra had given them. Moreover, in 1873, rather than incur the cost of building in that depressed year, they sold their vacant lot for $2,000. James Crowther, who was William Cawthra's lawyer, obviously approved of their decision because he personally lent the new purchaser $1,000, secured by a mortgage, in order to facilitate the transaction.

When Mrs. Cawthra moved into her new house in 1884, the opposite side of Jarvis Street was considerably more developed. In 1878, for example, Arthur R. McMaster had bought a large lot on the northeast corner of Jarvis and Wellesley Streets from his uncle, the Honourable William McMaster, who was then living on the Poplar Plains Hill and was presumably holding the Jarvis Street property simply as an investment. Arthur McMaster paid his uncle $5,325 for the land which had a frontage on Jarvis Street of 213 feet and on the north side of Wellesley Street of 287 feet. McMaster immediately built a substantial house for himself on his corner property which he was destined to

Roseneath, *the home of Chief Justice Sir Charles Moss on the east side of Jarvis Street, south of Isabella Street. Built in the 1870's, it has since been demolished, but its style of architecture survives in towns throughout southern Ontario.*— Toronto Old and New

occupy for only a few years. Similarly in 1878, Charles Moss, a lawyer well known in Toronto in that day, purchased a pleasant dwelling with a lofty tower room on the east side of Jarvis Street, south of Isabella Street, from John Laing Blaikie, a future president of the British American Life Assurance Company, to whom he paid $13,000. Later, as Chief Justice Sir Charles Moss, he called his ample Victorian house at 547 Jarvis Street, *Roseneath*. At the same time, Alexander

This comfortable Victorian house, with its open verandah, once stood at number 415 on the east side of Jarvis Street, north of Carlton Street. It was owned in 1891 by Alexander Nairn, a leading supplier of timber and ties to the railroads.—Toronto Old and New

Nairn, wharfinger and coal merchant, was occupying a comfortable, rambling house, also on the east side of Jarvis Street, but below Wellesley Street. With its covered front verandah and awninged main entrance, his house was typical of the architectural style of the seventies. Nairn, who had emigrated to Canada from Glasgow in 1857, held several large contracts with the railways for the supply of timber and ties, and built one of the finest docks on the waterfront for the use of his firm. By the 1890's, his house was numbered 415 Jarvis Street.

While today the street is wider and the trees fewer, this view of Jarvis Street looking south is unchanged from over a century ago. St. Andrew's Lutheran Church still occupies the southeast corner of Jarvis and Carlton streets, and farther south, at the Gerrard Street corner, the steeple of Jarvis Street Baptist Church looms above the chestnut trees.—Toronto Old and New

This peaceful street scene was taken at the end of Queen Victoria's reign from a point on Jarvis Street just north of Dundas Street. To the left, two Victorian ladies stroll beside a grassy verge, on the road a bicyclist and an early driver contend for the right of way, and in the distance the twin steeples of the street's landmark churches emerge from the treetops.—Metropolitan Toronto Library Board

As W. G. Storm was completing his designs for Mrs. Cawthra's house, Arthur McMaster died, and in 1882 the trustees of his estate sold his new house and property to Eliza Massey, the wife of Hart Massey, president and manager of the Massey Manufacturing Company. After having spent eleven years in semi-retirement in Cleveland, Ohio, Hart Massey had decided to move to Toronto with his family and help his son Charles establish a big, new plant in the city to manufacture his

150

Photographed in 1891, Dr. John B. Hall's coachman and brougham await his descent from his house at 326 Jarvis Street which he called Hahnemann Villa. *It was on the northwest corner of Jarvis and Carlton streets, and has been demolished. A contemporary writer noted, "although his practice is chiefly among the more affluent, the poor are never neglected."*—Toronto Old and New

highly successful farm equipment. The opening of the factory, which drew many of its employees from the existing Massey operation in Newcastle, Ontario, coincided with the Masseys' purchase of the spacious McMaster house. They paid $32,500 for it, a considerable price in those days, and gave back a mortgage to the McMaster trustees

Euclid Hall, *the residence of Hart A. Massey at the northeast corner of Jarvis and Wellesley Streets, as it appeared long ago. Today the house survives as the Keg Mansion, but the old conservatory and greenhouse areas have been preempted by a service station.—James Collection—City of Toronto Archives*

for $20,000. The fact that Massey, who was a devout Methodist, paid down only $12,500 for the twenty-five-room house was in no sense an admission that he was short of cash. It was simply the accepted way of doing business at that time. In fact, over the next three years (the mortgage remained outstanding until 1889) he poured another $13,000 into the place, adding a conservatory for his orchids, a greenhouse for his grapevines, and in the front hall, at the foot of a massive staircase,

152

an exotic fountain which splashed cheerfully into a pool of gold fish. The house was later called *Euclid Hall* by Massey's daughter Lillian, a name that was doubtless inspired by Cleveland's Euclid Avenue, an elegant street in that day.

A few years later, two of Hart Massey's sons acquired properties close to him. Chester D. Massey, the father of Vincent and Raymond, bought the property adjoining his father's place on the north. At that time he was vice-president of the family company, his younger brother, Walter E. Massey, holding the position of secretary and treasurer. Walter and his wife, formerly Susan Denton, bought a smaller lot on the west side of Jarvis Street in 1889, between Wellesley Street and today's Cawthra Square. It cost $5,875 and had a frontage of only forty-three feet. They built a house of moderate size for themselves on the site, with a stable behind it, and occupied the property in 1890.

The Masseys having completed the deployment of their family forces on both sides of Jarvis Street by that year, a volley from the Cawthra enclave farther up Jarvis Street was to be expected and it wasn't long in coming. James Crowther had died in April 1888, and the following July the executors of his estate transferred his house and property at the Gloucester Street corner to his daughter, Sarah Ellen Cawthra Mulock. She and her husband were living at that time on the east side of Avenue Road, between Yorkville Avenue and the then St. Paul's Methodist Church. Apparently, they immediately decided to relocate themselves on Jarvis Street on Sarah Mulock's inherited property because in 1888 and 1889 William G. Storm, who had built the neighbouring Cawthra house, was busy preparing a set of plans for Mulock which called for extensive renovations and additions to the existing Crowther house. William and Sarah Mulock were ensconced in their new home by 1891, when its number became 518, while next door, Mrs. William Cawthra (now Mrs. William A. Murray, she having remarried) was still holding to her spacious house at number 538.

Encouraged perhaps by the tempo of impressive building in that section of the street, George Horace Gooderham in 1890 purchased a parcel of land at the northwest corner of Jarvis Street and Cawthra Square, a few doors north of Walter Massey's place. Only in his twenty-third year, he built himself a house on the property of red sandstone in the Romanesque style which still survives today. At the same time, his father, George Gooderham, was adding the finishing touches to his own magnificent house in the same Romanesque manner at the corner of Bloor and St. George Streets. Today it is known as the York Club.

Hart A. Massey (1823-1896). While living at 515 Jarvis Street, Massey built and donated to the city the Massey Music Hall and the Fred Victor Mission. In later years, his estate, through a foundation, was to provide further benefactions, including Hart House and Massey College on the University of Toronto campus.—Metropolitan Toronto Library Board

After this sombre photograph was taken of Chester Massey's house at 519 Jarvis Street, adjoining Hart Massey's place to the south, a wing was added to the east, and the house substantially remodelled. It still stands today. Massey's understated plain picket fence provided a contrast with the ornamental iron fences of Mrs. Cawthra and her neighbours to the north.—James Collection—City of Toronto Archives

155

Walter E. Massey built this house between Wellesley Street and Cawthra Square in 1889. It lay across the street from the residence of his father, Hart A. Massey. After Walter Massey succeeded to the presidency of the Massey-Harris Company, he sold this place, which has since been demolished, in 1899 and moved up Jarvis Street to Mrs. David Smart's former house at the northwest corner of Isabella Street.—Toronto Old and New

There can be no doubt that Mrs. William Cawthra's arrival on Jarvis Street in 1884, and Hart Massey's highly visible ownership of the McMaster property at the same time, set the tone for the final development of Jarvis Street, especially on its west side where the

Cawthra land had laid dormant for so long. Just as William Cawthra's investment in Sam Jarvis's subdivision in 1847 had provided the faltering new Jarvis Street with a needed stimulant, so in its final stages, forty years later, a renewed Cawthra presence, dramatically projected by Mrs. Cawthra's house, influenced the style of architecture of upper Jarvis Street, and even its mode of life, in the closing years of the nineteenth century.

On the property immediately north of the Cawthra place, for example, on the opposite side of Isabella Street, Donald McDermid, of the contracting firm of McDermid and Ross, built himself a substantial house at 550 Jarvis Street similar in construction and design to the Cawthra mansion. He had purchased his corner lot in 1886 for $12,500. Completed the following year, his house was later owned by Mrs. David Smart when it was known as *Lindewald*. And next door to McDermid, at 566 Jarvis Street, John C. Fitch also built a large house of grey stone of which W. G. Storm was the architect. Like the McDermid and Cawthra estates, it was surrounded by spacious lawns with stables and a coach house at the rear. Earlier, Fitch had been in a partnership in Toronto with Sir William P. Howland which had held important interests in the milling industry. Sir William later filled the office of lieutenant-governor of the new province of Ontario from 1868 until 1873. In 1885, John Fitch was said to have received expressions of sympathy from hundreds of people throughout the city when word reached Toronto that his son, a young lieutenant with the Grenadiers, had been fatally wounded in the storming of Batoche during the Riel Rebellion.

On the east side of Jarvis Street, across the road from the McDermid and Fitch residences, James Carruthers, a leading Toronto grain merchant, also responded to the new trend in elegance when he retained Henry Langley as his architect. Langley designed and built a three-storey house for him in cut stone, and the place was completed at 545 Jarvis Street in 1889. "Among the many palatial residences on Jarvis Street," an observer in 1891 noted with restrained enthusiasm, "the home of Mr. James Carruthers, though not the most pretentious, is one of the most modern and ornate in the neighbourhood."

And a little farther north at 565 Jarvis Street, also on the east side, Joseph W. Flavelle purchased a property in 1894 from Mrs. Sarah Cawthra Murray. Mrs. Murray disposed of it under a power of sale in a mortgage she held that had fallen into default. Flavelle paid her $19,700, and in accordance with the practice of the time, she accepted a

Mrs. William Cawthra's Jarvis Street house, built for her in 1884 by William G. Storm, is shown here as it appeared in 1891. The stables and coach house at the rear, like the main house, were of cut stone. The front verandah was later removed and a large conservatory with a marble floor and mantelpiece added. In the distance, on the north side of Isabella Street, can be seen the substantial house built by Donald McDermid which was later owned by Mrs. David Smart, and, after 1899, by Walter E. Massey. Beyond it, a soaring gable of John C. Fitch's house is visible. All these houses have been demolished.—Toronto Old and New

This house of John C. Fitch mirrors the new elegance brought to Jarvis Street by Mrs. William Cawthra in the 1880's. Like her house, it was built of cut stone and designed by William G. Storm. Though added somewhat later, the curving drive, the spacious lawns, the ornamental fence were all vintage Cawthra. The house has since been demolished.—Toronto Old and New

mortgage from him for $15,000 as part of the purchase price. The new owner, the later Sir Joseph Flavelle, Baronet, immediately engaged David B. Dick to alter the house to his taste. Dick, a prominent Toronto architect, was later to undertake substantial commissions throughout the city for the William Davies Company of which Flavelle was the

159

Reflecting the new style of upper Jarvis Street, this house was built for James Carruthers, a Toronto grain merchant, by architect Henry Langley in 1889. It lay on the east side of Jarvis Street, somewhat incongruously next door to the older Victorian home of Sir Charles Moss. The Carruthers house was described as "one of the most modern and ornate in the neighbourhood" when it was built. It is now demolished.—Toronto Old and New managing director and a substantial shareholder.[9] He designed a number of new retail stores for the company's flourishing meat packing business, and built a few stables and wagon sheds as well.

As Jarvis Street was approaching its final stage of development, two Toronto writers extolled its qualities as they compared it with other residential districts in the city. C. P. Mulvany wrote in *Toronto Past and Present*:

> Of all the avenues extending south from Bloor Street to the Bay, the noblest are Church, Jarvis and Sherbourne Streets.* Church Street is somewhat less aristocratic, but has all the advantage of the magnificent church buildings in its course, the noble Cathedral of St. Michael, and that handsome though somewhat incongruous congeries of Gothic details, the "Metropolitan." Jarvis and Sherbourne are lined on either side through most part of their extent by the mansions of the upper ten. Of a summer it is pleasant to saunter down one of these streets while the thick verdure of the chestnut trees is fresh with the life of June, and the pink and white bunches of blossom are as beautiful as any of the exotic flowers in the lawns and gardens of the houses.

And in a similar vein, C. C. Taylor in *Toronto "Called Back"* wrote in 1886,

> In Rosedale are some elegant mansions, and here are the new and spacious grounds of the Athletic Association, with a grandstand and all suitable appointments.
>
> Sherbourne Street itself has become the residence of many leading merchants and manufacturers, and will impress a stranger most favourably.
>
> The streets intervening between Sherbourne and Yonge are Jarvis and Church, the former still retaining its character for beauty and style, and the latter steadily rising in importance, which will be enhanced by the new block paving. Both of these latter streets ought to be traversed, especially as sightseers invariably visit the Horticultural Gardens, and the Normal and Model Schools.

---

* The name Nelson Street for the road running south from Queen Street to the Bay was replaced in 1870 by the name Jarvis Street, to reduce the growing complexity of Toronto's street names. Thus Jarvis Street came to extend from Bloor Street to the Toronto waterfront.

While Queen's Park and St. George Street were also to become the milieu of a number of equally impressive residences, it was the breadth of Jarvis Street, with its sidewalks and ornamental fences and its great shade trees rising from grassy verges, that imparted to it something of the distinction of the Champs Élysées in Paris. The road itself, however, was relatively narrow, the original allowance of eighty feet being largely consumed by its treed sections and public walks.

The Vintage Years

When King Edward VII succeeded his mother in 1901, there were many people still living in Toronto who had witnessed the merry monarch's visit to the city in 1860 when he was Prince of Wales. He had received a tumultuous welcome, Toronto's population of 46,000 having swelled on the occasion by the thousands more who had poured into the city from the surrounding countryside to participate in the loyal celebrations.

Torontonians had taken the young prince to their heart, and they continued to follow his progress long after he had left the country, and throughout the declining years of his mother's reign. They never tired of relating anecdotes of his travels in Europe, particularly his visits to Paris, and liked especially to recount the occasion when he took his turn with the *bons vivants* of the French capital and appeared on stage one night in a performance of Sardou's *Fédora*. He played the role of a murdered prince while the immortal Sarah Bernhardt sobbed unrestrainedly over his silent deathbed. And all the fashions of dress for which he was responsible, largely the result of his own inattention to sartorial detail, were quickly followed in Toronto, like the soft, Cronstadt hat, the forgotten button on the bottom of a waistcoat, the accidental cuff that relieved the stovepipe monotony of trousers. It was during his amiable and urbane reign that Jarvis Street was to emerge from its shuttered Victorian gloom and attain the pinnacle of its elegance.

Neither Hart Massey nor Mrs. William Cawthra Murray, however, lived to see their street become the fashionable promenade of Edwardian society. Hart Massey died in 1896, and Mrs. Murray followed him to her grave the next year.

For Toronto, Hart Massey's death from natural causes on a blustery day in February was like the passing of a royal personage. A few days before he died at his house on Jarvis Street, the newspapers carried regular bulletins on his condition. When his end finally came, the city paused and fell silent. Paul Collins in his study of Hart Massey has recounted the impressive funeral that took place a few days later:

> It began with a quiet service at home for the family, joined by Mackenzie Bowell, now Prime Minister of Canada. A procession, estimated to have been over a kilometre long, moved from the home to Metropolitan Methodist Church where a public service was conducted. Hundreds of people lined the route of the procession and filled the large church, including 600 workers from the Massey-Harris Company. Telegrams poured in from religious, political and business leaders, acknowledging Hart's many contributions. As so often happens, Hart seems to have been more warmly regarded and his contributions more highly praised in death than during his lifetime. The newspapers that had often criticized him, now ran long accounts of his life, highlighting his business success and his charitable acts.[1]

In his lifetime, Hart Massey's public benefactions were legion. The most visible of his gifts to the city were Massey Hall on Shuter Street, soon to be succeeded by a magnificent new concert hall of the same name on King Street West, and the Fred Victor Mission at the southeast corner of Jarvis and Queen Streets. Both were monuments to sons who predeceased him, both were designed to reflect their interests during the tragically short span of their lives. In the case of Massey Music Hall, which was renamed Massey Hall in 1933, it was created to honour the memory of his son Charles, who had died of typhoid fever in 1884 at the age of thirty-six. Charles had been the dynamic force of the family business in Newcastle while his father lived in Cleveland, and it was also Charles who had encouraged his father to settle in Toronto and become involved in establishing the new Massey plant in the city. Charles had been devoted to music, he played the organ in church and organized a band from among his own employees in Newcastle. The new concert hall thus embodied his personal interests while serving the city's cultural needs. Work on the structure began in September 1893, and Hart Massey's grandson, Vincent Massey, who was then aged six, laid the cornerstone. Built at a cost of around $152,000, the hall was opened in June 1894, with a rousing performance of *The Messiah*. An ageing Hart Massey attended and presented the keys of the building to the mayor.

No sooner was that Massey edifice in place than the Fred Victor Mission was rushed to completion. It opened the following October. Hart Massey's youngest son, Frederic Victor, whom the new mission honoured, had died of tuberculosis in 1890 at the age of twenty-two. Imbued with deeply religious beliefs, he abhorred drinking, smoking, and the use of profane language, and had an overriding concern for the practical and spiritual needs of the destitute. The five-storey mission, which has now been replaced by a modern structure, cost $60,000 and provided overnight accommodation for more than 200 men, a hall to seat 500, together with a reading room and gymnasium.

Before these memorials were raised, Hart Massey had carried his company into an important merger with the successful A. Harris, Son and Company of Brantford, Ontario. They were vigorous competitors in some of Massey's implement lines, and after 1891, as the Massey-Harris Company Limited, the merged operation was steadily to increase its share of the international market.

After Hart Massey's death, his son Walter, at the age of thirty-three, was called upon to fill the vacant post of president of the Massey-Harris Company. He and his wife, Susan, continued to occupy the house they had built at 486 Jarvis Street, across the road from *Euclid Hall*, until 1899 when they sold the place to John H. Housser for $18,000. As befitted the new head of an international organization, Massey immediately moved north on Jarvis Street and took up his residence in the late Mrs. David Smart's extensive house at number 550. Mrs. Smart had acquired her property at the corner of Isabella Street from Donald McDermid, the contractor, in 1891. The Masseys now overlooked the Cawthra enclave, Walter's new house, which he renamed *Auburndale*, lying directly across Isabella Street from the late Mrs. William Cawthra Murray's landmark property.

In addition to his duties with Massey-Harris, Walter Massey had become increasingly interested in the operation of his Dentonia Park Farm on the eastern outskirts of the city. It was a model dairy farm of 240 acres whose rolling fields sustained herds of contented Jersey and Ayrshire cattle. In an age when the pasteurization of milk was little practised, Walter concentrated his energy on improving the quality of the city's milk. To this end he was instrumental in forming the City Dairy Co., Limited, as an outlet for his own pasteurized milk, and also to encourage other suppliers to maintain high standards of milk purification. The link between his farm and the successful City Dairy was emphasized in advertisements of that time:

CITY DAIRY CERTIFIED MILK
From Dentonia Park Farm
From Tuberculine Cows.
Certified by Milk Commission of
Academy of Medicine of Toronto
Certified Milk delivered in ice or protected from freezing
according to season—per quart 4 milk tickets.
Dentonia Milk delivered without ice or protection—
per quart three milk tickets.
CITY DAIRY CO.,
Limited
Toronto

In the light of his concern with the city's health, it is a sad irony that Walter Massey, like his older brother Charles, died of typhoid fever in 1901 at the age of thirty-seven. It is said that his death was caused by drinking water from a contaminated cooler while he was travelling on a railway car.

On Walter Massey's death, Chester Massey, now the only surviving son of Hart Massey, reluctantly assumed the presidency of the Massey-Harris Company. Plagued by a frail constitution and uncertain health, he was happy to be replaced a few years later, though he continued to occupy a seat on the company's board of directors. The last member of the family to occupy the president's office was Chester's oldest son, Vincent, who served with similar reluctance from 1921 until 1925.

Mrs. Hart Massey continued to reside at *Euclid Hall* until her death in 1908. In 1901, however, she transferred her ownership of the house to her daughter Lillian Massey Treble for the nominal price of $2,000. Lillian had married John Mill Treble, a King Street shirtmaker, shortly after her disapproving father's death, and Treble joined his wife and her mother at *Euclid Hall*.

Next door, Chester Massey's wife, Anna Vincent, died in 1903, and in 1907 Chester was married again in a private ceremony that took place in *Euclid Hall*. The house included among its many amenities a fine, electric organ. Chester's second wife, Margaret Phelps, was a cousin of approximately his own age. Raymond Massey in his personal memoir, *When I Was Young*,[2] vividly described his father's wedding. Raymond was only eleven years old at the time, nine years junior to his brother Vincent. He recalled his old grandmother, Mrs. Hart Massey, descending in an elevator from her quarters on the second floor, and the grim determination of Mr. Wheeldon, the organist from the Metropolitan

166

Church, to transform the wedding ceremony into a major musical concert. He finally relented, however, under the justifiable objection of the groom. Crowds of Massey relatives filled the ample rooms of *Euclid Hall*, though there was one conspicuous absentee: Vincent Massey. After referring to the many relatives who were on hand for the occasion, Raymond Massey added cryptically, "All, that is, but Vincent who didn't attend."

At the time of his father's second marriage, Vincent Massey, having graduated from St. Andrew's College in north Rosedale the previous year, was enrolled at the University of Toronto's University College. His first taste of undergraduate life, apparently, was discouraging.

In the early pages of his memoirs, *What's Past is Prologue,* he plainly identified the cause of his discontent. "The transition from school to university," he wrote, "was complicated by the existence of fraternities, societies that had spread into Canada from the United States."[3] Massey had earlier pledged himself to join a fraternity, but withdrew after having concluded that with the exception of two friends who were members, "the undergraduates were not people with whom I had many interests in common." This led to what he described as a crisis in his life when every conceivable pressure was exerted on him by the fraternity in an attempt to have him reconsider his decision. He remained unshakeable, however, and later congratulated himself on having remained free to find his friends in all areas of the university, although it is not entirely clear why membership in a loosely knit fraternity would have prevented him from forming other friendships on the campus. Be that as it may, there can be little doubt that the episode was painful, otherwise Massey would hardly have bothered recording it in his memoirs, which were written late in life.[4]

While the link between his distaste for fraternities and the building of Hart House may be tenuous, three years later, while still an undergraduate, he conceived the idea of having Hart Massey's estate finance the cost of constructing a great, new centre for male students on the university campus. When it was formally opened ten years later it was named Hart House. A beautiful building in the Collegiate Gothic style, it was designed by Sproatt and Rolph, a Toronto firm of architects. At the outset, it was described by Chester Massey as "a building for the University Young Men's Christian Association, also for the Students' Union, the two buildings to be connected by an Assembly Hall," but by the time the work had started in 1911, the original plan had been revised and expanded.[5] Vincent Massey was attending Balliol College, Oxford University, during the early period of the construction of Hart House, but when he returned to Toronto in 1913 he was able to follow its successive stages with an all-absorbing interest. At that time he was a junior lecturer in modern history at the university and dean of the new men's residence (Burwash Hall) at Victoria College which he had helped plan, and which, like Hart House, had been a gift of his grandfather's estate.

In 1915, Vincent Massey married Alice Parkin, a daughter of Sir George Parkin who earlier had been a principal of Upper Canada College. By then, Massey had moved from his father's house on Jarvis Street to the Massey-financed Burwash Hall in Queen's Park.

Meanwhile, farther up Jarvis Street, William Mulock's career had unfolded with quiet distinction. Elected to the Dominion parliament in 1882 under Edward Blake's Liberal banner, he had sat in opposition until 1896 when Sir Wilfrid Laurier finally led the Liberal forces to victory. Mulock, who represented North York, was immediately given a seat in the cabinet as postmaster general, and was instrumental in introducing a two-cent postal rate that was adopted by Canada and used throughout the British Empire. He was also responsible for securing Canada's interest in the Pacific Cable and a wireless telegraphy link with Great Britain. For his services, in 1902 King Edward conferred upon him the title of Knight Commander of Saint Michael and Saint George. Sir William retired from active politics in 1905 when he was appointed chief justice of the exchequer division of the High Court of Ontario. It was not until 1923, however, that he was to be named chief justice of Ontario, and the following year, chancellor of the University of Toronto.[6]

During the Edwardian era, Sir William's concerns with the administration of justice in no way stifled his inherited Cawthra instinct to invest in attractive land. Much earlier, around 1880, when he was practising law in Toronto, he had purchased a farm of several hundred acres on Yonge Street, a short distance from his early home in Newmarket. The holding was later increased and a fine country house built to replace the original dwelling. In 1909, still faithful to his Cawthra beliefs, when a large block of undeveloped township property became available for purchase on Toronto's northern outskirts, Sir William snapped it up. It lay on Yonge street north of Lawrence Avenue and, like his Newmarket farm, extended a considerable distance west of Yonge Street. Shortly after he acquired the property, he transferred it to Melrose Realty Company, Limited, a private company in which he and his family held the principal interest. At that time Herbert A. Clark, K.C., was president of the company by virtue of being

Knighted by King Edward VII in 1902, Sir William Mulock served in the Laurier government as postmaster general from 1896 to 1905, and as the first federal minister of labour from 1900 to 1905. Later, he became chief justice of Ontario. A legend in his own time, he died at his house at 518 Jarvis Street on October 1, 1944, at the age of 101. His house has since been demolished. This photograph was taken around 1904.—Private Collection

a partner in the firm of Mulock, Milliken, Clark and Redman, which was looking after the Mulock family interests at that time. In 1910, therefore, when the first plans of subdivision were being prepared, it was Clark's responsibility to select the names for the streets that were about to be laid out. He didn't find it difficult. As a devoted student of Sir Walter Scott's writings, he simply extracted from that rich mine many of the names that are now familiar to the residents of North Toronto, such as Melrose, Jedburgh, Deloraine, Falkirk, Selkirk, Bannockburn, and Marmion. The name St. Germain, however, equally well known in the district, was derived from the family who had owned part of the old farmlands that were acquired by Sir William.

Also during the Edwardian period, Toronto's King Edward Hotel and Royal Alexandra Theatre, both on King Street, were established by people who had a tie with Jarvis Street. The concept of the King Edward Hotel originated with Edward Aemilius Jarvis, a vigorous and imaginative investment banker. A grandson of Samuel Peters Jarvis, he was born in 1860 and lived for many years on Prince Arthur Avenue. Like his grandfather, he called his house *Hazelburn*, and later transferred the name to his farm near Aurora, Ontario. In his declining years, in an unfinished memoir, Jarvis recalled that he had been standing one day with Senator George A. Cox in a window of the old Central Canada Savings and Loan Company offices at the northwest corner of Victoria and King Streets. Cox, who was then the dominant financial figure in Toronto, lived at *Sherbourne Villa* on Sherbourne Street, the house that had been built originally by Thomas Gibbs Ridout when he was cashier of the Bank of Upper Canada. Their conversation had drifted around to the subject of the inadequacy of Toronto's hotel accommodation, both agreeing that the Queen's Hotel, now the site of the Royal York Hotel, and the Rossin House, then at the corner of King and York Streets, were "old firetraps," and should be replaced. Jarvis decided to investigate the idea further and obtained an expert opinion from the owner of the Windsor Hotel on New York's Fifth Avenue. He visited Toronto and after examining several sites in the city concluded that the proposed King Edward Hotel should be built on the land it now occupies. His recommendation was made subject to one condition, that Victoria Street be extended south from King Street so that the hotel would be accessible to carriages on three sides. This was ultimately done. Jarvis was successful in obtaining financial support for his scheme, not only from Senator Cox, but from George H. Gooderham as well. The necessary property was assembled by an ingenious arrangement under which the contributing owners accepted payment for their land in the form of a twenty-year annuity. Designed by Edward J. Lennox, the King Edward Hotel was opened in 1903 and was pronounced Toronto's most luxurious hotel. Its prestige was enhanced the following year when J. Pierpont Morgan of New York occupied its principal suite.

Farther west on King Street, the glittering new Royal Alexandra Theatre was opened to an entranced audience in 1907. It was organized and financed by the twenty-five-year-old Cawthra Mulock of 538 Jarvis Street. The youngest son of Sir William Mulock, he had received on his twenty-first birthday a substantial inheritance from his great-aunt, Mrs. William Cawthra Murray, that included the house she had built on Jarvis Street in 1884.

As the Edwardian era drew to a close, both the "Royal Alec" and the "King Eddie" were the focal point of Toronto society. On Saturdays, the young beaux liked to take their girls to the matinée performance at the Royal Alexandra Theatre and afterwards to the traditional tea-dance that was held on the mezzanine floor of the King Edward Hotel. The outbreak of World War I, however, brought most of these Edwardian traditions to an end, and for Jarvis Street, signalled the beginning of its decline as a prestigious residential district.

B.K. Sandwell, the editor of the Toronto *Saturday Night*, once quipped, "Toronto has no social classes, only the masses and the Masseys." With the exception of Vincent Massey, however, the Masseys never regarded themselves as being part of the *haut monde* of the city. Hart Massey was the great practitioner of the Methodist work ethic. Through the sweat of his brow and Godfearing adherence to his religious beliefs, he amassed considerable wealth. When his time came to depart, he bequeathed the greater part of his estate to charity. He seldom took his ease in softly lit Toronto drawing-rooms. If the light of the Lord shone upon him, that was enough. Likewise, his son Chester. After his father's death, and when he had put his responsibilities with the Massey-Harris Company behind him, he spent the rest of his life administering Hart Massey's estate, guiding its resources towards worthy objects. Both he and his sister, Lillian Massey Treble, were also always deeply involved in the work of the Metropolitan Church, and for years were among its principal benefactors. Throughout the city they were regarded with respect, admiration, even affection. But society leaders they were not. Vincent Massey, on the other hand, endowed by fate with money, and by nature with a good mind, high ambition, and

171

impressive dignity, devoted his career to politics and government service. It culminated in 1952 with his appointment as Canada's first, native-born governor general.

In the life of Jarvis Street at the turn of the century and until the early twenties, it was people like the Mulock family, with their formidable Cawthra background, who provided the district with its verve and style while the less colourful thoughts of the Masseys were focused upon useful, philanthropic work and the pursuit of religious excellence. No where is this contrast more strikingly illustrated than in the 1911 edition of Dau's *Blue Book*, the social directory of Toronto and Hamilton. The work listed the addresses of its subscribers, their club memberships and their "calling days," that is, the days upon which the matrons of both cities would be at home to receive their friends. Chester Massey claimed membership in only a single club, the Lambton Golf and Country Club, and that, we may be certain, was the result of his friendship with Albert W. Austin of *Spadina* who had formed the club in 1902 and was a fellow-member of the Metropolitan Church. In the case of Chester's son Vincent, who was then in his twenty-fifth year, his carefully selected memberships lay with the Toronto Golf Club, the University Club, and the Arts and Letters Club. As for their neighbour on Jarvis Street, Cawthra Mulock, who was then aged twenty-nine, he belonged to no fewer than eleven clubs: the Lambton Golf and Country Club, the National Club, the Ontario Jockey Club, the Toronto Club, the Toronto Golf Club, the Toronto Hunt Club, the Toronto Racquet Club, the York Club and in Montreal, the Mount Royal Club and St. James Club, and in Ottawa, the Rideau Club.

A month after he had celebrated his twenty-first birthday, Cawthra Mulock, on June 24, 1903, married Adèle Baldwin Falconbridge. She was a daughter of the chief justice of the King's Bench who would soon be knighted and known as Sir Glenholme Falconbridge. The marriage ceremony was performed at the Chapel of Our Lady of Lourdes on neighbouring Sherbourne Street. The *Globe* reporter who covered the event related that the wedding had taken place "in a very dark and threatening atmosphere, so far as the elements were concerned, but at the hospitable residence of the Chief Justice [80 Isabella Street] the sunshine appeared to surround the fair and youthful bride, as she stood in front of a large bank of white flowers to receive, with her husband, the congratulations of her many friends."

The *Globe* paid particular attention to the bride's wedding dress, which was of "richest cream satin," and noted that she wore "diamond necklet and magnificent spray of diamonds on the corsage." The generosity of the groom also attracted special notice. "The only bridesmaid was Miss Aimee Falconbridge," the reporter observed, "who wore white chiffon over turquoise blue silk, and pretty hat to correspond. Her gift from the groom was a diamond and sapphire ring, and little Miss Dorothy Anglin wore a muslin frock, with pretty hat, and a pearl heart as her gift." Mr. John D. Falconbridge, the bride's brother, was the best man. Later, the lieutenant-governor, Mortimer Clark, proposed the toast to the health of the bride and groom, and Cawthra Mulock and his wife then left the reception and drove to his father's farm near Newmarket where they were to spend a month before leaving for an extensive trip abroad. The newspaper article concluded, "Among the many presents from far and near was a cabinet of china from Sir Wilfrid and Lady Laurier."

For the next fifteen years, Cawthra Mulock's place at the corner of Jarvis and Isabella Streets was the setting for some of Toronto's most memorable entertainments. The house lent itself ideally to entertaining on a generous scale. There was a spacious ballroom with cloakrooms in the basement, two drawing-rooms on the main floor and another room on the south side of the house, known as the Red Room, which led into an extensive conservatory of marble. Cawthra Mulock, an early motoring enthusiast, kept his Pierce-Arrow touring car in a specially built brick garage behind his house. Among its appointments, the garage included a turntable so that the car could be rotated easily and thus left ready to be driven out.

His financial interests were almost as varied as his club memberships. "A fine stroke of constructive work was done," the *Toronto Daily Star* reported enthusiastically, "when he secured water-logged land on Ashbridge's Bay on which to erect the plant of the National Iron Works. Since then a large area has been reclaimed and other fine plants erected or sure to be in the near future."[7] Mulock was also the prime mover in establishing the Maple Leaf Milling Company and the Canada Bread Company. He was elected a member of the Toronto Stock Exchange in 1908 when he was twenty-six years of age, and his directorships, according to the *Star*, came to include the Confederation Life Association, the Imperial Bank of Canada, the Guardian Trust Company and the Penny Bank. In 1904, when Sir Joseph Flavelle had assumed the chairmanship of the Board of Trustees of the Toronto General Hospital, Cawthra Mulock joined the board after he had pledged $100,000 towards the cost of an out-patients' building for the old hospital at Parliament and Gerrard Streets. His subscription, however, became instead the catalyst for the great, new Toronto

General Hospital that was later built under Sir Joseph's guiding hand.[8] The Cawthra Mulock Out-Patient Department, with the name engraved on the external face of the building, still remains today a conspicuous feature of the section of the hospital that overlooks University Avenue.

Cawthra Mulock's colourful presence on Jarvis Street, however, turned out to be tragically brief. Just two weeks after the end of World War I, while he was visiting New York on a business trip, he was suddenly stricken with influenza. It turned to pneumonia, and his end came quickly in a New York hospital on Sunday, December 1, 1918. The next day the Toronto papers gave considerable prominence to his death. The *Toronto Daily Star*, for example, recalled that when he had turned twenty-one he had received an inheritance worth an incredible eight million dollars from his great-aunt, Mrs. William Cawthra Murray. The paper went on to relate that as soon as word of his death had reached the city on Sunday, Sir William Mulock had left by train for New York to arrange for his youngest son's remains to be returned to Toronto.[9] The funeral took place at Cawthra Mulock's house on Jarvis Street the following Tuesday afternoon. His wife, Adèle, and three young children survived him.

Notwithstanding their extensive coverage of the sad event, the Toronto papers did not foresee the effect it would soon have on the residential character of Jarvis Street. In March 1922, the trustees of Cawthra Mulock's estate sold his house and property at 538 Jarvis Street for $90,000 to Dr. Barnardo's Homes, an agency originally organized in England to provide homes for destitute children. The sale was significant for two reasons: it was the first Jarvis Street mansion to pass into institutional ownership, and second, its sale to Dr. Barnardo's Homes also revealed that large houses on Jarvis Street were no longer in demand for single-family use. True enough, the introduction of personal income tax during the war, rising property taxes, and the general cost of maintaining old and inefficient houses, undoubtedly contributed to the sudden lack of interest by private buyers in Jarvis Street. However, in the 1920's those factors probably carried less weight than the desire to withdraw from the city's downtown core. Rosedale, for example, with its surrounding ravines serving as protective moats, exerted a strong attraction. Other buyers were drawn to fashionable St. George Street; in the west end of the city, Parkdale, beside John G. Howard's High Park, was winning a new allegiance as the public transportation system improved, and on the hill overlooking the city,

This 1952 photograph of the Cawthra house at 538 Jarvis Street shows the conservatory addition, later corrupted by a modern façade. Occupied by Cawthra Mulock from 1903 until his death in 1918, the house was purchased by Dr. Barnardo's Homes, then by the Salvation Army, who sold it to a developer in 1956 when it was demolished.—Metropolitan Toronto Library Board

beside Upper Canada College, rapidly developing Forest Hill Village was, perhaps, the most popular new district of all.

It was not long before Hart Massey's *Euclid Hall* followed the Cawthra Mulock house into the public domain. When Lillian Massey Treble died in 1915, she left the house to the Board of Regents of Victoria University, and in 1928 they sold it for $60,000 to Ryan's Art Galleries Limited. And next door, Chester Massey having died in 1926, his fine home was sold for $45,000 in 1929.

In his declining years, Chester Massey's interests had been focused mainly upon the work of the Methodist Church. He lived to see it become part of the new United Church of Canada. He also lived to see his youngest son, Raymond, firmly established in his stage career, and

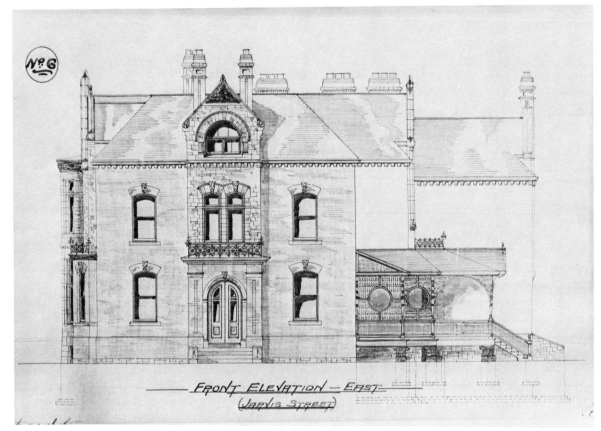

In 1888, Sir William Mulock commissioned William G. Storm, R.C.A., to prepare plans for extensive alterations and additions to the old James Crowther house at the corner of Jarvis and Gloucester streets. This is Storm's design for the front elevation of the remodelled Mulock house, overlooking Jarvis Street. The house was demolished in 1956.—Horwood Architectural Drawings Collection, Archives of Ontario

his son, Vincent, though unsuccessful in his attempt as a Liberal to win a seat in the House of Commons in the election of 1925, appointed the following year as Canada's "Envoy Extraordinary and Minister Plenipotentiary" to the United States.

In the normal course, one would not have thought Sir William Mulock would have remained for long in his house at 518 Jarvis Street after his son's property next door had been sold to Dr. Barnardo's Homes. When the sale was made in 1922, he was in his eightieth year,

176

the time of life when a man would not be criticized for choosing to escape from the din of Dr. Barnardo's children playing beneath his windows. In an astonishing feat of forbearance and longevity, however, he remained, and lived to celebrate his one hundred and first birthday, on January 19, 1944, in the house he had built over half a century before. On his birthday (it was mistakenly thought to have been his one hundredth anniversary), Prime Minister Mackenzie King joined "The Grand Old Man of Canada" for breakfast, and a congratulatory message arrived from King George VI that referred to him as "The oldest member of my Privy Council." Later in the day, over 800 people crowded into Sir William's house to pay him their respects and to drink to his good health.

The following month, Vincent Massey, who was visiting Canada briefly after a long absence in London as High Commissioner for Canada, called on Sir William at his house. He found him "sitting at his bridge table, which was prepared for a game, dressed in a very loud check suit and engaged in extracting a cigar from a box, which he refused to allow me to light for him." Massey naturally found him looking much older than when he had last seen him, but concluded that his mind "seemed entirely clear."[10]

Sir William Mulock's end came on Sunday morning, October 1, 1944. The *Globe and Mail* reported the next day that he had "died peacefully after several months of gradually increasing weakness." His funeral service was held at St. Paul's Church, at the head of Jarvis Street, the following Wednesday afternoon, and both Canon F. H. Wilkinson, the rector of St. Paul's, and President H. J. Cody of the University of Toronto, officiated. Dr. Cody, a former distinguished rector of the church, had also been a neighbour of Sir William's on Jarvis Street since the 1890's.

It didn't take long for Sir William Mulock's house to follow Cawthra Mulock's place into the realm of institutional ownership. The following year, in April 1945, Colonel the Honourable William Pate Mulock, Sir William's grandson and executor of his estate, sold the house to the governing council of the Salvation Army, Canada East. While it was a wartime sale to a charitable organization, the $25,000 price that was realized provided further evidence, if such was needed, that the appeal to single families of the glorious, old homes of Jarvis Street had ended.[11] Before the sale could be completed, however, there arose a curious legal quirk, involving the Prime Minister of Canada, that had first to be resolved.

Under his will, Sir William Mulock had left Prime Minister Mackenzie King, whose political mentor he had once been, a cash bequest of $50,000. Sir William had also provided that the legacy was to be a "charge" upon all his real estate, including his residence at 518 Jarvis Street. It therefore became necessary for Mackenzie King to sign a release to be registered against the property by the executor of the estate. This he did, on March 2, 1945, in the presence of Arnold D. P. Heeney, then clerk of the privy council and secretary to the cabinet. A few minutes after the Prime Minister's release was registered, on April 13, Sir William's house was transferred to the Salvation Army.[12]

In 1946, a few days before Christmas, *The Globe and Mail* visited Jarvis Street to observe the first stage of the post-war onslaught that was to transform the character of the street and incorporate it into the downtown extension of Mount Pleasant Road:

> Long past its prime, and stripped of its youthful grandeur, Jarvis Street is in the process of losing one of its few remaining adornments, the tall, stately trees which line the too-narrow roadway. When the operation is completed, the thoroughfare of checkered history will be widened as part of a new north-south traffic artery.
>
> During the past two decades, Jarvis Street has been deserted by many of its old and respected residents and its 13 licensed hotels, eight of them in one block, have spread its shady reputation as the heart of the city's tenderloin district far beyond Toronto's borders. In the Jarvis-Dundas area policemen patrol their beats in pairs, and twice within the past year pitched battles between police and frequenters of the area have occurred on the street. Bootleggers, prostitutes and dope peddlers have made their headquarters in its big, old rooming houses and apartments.
>
> Yet Jarvis Street, even in its worst days, has housed the Dominion offices of the Church of England and establishments of the Salvation Army, Red Cross, Dr. Barnardo's Home, the YWCA, a maternity hospital, CBC broadcasting studios and the Nisei co-operative residence for Japanese-Canadians.[13]

As the realignment and widening of Jarvis Street neared completion in 1948, the Salvation Army moved to acquire the balance of the land surrounding Sir William Mulock's property. First, in April 1948, they purchased for $12,000 the former house and property of Sir William's eldest son, William, from his estate. The house fronted on Gloucester Street and adjoined the rear of Sir William's property.[14] Next, in July 1948, the Salvation Army bought Cawthra Mulock's former house from Dr. Bernardo's Homes. They paid $70,000 for it, $20,000 less than it had cost Dr. Barnardo's in 1922.[15] As a result, for a total outlay of $107,000, the Salvation Army obtained control of the Gloucester-Isabella block on Jarvis Street, together with the additional Mulock property lying behind it on Gloucester Street. It was a shrewd piece of land assembly, expertly timed as the new Jarvis Street was emerging. Soon after, the Salvation Army established its territorial headquarters at 538 Jarvis Street, in Cawthra Mulock's once-fabulous house. The famous basement ballroom that had softly echoed the strains of Franz Lehar and Victor Herbert, was now to reverberate instead to the crash of drums and rattle of tambourines. But investment time passes quickly, and in 1956, just eight years after the Army had consolidated its position in the old Cawthra enclave, it sold the entire parcel to an apartment developer for $585,000—a profit of $478,000 on its original outlay.[16] Clearly, in that transaction, the angels were on the side of the Army.

After the large mortgage that the Salvation Army had accepted from its purchaser was paid off in full in 1958, the Army moved down Jarvis Street and bought for $86,000 its present property at the southwest corner of Jarvis and Shuter streets.[17] It is now the site of its Harbour Light Centre.

There was a double irony in the series of transactions that brought Harbour Light to Shuter Street, and two eleven-storey apartment buildings to the former Cawthra enclave. By the purchase and sale of the Gloucester-Isabella block, the Salvation Army had demonstrated that it was indeed possible to extract a further profit from a piece of Cawthra land, even after the Cawthras were finished with it. In addition, having thus helped extinguish the notable Cawthra and Mulock houses on upper Jarvis Street, the Salvation Army had then reinvested its profit at the intersection where Jarvis Street had had its beginnings, where Sam Jarvis's house had been razed in 1847 to make way for modern Jarvis Street, where "the heart of the city's tenderloin district" then lay.

CHAPTER ELEVEN

Afterglow

When John G. Howard prepared his first plan of subdivision, which covered only the forty acres of Sam Jarvis's *Hazelburn* farm lying between Queen and Gerrard Street, he adhered closely to the concept of the subdivision that Sam had announced in the *Globe* in 1845. In his advertisement, Sam had stated that his new building lots would be found "peculiarly eligible for the residences of private families, of persons engaged in commerce or of mechanics." In his mention of mechanics, Sam was recognizing the emergence of a new class of prospective householder, the less-educated but skilled manual workers. Under Howard's plan, therefore, in a direct appeal to that important new market, the lower part of Jarvis Street, from Queen to Shuter Street, was divided into numerous low-priced lots, of shallow depth and narrow frontage. Seventeen of these, doubtless designed for commercial use, had their twenty-six- to twenty-eight-foot frontages on Queen Street, on both sides of Jarvis Street. North of Shuter Street, however, where an ancient creek once meandered across Sam's property, the lots, running east and west, were laid out on a more generous scale. Typically, they had a depth of about 250 feet and a frontage on Jarvis Street of fifty feet. Howard calculated that they would sell for an average price of £250. Beyond Gerrard Street, north to Bloor Street, there were no early registered plans. New purchasers were required to make their selections from the surveys Howard maintained for inspection in his office. Thus, the earliest development of Jarvis Street was largely concentrated below Gerrard Street, and the century-long character of the street, with the "mechanics" at the bottom and the more affluent residents farther up, was established at the very beginning.

Today, only a few lineaments of the street's early face are discernible. On Queen Street, for example, the store premises that extend west from

Jarvis Street to Mutual Street still maintain their narrow frontages. To the east of Jarvis Street, however, the modern Moss Park Armoury has devoured the entire block from Queen to Shuter. As a result the little lots and dwellings that were once occupied by the "mechanics" have disappeared.

North of Shuter Street, in clear diagonal view of Harbour Light, a series of terrace houses, recently restored, create the fleeting illusion that time has stood still on Jarvis Street. In the range of numbers from 207 to 213, and from 215 to 219, one can still obtain a clear perception of Toronto's typical terrace houses of the 1850's. Constructed of yellow and pink brick, with unusual details of stone and woodwork, with antique basement areaways surmounted by iron railings, the houses overlook miniature verges of pale grass, each with diminutive trees, all evocative of the glories of old Jarvis Street.

Farther up, at the northeast corner of Dundas Street, the new, commemorative Sir William Mulock Building, housing various federal government offices, now dominates the famous intersection where policemen in the 1940's patrolled "their beats in pairs" for their own protection. Across the road from the Mulock building, on the west side of Jarvis Street, the old Warwick Hotel still survives as one of the "13 licensed hotels, eight of them in one block" that *The Globe and Mail* had viewed darkly in 1946. The Warwick's closest hotel neighbour now, the Westminster Hotel, lies to the north on the same side of the street, separated from the Warwick by a formidable buffer, the towering, new Simpsons-Sears building. Like the Warwick, the Westminster Hotel also enjoys the close proximity of a new government building: directly across the road, on the east side of Jarvis Street, the Family Division of the Provincial Court projects its conciliatory image from a handsome structure of grey stone. Now, it would seem, under the pervasive influence of these new government offices, to say nothing of the "O" Divisional Headquarters of the Royal Canadian Mounted Police just south of Dundas Street, the district's former "shady reputation" has faded, and urban normalcy has been restored.

In the block extending north from Dundas to Gerrard Street, a few tattered old houses still remain. Elaborate keystones in the window arches of one house, or a finely ornamented front door, smiling self-consciously across a bleak porch in another, richly carved stone columns in still another, all remind us that this early section of Jarvis Street once belonged to the second category of householder mentioned in Sam Jarvis's advertisement, "the persons engaged in commerce," as opposed to the "mechanics" who were accommodated to the south, or the "private families" who were to bloom yet farther north.

In the 1860's, for example, Charles Scadding, Dr. Henry Scadding's older brother, occupied a house on the present site of Harbour Light, on the threshold of the domain of the then-rising men of commerce. At that time, Charles Scadding was the treasurer of the Home District Savings Bank. Farther up Jarvis Street, also on the west side, George L. Beardmore owned a house just below Gerrard Street. A tanner and leather merchant, the elegant, Victorian Beardmore Building on the south side of Front Street East still survives as a significant architectural link with his early residence on Jarvis Street. Elsewhere on the west side of the street, in the same block, Patrick Foy, a successful wholesale grocer, had early acquired a property and built himself a house, and close to Shuter Street, Henry Rowsell, well-known in his day as a printer, stationer and bookseller, maintained his home for many years.

On the east side of Jarvis Street, a few doors below Gerrard Street, James Austin, like his Irish partner Patrick Foy, had also been an early purchaser of land. He built his two-storey, red brick house in 1852 with the assistance of a mortgage loan from William Cawthra. By 1865, however, his affairs had prospered to the extent that he bought at auction eighty acres of the Baldwin property on the Davenport Hill where in 1866 he built himself a new *Spadina* on the earlier site of two smaller Baldwin houses of the same name.[1] His house, to the east of *Casa Loma*, still survives and, like *Mackenzie House* and John G. Howard's *Colborne Lodge*, is now destined to be preserved, with its original pre-Confederation furnishings, as a living museum under the management of the Toronto Historical Board in co-operation with the Ontario Heritage Foundation.

After he had settled into his new *Spadina*, Austin became president of the Consumers' Gas Company of Toronto and the first president of The Dominion Bank, positions he was to hold for many years. In them, he found himself associated with a number of men who had been connected with the Jarvis Street of his day. When The Dominion Bank was established in 1871, for example, James Crowther was a founding director, and the bank's first lawyer. It will be recalled that he had built his house on the Jarvis-Gloucester corner in 1866, at the same time that Austin was building *Spadina*. Moreover, young William Mulock, having married Crowther's daughter in 1870 and having joined his father-in-law's firm of Bell and Crowther, was deputized the day The

Dominion Bank opened its first office, on February 1, 1871, to supervise the transfer of $100,000 in gold, in a rickety cart, from the vaults of the Bank of Toronto to the new bank at 40 King Street East. Also in later years, associated with James Austin on the board of directors of the Consumers' Gas Company of Toronto, at one time or another, were William Cawthra, who had provided the financing for the construction of Jarvis Street, Samuel Platt, who lived a few doors north of Austin on Jarvis Street in the 1860's, and two presidents of the gas company, E. H. Rutherford, who served from 1867 to 1874 and whom James Austin succeeded, and John L. Blaikie who held the office from 1906 to 1912. In the 1860's, both Rutherford and Blaikie lived as close neighbours just north of Carlton Street, on the west side of Jarvis Street, on part of the land that John Ewart had purchased from a troubled Sam Jarvis in 1843. John Ewart, an important builder in his day, chose later to live in the Dundas-Gerrard block of Jarvis Street where his widow, Jane, was a next-door neighbour of George L. Beardmore.

After the residential sections north of Shuter Street had been largely settled, two historic churches made their appearance on Jarvis Street. At its familiar location on the northeast corner of Gerrard Street, Jarvis Street Baptist Church was completed and dedicated in 1875. Designed in grey stone by the Toronto architect Edmund Burke in the Gothic Revival style, the church is still well maintained and, somewhat incongruously, displays a small plaque on the wall by its entrance which assures the passerby, "I am not ashamed of the Gospel of Christ. *Romans* 1:16." In the 1890's, the church became celebrated as a result of the work of Dr. Augustus Vogt, its distinguished organist and choirmaster. He organized Toronto's original Mendelssohn Choir, and in his lifetime achieved international renown as a choral conductor. He was a later principal of the Toronto Conservatory of Music and dean of the University's Faculty of Music.

Farther north, at the southeast corner of Jarvis and Carlton Street, the beautifully preserved St. Andrew's Latvian Lutheran Church now occupies the earlier St. Andrew's Presbyterian Church that was dedicated in 1878. Designed by Langley and Burke in distinctive Credit Valley pink and grey stone, for many years it was adjacent to the Toronto Collegiate Institute. Now, the Allan Gardens have been extended from Sherbourne Street to Jarvis Street and include the old school site, and an impressive parkland setting has been created beside the old St. Andrew's Church.

The steeples of Jarvis Street Baptist Church and St. Andrew's Latvian Lutheran Church, when viewed from Dundas Street looking north, or from Wellesley Street looking south, provide a rare vista of Jarvis Street as it appeared over a century ago. Though the street is now wider, its verges gone, and the existing trees pale in comparison with the great, flowering chestnuts and elms that once sheltered the roadway, it is still possible to recreate the distant scenes of Queen Victoria's time when broughams and victorias moved silently through the gaslit street, and ladies with their silk-hatted gentlemen strolled leisurely along the shaded sidewalks.

Above the corner opposite St. Andrew's Latvian Lutheran Church, the present CBC Radio Building is the dominant structure in the block extending from Carlton to Maitland Street. Included in the CBC complex is the old *Northfield* house, now the home of the executive offices of the CBC's Ontario Region, that was built in the Georgian style by Sir Oliver Mowat in 1856. As the name of his house implied, only open fields swept north to Bloor Street when he first occupied it. In placing his substantial house where he did, Mowat led the way in the development of upper Jarvis Street, and provided early proof of the first category mentioned in Sam Jarvis's advertisement that his lots would be found "peculiarly eligible for the residences of private families" as well as for men of commerce or "mechanics." Mowat's *Northfield* was among the first houses built on Jarvis Street that attained the grace and style of a so-called private family residence.

Sir Oliver Mowat, later a Father of Confederation, long-time premier of Ontario, and then lieutenant-governor, acquired the land for *Northfield* from his father-in-law, John Ewart. Mowat had married Ewart's daughter Jane in 1846, three years after Ewart had bought the property from Sam Jarvis. It had a frontage on Jarvis Street of nearly 1,200 feet, and it was subdivided by Mowat and his brother-in-law George Ewart in 1861. Their registered plan extended from Carlton Street to Maitland Street. In the same year, Mowat sold *Northfield* to E. H. Rutherford.

Before Mowat moved from *Northfield*, a few smaller houses had been built south of his place, down to the Carlton Street corner. In 1861, one of them was occupied by J. Herbert Mason, who was then the secretary and treasurer of the Canada Permanent Building Society, a company he had organized in 1855 when he was twenty-eight years old. Mason later became president of the society and a founding director of the Confederation Life Association. In 1888, he presented Upper

Canada College with $1,000 for "the funding of 2 medals, to be awarded annually to the pupils most distinguished for excellence of character." Today, the J. Herbert Mason medals remain among the most coveted awards at the school. In later years, Mason occupied a larger house on Sherbourne Street which he called *Ermeleigh*.[2]

Today's CBC Radio Building was from 1898 to 1927, the principal home of Havergal Ladies' College, which was both a boarding and day school. In 1913, the school acquired *Northfield* and changed its name to *Coverley House*. Throughout its sojourn on Jarvis Street, Havergal added much to the ambience of the district, especially on Sunday mornings when, led by a determined mistress, the girls were to be seen walking decorously in pairs up Jarvis Street on their way to attend divine service at St. Paul's Anglican Church on Bloor Street. For many years, the rector of the church, Canon Henry John Cody, was their chaplain; and when the great, new St. Paul's was dedicated in 1913, the Havergal girls recognized the occasion by presenting the church with a prayer desk for its chancel.

In 1923, as construction was under way for a new home for Jarvis Collegiate Institute in its planned move north from below Carlton Street to Wellesley Street, the board of Havergal College decided that the time had come for them to move north, too. The momentum generated by their decisions, however, carried Havergal College much farther north than the minuscule distance that was involved in the collegiate's move to its new home. In fact, Havergal College picked up its skirts and kept running until it dropped exhausted in the open fields of north Avenue Road, close to Lawrence Avenue. There, in 1927, on the east side of Avenue Road, which was then a rough, dirt thoroughfare, the new school received its first pupils.

Across the road from the CBC's Radio Building and a short distance north of the Hampton Court Hotel, two adjoining houses, rich in legend, exist today as Jarvis Street's Odd Couple. They are the Celebrity Club and the Red Lion Tavern. They wear a shy, regretful air like two genteel old ladies who have fallen from their station. Both are architectural anomalies. Both had a long connection with the Honourable Edward Blake, Q.C. Take, for example, the discrepancy involved in their street numbers. The red brick dwelling occupied by the Celebrity Club has 449 as its number, while its immediate neighbour on the north, the Red Lion Tavern of yellow brick, boasts a much higher number, 467. This break in the normal sequence of house addresses occurred over three-quarters of a century ago. And to

Havergal College as it appeared around 1913. CBC Radio has occupied the old school building at 354 Jarvis Street since 1945, but long before that Havergal College had moved to a new site on Avenue Road at Lawrence Avenue purchased in 1923—Havergal College.

complicate matters further, the Red Lion Tavern was once a semi-detached house, with two separate front entrances. Until recently it was known as 467-469 Jarvis Street. In its original state, the Blake family opened and closed the interior of the twin dwelling like an accordion, knocking down walls and patching them up again in response to the varying needs of their family. It was a setting in which Lewis Carroll would have felt at home. In these two (or three) houses, at different times and in various combinations, the Honourable Edward Blake resided with his wife and children, his son Edward Francis Blake, after

186

he had married and as a lawyer had a separate household, and Blake Senior's son-in-law, Professor George M. Wrong, the colourful head of the History Department at the University of Toronto.

The Honourable Edward Blake was a brilliant lawyer, a political idealist, and a man of uncompromising integrity. In his time, he was a premier of Ontario, a leader of the Liberal Party in Ottawa, a chancellor of the University of Toronto, and to cap it all, a member of the British House of Commons where he was allied with the Irish Parliamentary Party. As a member of the British Parliament, he was one of a committee of fifteen appointed to investigate South African affairs and the causes of the Transvaal raid. His cross-examination of Cecil Rhodes was later described as "a masterly piece of work." Lord Rosebery, who succeeded Gladstone as Prime Minister in 1894, once referred to Blake as "the most brilliant orator and one of the most capable statesmen of Canada." During the course of his career, the Honourable Edward Blake refused a knighthood, the chancellorship of Upper Canada, the chief justiceship of Ontario, and finally the chief justiceship of Canada.

With his brother, the Honourable S. Hume Blake, Q.C., who for a time was vice-chancellor of the Ontario Court of Chancery, Edward Blake had earlier practised law in Toronto. Their firm became widely known as Blake, Lash and Cassels. The brothers both married daughters of the Right Reverend Benjamin Cronyn, the first Bishop of Huron, and both men also brought their wives to live on Jarvis Street, S. Hume Blake for many years occupying a house on the west side of the street, below Gerrard Street.

In 1892, when Blake accepted the nomination to seek election to the British House of Commons, his brother, as trustee under an earlier marriage settlement between Edward Blake and his wife, transferred both the Blake properties on upper Jarvis Street to the Toronto General Trusts Company, of which Edward Blake was the president. House number 449, today occupied by the Celebrity Club, was shown as having a frontage on Jarvis Street of forty feet, and the property next door, numbered 467 and 469, now entirely occupied by the Red Lion Tavern, enjoyed a frontage of a hundred feet. In 1896, when his father was abroad, Edward Francis Blake bought the present Celebrity Club property from the Toronto General Trusts Company. A sketch attached to the deed reveals that the house then had a width of only twenty feet, a surprising dimension for a dwelling in that section of Jarvis Street, just below Wellesley Street. In any event, in 1897 young

Blake called in the Toronto architect, David B. Dick, to make substantial additions and alterations to his new house, and these changes are reflected in the present structure. After young Blake's death, his father purchased the enlarged house from his son's estate in 1907 and later occupied it himself.

Meanwhile, while Edward Blake was in England, the south half of the present Red Lion Tavern, number 467, was retained as his principal residence in Toronto, and this state of affairs appears to have been continued at least until he bought his son's house next door in 1907. It was around that time that Professor and Mrs. George M. Wrong and their family of four children took up their residence at 467 Jarvis Street, and they remained there at least until 1921. It was, therefore, from the house that has survived today as the Red Lion Tavern that George M. Wrong departed on a fine day in June 1915, to journey to Kingston to fulfil an important engagement. Vincent Massey has recorded the purpose of his trip. After speaking of his fiancée, Alice Parkin, Massey wrote:

> Our formal engagement was very brief, and in June 1915 we were married in St. George's Cathedral at Kingston where Alice's sister, Maude, the wife of a professor at Queen's University, lived. One of the officiating clergymen was my chief, George Wrong, who was in holy orders. My brother, Raymond, who as a gunner officer was taking a course at Kingston, was a resplendent best man. The wedding, as befitted a war-time marriage, could not have been simpler—8.30 A.M., informal dress, only a handful of persons present, no wedding breakfast. Alice and I contented ourselves with a picnic meal *à deux* by the roadside, many miles from Kingston. It was a "quiet wedding," but for us it was the prelude to thirty-five years of complete happiness.[3]

Just beyond the Red Lion Tavern and the Celebrity Club, the north and south limits of the grounds surrounding Jarvis Collegiate Institute are still marked by a fine, ornamental iron fence which was mercifully preserved when the existing houses on the site, including Thomas Long's *Woodlawn*, were demolished to make way for the new school. To the north, on the opposite side of Wellesley Street, a corner service station now occupies that part of Hart Massey's *Euclid Hall*, which once supported his exotic greenhouse and conservatory. While the old Massey house, since it was bought by Ryan's Art Galleries, has seen service as an art and antiques gallery and as a restaurant, its most memorable use occurred when Ryan rented space for a primitive broadcasting studio to the new Toronto radio station, CFRB, over fifty years ago. After a tenancy of four years, the station moved in dramatic circumstances to a new location on Bloor Street near Yonge Street. William Baker, who as a young engineer had helped launch the station, later described CFRB's hurried departure from *Euclid Hall*:

> We were all set to end our shows at the Massey place one night and come on the air from the new location on Bloor Street the next morning, but we figured to take a few days getting our equipment out of the old place, after that. Then Tommy Ryan, who owned the Massey building, came in and said if we did not have everything out by midnight, when our lease was up, we'd have to pay another full year's rent. The station was not making a profit yet, so that night, as the last newscast was being broadcast at 11 o'clock, we were taking out the screws holding the control panel to the floor.
>
> When we signed off at 11:06, one of us went behind the panel and cut all the wires, and we rushed all the equipment out the door. We were away by midnight, but the place was a shambles.[4]

Across Jarvis Street, at the north east corner of Cawthra Square, the Romanesque house that George H. Gooderham built as a young man in 1891 has miraculously survived. Gooderham left Jarvis Street in 1906 after having occupied the house, which is numbered 504, for fifteen years. He moved to a larger place on St. George Street, and while he was living there served as commodore of the Royal Canadian Yacht Club from 1918 to 1930, an unprecedented twelve years. His Cawthra Square house was purchased in 1908 by Leo Frankel, and was made available by the Frankel family in 1946 to the Big Brothers of Metropolitan Toronto in whose work Leo Frankel had been keenly interested. The Big Brothers disposed of the house in 1975. Undoubtedly, the benign ownership of the former Gooderham house by Frankel and then by the Big Brothers combined to save the unique house from the carnage that ravaged upper Jarvis Street after World War II.

As with all streets, the story of Jarvis Street is one of arrivals and departures. Many arrived, prospered, and then departed, moving on to larger homes or more congenial districts. Sir Joseph Flavelle, like George H. Gooderham, was one of these. As noted earlier, Flavelle purchased his house at 565 Jarvis Street in 1894. His affairs prospered brilliantly, and after a sojourn of only eight years, he hurried away to

The Reverend Canon H.J. Cody posed for this picture in 1913 while the chancel of the new St. Paul's Anglican Church on Bloor Street was still under construction. He was rector of the church for thirty-three years and lived at 603 Jarvis Street for over fifty years. He was forced to move in 1947 when his house was demolished to make way for the Clifton Road Extension.—James Collection, City of Toronto Archives

190

take up his residence in his baronial *Holwood*, the new house he had built for himself in 1902 in Queen's Park, just south of today's Royal Ontario Museum.

On the other hand, a few men who would have liked to have lived out their lives on Jarvis Street couldn't. Among them was Canon H. J. Cody. He had lived at 603 Jarvis Street for over fifty years. His place was a few doors south of Bloor Street, on the east side of Jarvis. On June 15, 1947, when he was in his seventy-ninth year, he signed a deed to his house in favour of the city of Toronto.[5] Shortly later, he moved to Dale Avenue in Rosedale. His Jarvis Street house was required by the city for demolition in connection with the building of the Clifton Road Extension which joined Mount Pleasant Road to Jarvis Street and created a new north-south traffic artery.

Regarded in his time as one of the great preachers of Canada, Canon Cody was the rector of St. Paul's Anglican Church for thirty-three years. Except for St. James's Cathedral, his church was the oldest Anglican parish within Toronto proper. It was as a result of his popular ministry that St. Paul's was able to build its new church on Bloor Street with a seating capacity of 3,000 people. Just before it opened, the final service in the old church next door was held on Sunday, November 23, 1913. The sermon naturally was preached by the rector, the Venerable Dr. Cody, Archdeacon of York, and he confined his remarks to a review of the history of St. Paul's to that day. As his fame spread, he was given the honour of preaching in Westminster Abbey, and in 1922 he preached before King George V and Queen Mary in the Buckingham Palace Chapel. After a long association with the University of Toronto, he became its president in 1932, and in 1945 succeeded Sir William Mulock as chancellor. Following the end of World War II, Vincent Massey returned to Canada upon completion of his eleven-year tenure in England as Canadian High Commissioner. After a year of quietude and reflection at *Batterwood*, his country place near Port Hope, Massey was available for new appointments. In 1947, as Canon Cody was uprooting himself from Jarvis Street, he also stepped aside as chancellor of the university so that Massey, his former neighbour, could succeed him. For fifty years, Cody had lived within the sound of the sexton's bell at St. Paul's. He died in Rosedale in 1951, just beyond its hearing. He was in his eighty-third year.[6]

Canon Cody's departure from Jarvis Street severed the last link in a long chain of outstanding people who had made their homes there and had seen its greatest days. Before he left he had watched the great trees being cut down, some familiar houses around him being demolished. Soon there would be more. Their windows would be dark and undraped for a while, then their iron fences would disappear, their gardens would gradually fill with planks and heaps of brick, and their hedges would be trampled down. As he watched them die as they had lived with a quiet and noble dignity, somehow it seemed the street that had been born in despair a hundred years before had finally come full circle.

Notes

Abbreviations

PAC — Public Archives of Canada
PAO — Public Archives of Ontario
MTL — Metropolitan Toronto Library
TPL — Toronto Public Library

CHAPTER ONE: THE KING'S MEN

1. *Political Writers and Speakers* (Cambridge: The Cambridge History of English Literature, 1934), Vol. II, Ch. 2. See also William Hazlitt, *Character of the Late Mr. Pitt*, Selected Writings (Penguin English Library, 1970).

2. The Honourable William Renwick Riddell, *The Life of John Graves Simcoe* (Toronto: McClelland and Stewart Limited, 1926), pp. 80 and 90. Simcoe did, however, take part in the committee discussion of the Constitutional Act.

3. *Ibid.*, p. 81.   4. *Ibid.*, p. 162.

5. North Callahan, *Flight from the Republic, The Tories of the American Revolution* (Indianapolis: The Bobbs-Merrill Co. Inc., 1967), p. 102.

6. Mary Beth Norton, *The British-Americans, The Loyalist Exiles in England, 1774-1789* (Boston: Little, Brown & Co., 1972), p. 127.

7. Quoted in Julia Jarvis, *"In Good Faith: The Story of Some Jarvises"*, MTL, Baldwin Room.

8. *Country Life Magazine*, England, July 12, 1962.

9. PAO, Russell Papers.

10. Mary Agnes Fitzgibbon, *The Jarvis Letters* (Niagara Historical Society Family History No. 8, 1901), p. 26.

11. *Letters from the Secretary of Upper Canada and Mrs. Jarvis to her father, the Rev. Samuel Peters, D. D.*, (Women's Canadian Historical Society of Toronto, Transaction No. 23, 1922-1923) p. 17.

12. *Ibid.*, p. 18.   13. *Ibid.*, p. 23.

CHAPTER TWO: NEHKIK

1. PAC, William Jarvis Papers, quoted in *Mrs. Simcoe's Diary*, edited by Mary Quayle Innis (Toronto: The Macmillan Company of Canada Limited, 1965), p. 8.

2. Women's Canadian Historical Society of Toronto, Transaction No. 23, *op cit*, p. 27.

3. André Maurois, *Chateaubriand* (New York and London, Harper & Brothers, 1938), p. 39.

4. PAO, Russell Papers, quoted in Edith G. Firth, *The Town of York, 1793-1815* (Toronto: University of Toronto Press, 1962), p. 9.

5. Women's Canadian Historical Society of Toronto, Transaction No. 23, *op cit*, p. 32.

6. William Kirby, F.R.S.C., *Annals of Niagara* (Toronto: The Macmillan Company of Canada, 1927), p. 6.

7. Percy J. Robinson, M.A., *Toronto During the French Régime* (Toronto: The Ryerson Press, 1933), p. 221. See also *More About Toronto* by the same author (Ontario History, Vol. XIV, 1953, No. 3) in which he presents additional evidence that "Toronto was the name given to the Huron Country after the expulsion of the Hurons in 1649-50, and perhaps before."

8. Women's Canadian Historical Society of Toronto, Transaction No. 23, *op cit*, p. 44. In *Toronto in 1810* (Toronto: The Ryerson Press, 1970), p. 63, Eric W. Hounsom, after examining a carpenter's drawing for a large house in Newark he found amongst the Jarvis Papers, mistakenly concluded that the house had been built in 1794. The Jarvis correspondence of that period makes it clear that no such house was ever built.

9. PAO, Simcoe Papers, quoted in Edith G. Firth, *op cit*, p. 25.

CHAPTER THREE: CAROLINE STREET

1. PAO, Ridout Papers, quoted in Edith G. Firth, *op cit*, p. 239.

2. Women's Canadian Historical Society of Toronto, Transaction No. 23, *op cit*, p. 46.

3. TPL, Peter Russell Papers, quoted in Edith G. Firth, *op cit*, p. 46.

4. While Jarvis's correspondence shows that he acquired his corner Lot 12 from John Coon in February 1798, and Lot 11 from Samuel Backhouse

shortly after (before Crown grants had been issued to either of them), it was not until November 1, 1811, that Jarvis got around to registering Crown grants in his own favour of both these parcels. It will be recalled that he also delayed registering his Crown grant of the one-hundred acre Park Lot 6 that he had acquired around 1793 until November 1, 1811. But these transactions are models of conveyancing practice when contrasted with the mystery surrounding his acquisition of Lot 3 at the northeast corner of Caroline and Duke Streets, and Lot 10 lying to the east of his original property on the south side of Duke Street.

In the case of Lot 3, which measured 198 feet square and contained approximately one acre, the property was granted by the Crown to Peter Penning on June 10, 1801. Penning, whose name also appears in the records of York as Peter Piney or Pining, was one of Berczy's German settlers in Markham. The records of the registry office are innocent of any transfer of Lot 3 from Penning to Jarvis and yet in 1816 the secretary, apparently enjoying the full fruits of ownership, appears on the title for the first time when he transfers the property to his son, Samuel Peters Jarvis. It is certain that William Jarvis gained control of Lot 3 long before that date because in a schedule of his personal worth prepared in 1803 he listed "One small house on an acre Lot opposite the Secy's office—£125." His office at that time was on the ground floor of his house, at the northwest corner of the structure, directly across from Lot 3. If it was on this parcel that Archibald Thomson was building a small house in April, 1798, it could only have been accomplished with the prior approval of the not-yet registered owner, Peter Penning. Later, in 1801, when the original Crown grant in Penning's favour was registered, Jarvis may have overlooked registering the further, critically important deed in his own favour from Penning—or perhaps he had simply lost it.

Similarly in the case of Lot 10. Like Jarvis's original Lots 12 and 11, it contained one-fifth of an acre and occupied a frontage on the south side of Duke Street of 66 feet with a depth of 132 feet. This lot had been granted to John Henry Kahman by the Crown on May 17, 1802. Kahman, who was a Loyalist, and latterly a blacksmith with the Indian Department, died in 1810. Again according to the records of the Registry Office, Jarvis does not appear on the title until 1816 when he transferred the lot, as absolute owner, to his son. No deed from Kahman or his executors in favour of Jarvis had ever been registered.

The unusual nature of these personal land transactions would appear to lend pith and substance to Russell's concerns over the efficiency of the secretary which led him to launch an inquiry into his office in the summer of 1797.

5. TPL, William Jarvis Papers, quoted in Edith G. Firth, *op cit*, p. 224.

6. TPL, Jarvis Papers, B. 53, No. 69.

7. Marion MacRae, *MacNab of Dundurn* (Toronto: Clarke, Irwin & Company Limited, 1971), p. 20.

8. Willcocks was a cousin of the Honourable Peter Russell and later became Dr. W.W. Baldwin's father-in-law. An incorrigible land speculator, he died leaving a number of large properties throughout the province. Lake Willcocks in the Township of Whitchurch, and Willcocks Street in Toronto, were both named for him.

9. Women's Canadian Historical Society of Toronto, Transaction No. 23, *op cit*, p. 50.

10. Edith G. Firth, *op cit*, p. 162.

11. Ontario Historical Society, Papers and Records, Vol. XXX, 1934, p. 5.

12. Women's Canadian Historical Society of Toronto, Transaction No. 23, *op cit*, p. 56.

13. TPL, Early Toronto Papers, quoted in Edith G. Firth, *op cit*, p. 198.

14. PAC, William Jarvis Papers, quoted in Edith G. Firth, *op cit, p. 256.*

CHAPTER FOUR: THE RESIDUE OF PEACE

1. Matilda Edgar, *Ten Years of Upper Canada in Peace and War, 1805-1815, Being the Ridout Letters* (Toronto: William Briggs, 1890), p. 22.

2. *The Canadian Magazine*, Vol. XXVI, March, 1906, p. 450.

3. PAO, Baldwin Papers, William Jarvis to Quetton St. George, January 25, 1808.

4. PAO, Baldwin Papers, William Jarvis to Quetton St. George, April 11, 1808.

5. PAO, Baldwin Papers, William Jarvis to Quetton St. George, May 6, 1808.

6. TPL, William Jarvis Papers, B. 55, No. 41, "Schedule of the Debts owing by Wm. Jarvis Esq. Secy & Register of the Province of Upper Canada, Dec. 26, 1808."

7. PAO, Ridout Papers, quoted in Edith G. Firth, *op cit*, p. 82.

8. *Ibid.*, p. 287.

9. George F. G. Stanley, *Canada's Soldiers* (Toronto: The Macmillan Company of Canada Limited, 1960), p. 155.

10. PAC, C688c, p. 84; printed in Wood, Select British Documents of the Canadian War of 1812, 11, 193-6, quoted in Edith G. Firth, *op cit*, p. 318.

11. D. B. Read, Q.C., *The Lieutenant-Governors of Upper Canada and Ontario, 1792-1899* (Toronto: William Briggs, 1900), p. 102.

CHAPTER FIVE: A MEETING AT ELMSLEY'S FARM

1. Strachan purchased Front Town Lots 9 and 10 from the estate of Robert Isaac Dey Gray, a former solicitor-general. Gray had purchased them in 1802 from Hannah and William Jarvis.
2. Austin Seton Thompson, *Spadina, A Story of Old Toronto* (Toronto: Pagurian Press Limited, 1975), *passim.*
3. TPL, Jarvis Papers, B55, S 109, N. 101.
4. PAO, Ridout Papers, quoted in Edith G. Firth, *op cit*, p. 90.
5. In 1828, York's *Canadian Freeman* carried a lurid account of the Jarvis-Ridout duel which had been written by a "Relative" of John Ridout who is said to have been his mother. It was bitterly critical of Jarvis and Boulton. Sam Jarvis replied on March 14, 1828, by publishing privately "A Contradiction of the Libel Under the Signature of 'A Relative,' published in *The Canadian Freeman* of 28th February, 1828." His "Contradiction" took the form of several letters which were written to him at his request by various people involved in the "unhappy affair," like Fitzgibbon, together with two prepared statements concerning the duel itself which James E. Small and Henry J. Boulton were asked to confirm in the presence of Sam's friend, Colonel James Fitzgibbon, and his cousin, Sheriff William Botsford Jarvis of *Rosedale*. To lend authority and credibility to the statements, they were marked "Certified" by both Fitzgibbon and W. B. Jarvis.
6. The fact that John Ridout fired prematurely has been attributed by Ridout apologists to the inaudibility of the count, and also to Ridout's nervousness and excitement, a condition arising from his youth. Neither explanation is convincing. He was a mature eighteen-year old who had served in the navy when he was only thirteen, had benefited greatly from the tutelage of two able older brothers, and though alone, hadn't hesitated to attack Jarvis on King Street while Sam was in the company of a friend.

   Two further explanations of Ridout's errant conduct are more plausible. First, he may have convinced himself in advance that he was at a disadvantage in terms of his shooting skill. (It was at his request that the duelling distance was reduced from twelve to eight paces.) To offset that handicap, he might have decided to try to hit Sam first, thereby minimizing or eliminating the chance of injury to himself—better to face a scandal as a result of having fired first, than sacrifice his life to a man whom he believed to be the better shot. Second, he might have been influenced by the well-known duel fought by Dr. Baldwin in 1812. In that incident, Dr. Baldwin had intentionally fired wide after his opponent, his arm unraised, had urged him to fire. Ridout thus fired first and wide and then walked away in an attempt to reduce the duel to a light-hearted formality. After all, Ridout was William Jarvis's godson, and in the eyes of the law, at the age of eighteen, he was only a child. He might have gambled, therefore, that having fired first, before Sam fired at him, Sam would accept his proferred truce and, being uninjured, would not insist upon having his shot. If that had been Ridout's line of reasoning, subsequent events obviously proved it a fatal miscalculation.

7. Down to the present day, Jarvis apologists have insisted that Sam Jarvis didn't intend to injure Ridout, that his hand had been shattered by Ridout's stick, and he couldn't therefore control his pistol. In addition, they argue, Ridout's early shot "nicked" Sam's neck-cloth.

Under the duelling code, the encounter had to occur in fair and equally advantageous conditions. Had Jarvis's hand been seriously impaired by a blow from a stick, or his eye closed, the duel would simply have been delayed, without loss of honour, until conditions of equality were restored. It is inconceivable, had his hand been seriously injured the previous Wednesday, that Sam would have extended a challenge on Friday for a meeting early the following morning.

The statement that Jarvis didn't intend to injure Ridout is also at variance with the certified statements signed by the two seconds. If the rules of the code were being followed strictly, and the statements suggest that they were, the only certain way Sam could have avoided injuring Ridout was not to have fired at him at all. If Sam had intentionally fired wide, under a strict interpretation of the rules, his action could have been taken as an admission of guilt, or as an apology.

The statement concerning Sam's neck-cloth as having been "nicked" by Ridout appears in John Carroll, D.D., *My Boy Life* (Toronto: William Briggs, 1882), p. 125. Based upon his recollection of the affair, which occurred when he was eight years old, many of his statements are in conflict with the accepted facts of the case. His summation of the duel, however, was sympathetic to Ridout of whom he wrote that "he was put back at eight paces and deliberately shot at . . ." and that he had been "led as an ox to the slaughter."

From Jarvis's standpoint, the real significance of Ridout's premature shot, whether it "nicked" his neck-cloth, his breeches, or went wide, would have been that it constituted a heinous breach of the duelling code. Had Ridout survived, he would have been an object of ridicule and odium throughout the town. The early shot by Ridout could only have intensified Jarvis's feelings of contempt—that is why he was at pains to describe the meticulous care he took to comply with the code when he returned Ridout's fire, in contrast to Ridout's dishonourable early shot. To Sam, a soldier and sportsman, the rules of the code would have been paramount.

8. Payment of Dr. Widmer's account was authorized by the magistrates on November 1, 1817. Widmer later became celebrated as the "Father of Surgery in Upper Canada."

9. Edith G. Firth, *The Town of York, 1815-1834* (Toronto: University of Toronto Press, 1966), p. 261.

10. *Canadian Law Times* (1915) Vol. 35, p. 726. In his article Judge Riddell discusses several early duels including the Jarvis-Ridout affair in which his remarks appear based largely upon the verbal account given him by Sam Jarvis's grandson, Edward Aemilius Jarvis, who also showed him the legendary pistols. Riddell does not seem to have been aware of the underlying financial difficulties of the Jarvis family in 1817, and the resulting pressures on Sam.

11. TPL, S. P. Jarvis Papers, unbound.

12. A. M. Carey, *English Irish and Scottish Fire Arms Makers* (Thomas Crowell Co., 1854), and Colonel Robert Gardner, *Small Arms Makers* (New York, Crown Publishers Inc.).

13. R. M. and J. Baldwin, *The Baldwins and the Great Experiment* (Toronto: Longmans, Canada Limited, 1969), p. 104.

14. MTL, W. D. Powell Papers, Mrs. W. D. Powell to George Murray, August 3, 1818.

15. TPL, S. P. Jarvis Collection Miscellaneous Papers, B69, pp. 44-45.

16. J. Ross Robertson, *History of Freemasonry in Canada* (Toronto: George Morang & Co. Ltd., 1900), Vol. I, p. 465.

CHAPTER SIX: NEHKIK BECOMES A CHIEF

1. MTL, W. D. Powell Papers, Mrs. W. D. Powell to George Murray, October 2, 1818.

2. TPL, Jarvis Papers, B55, S109, No. 31. This twelve-page document, entitled "Draft on Secretary Jarvis," is unsigned and undated, but was clearly written by Sam Jarvis, after Sir Peregrine Maitland had left the province in 1828, as the basis for a further application "for compensation for a more adequate living." After reviewing the circumstances of his father's loss of fee income over the years and the hardships he thereby suffered, Sam states, referring to himself, "He holds now the office of

Clerk of the Crown in Chancery and is Deputy Secretary of the Province, the accumulated Benefice barely sufficient to feed and Clothe his large family—The kindness of the late Lt. Gov Sir P M procured for him £1,000 pounds as part compensation for the Injury suffered by his father." See also Petition of S. P. Jarvis to Governor in Council, April 2, 1822, PAC., RG 1, E3, Vol. 101, pp. 267-272, and Extract from a Report to the Executive Council, October 6, 1827, wherein reference is made to the earlier payment of £1,000 to S. P. Jarvis, PAC., RG 1, E3, Vol. 41, p. 14.

3. MTL, Correspondence of Mrs. W. D. Powell, *op. cit.*

4. The mortgage for £200 was registered by Dr. Widmer on August 22, 1826 as No. 5686, and was discharged by Sam Jarvis on April 8, 1829.

5. TPL., TR 920—071—J13-21, *Statement of Facts, relating to the Trespass on the Printing Press in the possession of Mr. William Lyon M'Kenzie, in June 1826*. Written by Samuel P. Jarvis, and sworn to by the other seven press wreckers, the main purpose of this thirty-two-page pamphlet, published in 1828, was to counter the allegations made by Mackenzie and others that the raid had been conducted "under the direction, or with the knowledge or sanction of the Executive Government." The action of the wreckers had been a great embarrassment to the government, and because of Sam Jarvis's leading role in it, the raid had proved an equal embarrassment to him, indeed, he admitted its "impropriety, so far as Society is concerned, and still more its folly."

But Sam's *Statement of Facts* had a chilling side-effect. In it, he cited the *Advocate*'s reference to himself as a "Murderer," and pointed out in his own defence that after the Ridout duel he had surrendered himself unhesitatingly to the officers of Justice, "I endured imprisonment," he went on, "and was readily acquitted by a Jury of my Countrymen. The whole melancholy story has been long given to the World." It was this statement that fell under the critical gaze of a "Relative" of the late John Ridout, believed to have been old Mrs. Thomas Ridout, and led her to publish in the *Canadian Freeman* her own unflattering version of the events at Elmsley's Farm. As noted in the preceding chapter of this book, Sam Jarvis then leaped into print again with his own *Contradiction* of Mrs. Ridout's "Libel." All in all, 1828 was a trying year for Sam Jarvis. But that was not all. Under goading from Francis Collins, the intransigent editor of the *Canadian Freeman*, published in York, the government that year also prosecuted Henry J. Boulton and James E. Small for their role in the 1817 duel. Both were acquitted.

6. William Dawson LeSueur, *William Lyon Mackenzie: A Reinterpretation*, edited by A. B. McKillop (The Carleton Library No. 111, Macmillan of Canada, Limited, 1979).

7. D. B. Read, Q.C., *The Lieutenant-Governors of Upper Canada and Ontario, 1792-1899*, op cit, p. 157.

8. Anna Brownell Jameson, *Winter Studies and Summer Rambles in Canada* (Toronto: Thomas Nelson and Sons Limited, 1943), p. 236 *et seq.*

CHAPTER SEVEN: SAM'S STREET

1. George F. G. Stanley, *Canada's Soldiers, op cit*, p. 198 *et seq.*

2. J. M. S. Careless, *The Union of the Canadas* (Toronto: McClelland and Stewart Limited, 1967), p. 8.

3. Douglas Leighton, Huron College, *The Compact Tory as Bureaucrat: Samuel Peters Jarvis and the Indian Department, 1837-1845*, a paper presented to the annual meeting of the Canadian Historical Association at Quebec City in June, 1976.

4. PAO, Jarvis-Powell Papers, 1843-1848.

5. *Ibid.*   6. *Ibid.*   7. *Ibid.*   8. *Ibid.*

9. Sam's mortgage for £4,300 to the Bank of Upper Canada was dated August 21, 1843, and registered December 2, 1844 as No. 23632. It was discharged on July 18, 1856 (No. 63289).

10. Frederick H. Armstrong, *Handbook of Upper Canadian Chronology and Territorial Legislation* (Centennial Publication, Lawson Memorial University, University of Western Ontario, 1967).

11. See *Paul Kane's Frontier*, edited by J. Russell Harper (Toronto: University of Toronto Press, 1971), p. 52.

12. Janet Carnochan, *Inscriptions and Graves in the Niagara Penninsula*, Niagara Historical Society, Number 10, *The Times*, Niagara, Ontario, The Hamilton Graveyard, p. 25.

13. The Toronto *Telegram*, May 14, 1935.

14. The deed to the "11 acres, 2 rods and 3 perches" on Jarvis Street purchased by William Cawthra for £4,000 was dated and registered on August 18, 1847 as No. 29804. The renewed mortgage for £4,000 was similarly dated and registered, its number being 29805. John G. Howard's Journal records receipt of a payment from William Cawthra, on August 18, 1847, of only £2,372.7.3 for "11a.2R.3P," which would suggest that the £4,000 price recited in the deed was in fact reduced by the amount outstanding on the earlier Jarvis mortgage which was then simply renewed by Cawthra in its original amount.

CHAPTER EIGHT: THE DEATH OF SAM JARVIS

1. J. Douglas Stewart and Ian E. Wilson, *Heritage Kingston* (Agnes Etherington Art Centre, Queen's University, Kingston, Ontario, 1973), p. 122.
2. PAO, Jarvis-Powell Papers, S. P. Jarvis's Travel Diaries, 1066.
3. *Ibid.*, 1065 and 1067.
4. PAO, Jarvis-Powell Papers, 536(a).
5. PAO, Jarvis-Powell Papers, 542.
6. William Dawson LeSueur, *William Lyon Mackenzie: A Reinterpretation*, *op cit*, p. 363.
7. PAO, Jarvis-Powell Papers, S. P. Jarvis's Travel Diaries, 1074 and 1075.
8. For the last Will and Testament of Samuel Peters Jarvis see General Register for the County of York (1875), Number 213.

CHAPTER NINE: TORONTO'S CHAMPS ÉLYSÉES

1. For a definitive history of the school, see Harvey Medland, *Minerva's Diary, A History of Jarvis Collegiate Institute* (Belleville, Ontario: Mika Publishing Company, 1979).
2. MTL, T. A. Reed Papers, H.50.
3. MTL, *Ibid.*, H.57   4. MTL, *Ibid.*, H.57
5. The Jarvis deed to Thomas Long, under which he assumed the $20,000 mortgage, was dated July 2, 1888, and was registered in the Registry Office for the City of Toronto on October 4, 1888 as No. 3909M.
6. William G. Storm is shown as having prepared plans for Mrs. Cawthra's house in *A Listing of the J.C.B. and E.C. Horwood Collection of Architectural Drawings and Related Materials in the Archives of Ontario*, published recently by the Ontario Ministry of Culture and Recreation. The names of other architects who were responsible for designing some of the houses discussed in this chapter were also gleaned from this list.
7. Harvey Medland, *Minerva's Diary, A History of Jarvis Collegiate Institute, op cit*, pp. 50 and 96.
8. Eric Arthur, *Toronto, No Mean City* (Toronto: University of Toronto Press, 1964), p. 147.
9. For a definitive biography of Flavelle, see Michael Bliss, *A Canadian Millionaire, The Life and Business Times of Sir Joseph Flavelle, Bart. 1858-1939* (Toronto: The Macmillan Company of Canada Limited, 1978).

✧ NOTES ⸙

CHAPTER TEN: THE VINTAGE YEARS

1. Paul Collins, *Hart Massey* (Toronto: Fitzhenry & Whiteside Limited, 1977), p. 53.

2. Raymond Massey, *When I Was Young* (Toronto: McClelland and Stewart Limited, 1976), p. 68 *et seq*.

3. Vincent Massey, *What's Past is Prologue* (Toronto: The Macmillan Company of Canada Limited, 1963), p. 16.

4. Some light was thrown on Massey's difficulties with the fraternity system many years later by the Reverend Dr. D. Bruce Macdonald, who had been headmaster of St. Andrew's College during Vincent's attendance there from 1902 to 1906. In the summer of 1938, after he had retired from St. Andrew's and was serving as chairman of the Board of Governors of the University of Toronto, he recalled to the writer (whose headmaster he had also been) that Massey had wished to join the Kappa Alpha Society when he entered the university, but had failed to receive an invitation. Since Dr. Macdonald had belonged to that fraternity when he was an undergraduate, Massey blamed him bitterly for having influenced the fraternity against him, an accusation that Dr. Macdonald emphatically denied. Vincent's younger brother, Raymond, who had also attended St. Andrew's briefly under Dr. Macdonald, later joined the fraternity in question.

   When Vincent Massey graduated from St. Andrew's in 1906, all was sweetness and light. He had been a good student. He had served on the executive of the Literary Society, he was one of the three officers of the Cadet Corps the year it was formed, and he was also an editor of the school magazine, *The Review*, to which in his final year he contributed a rousing poem in celebration of the school which ended, "Vivat, Saint Andrew!" Moreover, when he left, it was arranged that he would return in the fall as a junior housemaster while he was in attendance at the university. Apparently, the fraternity "crisis," as he called it, ended that arrangement abruptly, and led Massey, long after Macdonald's death, to attack the St. Andrew's College of Macdonald's day in his autobiography, *What's Past is Prologue* (p. 14). Today, portraits of both Macdonald and Massey hang in the Great Hall of Hart House.

5. Ian Montagnes, *An Uncommon Fellowship, The Story of Hart House* (Toronto: University of Toronto Press, 1969).

6. William James Loudon, *Sir William Mulock* (Toronto: The Macmillan Company of Canada Limited, 2932).

7. *The Toronto Daily Star*, December 2, 1918.

8. Michael Bliss, *A Canadian Millionaire, op cit*, p. 144.

9. *The Toronto Daily Star, op cit.*

10. Vincent Massey, *What's Past is Prologue, op cit*, p. 397.

11. The Mulock deed to 518 Jarvis Street in favour of the governing council of the Salvation Army, Canada East, was dated April 9, 1945, and was registered on April 13, 1945, as Number 52541 EP.

12. Mackenzie King's Release was registered against the property at 518 Jarvis Street on April 13, 1945, as Number 52539 EP.

13. *The Globe and Mail*, December 21, 1946.

14. The Mulock deed to the Gloucester Street property in favour of the governing council of the Salvation Army, Canada East, was dated February 28, 1948, and was registered on April 19, 1948, as Number 62861 EP.

15. The deed to 538 Jarvis Street from Dr. Barnardo's Homes to the governing council of the Salvation Army, Canada East, was dated July 27, 1948, and was registered on the same date as Number 63827 EP.

16. The deed from the governing council of the Salvation Army, Canada East, in favour of Brookmere Investments Limited, was dated June 22, 1956, and was registered on June 28, 1956, as Number 99026 EP. The accompanying Land Transfer Tax Affidavit showed that $70,000 was paid in cash with the $515,000 balance being secured by a mortgage, which was discharged in 1958 by instrument Number 109090 EP.

17. The property at the southwest corner of Jarvis and Shuter Streets was purchased by the General Council of the Salvation Army, Canada East, from J. Charles Ingwer. The deed was dated November 5, 1958, and was registered the same month as Number 109641 EP.

CHAPTER ELEVEN: AFTERGLOW

1. Austin Seton Thompson, *Spadina, A Story of Old Toronto, op cit. passim.*

2. Henry James Morgan, *The Canadian Men and Women of the Time: A Hand-book of Canadian Biography* (Toronto: William Briggs, 1898), p. 609.

3. Vincent Massey, *What's Past is Prologue, op cit*, p. 46.

4. *The Toronto Daily Star*, February 18, 1977.

5. Henry J. Cody sold 603 Jarvis Street to the Corporation of the City of Toronto for $42,000, in his capacity as executor of the estate of the late Florence L. Cody. The deed was registered as number 60367 EP on July 14, 1947. The property had a frontage on Jarvis Street of 106' 6½'' and a depth of 286' 5''.

6. See *The Globe and Mail*, April 28, 1951.

Index